MENNO MOTO

MENNO MOTO

A JOURNEY ACROSS THE AMERICAS
IN SEARCH OF
MY MENNONITE IDENTITY

CAMERON DUECK

Biblioasis
Windsor, Ontario

FIRST EDITION

Library and Archives Canada Cataloguing in Publication

Title: Menno moto : a journey across the Americas in search of my Mennonite identity / Cameron Dueck.
Names: Dueck, Cameron, author.
Description: Series statement: Untold lives
Identifiers: Canadiana (print) 20190238755 | Canadiana (ebook) 20190238763
  ISBN 9781771963473 (softcover) | ISBN 9781771963480 (ebook)
Subjects: LCSH: Dueck, Cameron—Travel—America. | LCSH: Mennonites—Canada—Biography. | LCSH: Mennonites—Travel—America. | LCSH: Mennonites—America—Social conditions. | LCSH: Mennonites— America—Social life and customs. | LCSH: Motorcycle touring—America. | LCSH: America—Description and travel. | LCGFT: Autobiographies.
Classification: LCC BX8143.D84 A3 2020 | DDC 289.7092—dc23

Edited by Janice Zawerbny | Copy-edited by Chandra Wohleber
Cover designed by Natalie Olsen | Interior designed by Zoe Norvell

Published with the generous assistance of the Canada Council for the Arts, which last year invested $153 million to bring the arts to Canadians throughout the country, and the financial support of the Government of Canada. Biblioasis also acknowledges the support of the Ontario Arts Council (OAC), an agency of the Government of Ontario, which last year funded 1,709 individual artists and 1,078 organizations in 204 communities across Ontario, for a total of $52.1 million, and the contribution of the Government of Ontario through the Ontario Book Publishing Tax Credit and Ontario Creates. This is one of the 200 exceptional projects funded through the Canada Council for the Arts' New Chapter program. With this $35M investment, the Council supports the creation and sharing of the arts in communities across Canada.

PRINTED AND BOUND IN CANADA

For Leonard Dueck

my legendary father,
a pioneer
and adventurer

Contents

Author's Note

This is a book of non-fiction. The story it tells is true to what my eyes saw, my ears heard, and my mind remembered. Many of the conversations were translated from Plautdietsch to English in my note-taking, and I remained as true to the original meanings as I understood them to be. Some people's names have been changed or Germanized in order to reduce confusion as there are many Mennonite men named John or Peter, and Loewen is a very common family name. For example, Johann, my great-grandfather, was actually named John W. Dueck. In some cases, such as conversations involving numerous people, I have combined characters. However, when dealing with controversial or strong views, I did my best to attribute them to the people who shared them.

Prologue

The Mennonites were nearly there.

"God has given us a new home in Canada, a place where we can live our own way, undisturbed, without the Russians telling us what to do," Pa said.

Johann, who had to stand on his tiptoes to see over the railing of the ship, nodded. This dream, the utopia they talked about so often, had helped push, pull, and lure them on, for mile after thousands of miles.

"What will it be like, Pa?"

"It will be good. Good farming, a good life," Pa said as he looked at the clearings on the riverbank. Rough wooden cabins surrounded by tethered horses that stamped their hoofs in frustration at the clouds of flies and mosquitoes. Many of the Mennonites on the ship were unable to afford their own land in Russia, and the opportunity to achieve this in Canada, a country newly formed and optimistic in the 1870s, had them beaming. Everyone wanted land. The young men, as soon as they were married, wanted land. Johann wanted land, or at least Pa said he would in a few years' time, once he was old enough. Now there would be plenty of rich farmland for all. They could start over, doing things the old way.

"But most important of all, you will never have to be a Russian soldier." Pa tousled Johann's light brown hair, but his eyes did not stop roving the riverbank.

Russia was thousands of miles behind them now, but the fear was still close, like the soot the trains and ships of their journey had spewed into the sky, which clung to them and besmirched their clothing long after they'd disembarked. Fear that the Russians would take away their way of life along the Molochna River and shut their small village schools. Fear that the Russian language would replace the flat guttural Plautdietsch they spoke at home, and the proper German that the preachers and teachers used. And that, once they spoke Russian, the young boys would be marched off to war, wearing those horrible uniforms, carrying guns, as dictated by the new laws introduced a few years earlier. The slow peaceful farm life that had become synonymous with Russia's Mennonites had come to an end.

So Pa sold everything—the horses, the machinery, the entire farm—cheap to those who were staying in Russia. Everything except the bedding, a few small pieces of furniture, and a change of clothes for each family member. Pa's mouth still tightened into a pointed, bitter pout when he thought about it. All those years of work, building up the farm, to have to give it all up because Russia had broken its promise to the Mennonites.

It had taken them two months of trains and ships and waiting and transfers. The toasted *zwieback* they'd brought were almost gone, and the few rolls that were left had gone stale. Every morning Johann ate one of the *zwieback*, sometimes with a dab of butter.

"It's the last bit, we're almost there," Pa reassured Mutta. "Just a little bit farther."

"Then the real work will start," Mutta said. She was exhausted. Heinrich, their sickly toddler, had spent much of the last few months in her lap, listless and becoming weaker every day. And Johann noticed Mutta's lap had become smaller as her belly had become larger over the course of the journey—another child was on its way.

But now they were on the last part of the journey. The *International* was a flat-bottomed, double-decked sternwheeler with grubby white topsides and two tall, blackened smokestacks. They had boarded the ship in the United States and sailed down the Red River, into Canada.

The riverbanks were a tangle of green forest that leaned in on the narrow river. The branches scraped and slapped and tickled across the steamboat, robbing one man of his hat as they chugged northward. Elms, oaks, maples, and poplars crept to the river's edge and kissed above the water. But the better the shade, the bigger the mosquitoes. They'd known mosquitoes in Russia, but not this big, not this thirsty. The men waved their hats, the women slapped at fleshy backs, and the children scratched until they bled. It would be a good story, another one about Mennonite perseverance that they could tell during the long evenings on their new farms.

The dark-skinned, long-haired crew of the ship spat out their curses in a babble of tongues. Several wore beaded leather thongs in their hair. Some of them wore buckskin shirts and smelled of campfire smoke and life in the woods.

"They're those Indians, the ones we heard about," Pa said when Mutta asked if he was sure they were in good hands. The agents who had arranged their passage, patching together ship-to-train-to-carriage-to-riverboat, had told them about the Indians who lived on the land. Their land.

"They're no good at farming, I heard," Pa said.

One of the Indians wore a red sash around his waist and winked at Johann when he caught him staring. They had a reckless, can-do air about them that made Johann want to copy them and spit tobacco juice over the railing and laugh, open throated, like these *weltmensch*.

"Johann," Pa called. "Those are not our people. You stay here, with the rest of us."

In the afternoon of the third day Johann was on the forward deck when the *International* slowed, stopped, and its great dripping wheel went into reverse. The ship crab-crawled across the current towards a muddy bank. A smaller river joined the Red River right where the helmsman was aiming the *International*. This was Canada, the place they'd talked about for two years, where the Queen had promised the Mennonites land and peace and freedom.

There was no dock or town, just a break in the trees. Then, through the trees, on a slight rise, Johann saw wagons and horses, stacks of gleaming raw lumber. Several long, low buildings that shone with newness. And on the riverbank, where the earth had been torn by trampling horses, a group of men, shirtsleeves rolled up, muddy to their knees, waving their hats.

The ship listed to starboard as more than three hundred silent Mennonites pressed against the railing for a glimpse of their new land. Hours earlier, as they passed a few open fields and signs of development, the men had eagerly taken note of the greenness of the pasture, the thickness of the oak trees. Now they silently stood along the rail and nervously cleared their throats as they stared at the riverbank.

Long warps were run out and wrapped around the tree trunks. A gangplank landed just short of the shore with a splash. The young men leapt across the muddy gap onto the bank. Extra planks were found and tied together with a few logs to reach dry land.

And then it was Johann's turn. He followed Pa down the steep gangplank. The rich mud clung to his shoes as he struggled up the riverbank, into the trees, to a place where they could start over.

CHAPTER 1

Canada

The Red River

The faces around the campfire were all familiar to me. Not only because I'd known them my entire life, but because many of them looked like me. Most had a prominent hooked nose and a body short in stature that, with age, carried the round Dueck belly. Our Mennonite genes still ran strong three and four generations after Johann had brought us here.

Here, on the riverbank where my great-grandfather had stepped ashore on August 1, 1874, after his long voyage from Russia. Johann's feet had slipped in the same cloying black mud that now stuck to my motorcycle boots. Here, where the Rat River, a sloughy and overgrown tributary, weakly joined the Red River in southern Manitoba. Now it was a popular fishing spot marked by crushed beer cans, a few tangled balls of fishing line, and a thousand boot prints in the mud. Not a very impressive place for the Mennonites to have begun their wanderings across two vast continents of virgin land to leverage accommodating governments and elicit promises to be left alone. Free to live our own way, to start a whole new saga of moves and migrations, bitter feuds and fresh departures.

The riverbank that had been Johann's point of arrival would be my point of departure and my family had come to say goodbye. I had pitched my tent on the bank, ready to be away early the next morning. There were no riverboats to take me south, so instead I'd steer my motorcycle down the highway, across the United States border just a few hours from there, and then keep riding.

I was going on an epic journey to find out who I was. I didn't say that, though, at least not out loud. When people asked why I wanted to ride a motorcycle the length of the Americas, all the way to Argentina, I answered that I liked adventure and that I wanted to learn more about Mennonite culture. My culture. I knew there were tens of thousands of my people down south, and I'd never been, so I wanted to go take a look.

Johann had come to Canada, he had been allowed into Canada, because he was a Mennonite and being a Mennonite in Russia had become dangerous. Calling myself a Mennonite meant something to me, but I wasn't sure what. There was the Christian faith part of the culture, a cornerstone to be sure, but I was more interested in the culture itself. The thing you describe when someone asks, "Where are you from?"

Deep down, so deep I wasn't sure I could even admit it to myself, I was setting off to find out if I was still a Mennonite. I wanted to find out if my definition of Mennonite was still relevant. I called this my culture, but I'd lived outside of its communities for most of my adult life. How much of the culture had remained in me? How Mennonite was I, after all these years?

I had left my own Mennonite community two decades ago. Not wilfully or consciously, but because opportunities and wanderlust drew me away. I became a journalist and travelled widely, and wildly. At first my family thought I'd return after a few years, but with time that became less likely. I loved the diversity and excitement of New York, London, Hong Kong, and all the cities in between. I'd found my calling, I was living my dream.

I left the community simply by choosing new opportunities over the safety of a familiar community. My father expressed concern that I was losing my religion, but no one tried to prevent me from leaving. My family listened to my stories with interest, and always welcomed me back when I returned to the farm for holidays. They visited me in different cities, and told their friends about my adventures. But there was also a slight hesitance to their enthusiasm, as leaving, exploring a different life, meant leaving a life that was intrinsically linked to our religion. To being Mennonite. Other cousins, nephews, and nieces also left, but few wandered so far or took up a lifestyle so foreign to that of their community. So I became a sort of curiosity back home: the guy who moved to Asia.

But when people in Hong Kong, New York, or anywhere else I made my home, asked me the origins of my last name I always explained it, and myself, as Mennonite. It was a very convenient label. I wasn't just another Anglo-Saxon male, I was a Mennonite. It gave me a story to tell, because if a Mennonite travels far enough away from Manitoba he becomes exotic.

"Menna…what's that?"

"A Germanic Christian culture. Sort of like Amish, but with a broader spectrum of conservatism."

"So, you grew up riding a horse and buggy?"

"*I* didn't, but some Mennonites do. My family is pretty normal, you wouldn't know they're Mennonites if you met them. But we have our own language and foods. So it's a culture and a religion. I'm Russian Mennonite, because my family came to Canada from Russia."

"Russian? I thought you said it was German."

"It's a long story."

If they bought me a drink I might get into the story, going back to Germany and the Low Countries, then Prussia and Russia, and eventually the move to the Americas. People always found it fascinating—who really knows their family history these days—so I loved to tell the story. In fact, I just loved telling stories about growing up on a Mennonite turkey farm in the Canadian Prairies, and people from Barcelona to Bangkok knew the names of my siblings and the fact that I had attended a three-room country school. These were all cornerstone details of my story—the story about me being a Mennonite.

I no longer lived a traditional Mennonite lifestyle—I was not a farmer, nor a member of a tight, church-centred community.

In fact, pacifism was one of the few bits of the religion I still called my own. I worried that by leaving the religion I'd given up my right to claim a Mennonite identity. But my family name was unmistakably Mennonite, I could still carry on a halting conversation in Plautdietsch and I liked to eat *foarmaworscht*, our locally-made smoked pork sausage. Was that enough?

Some parts of Mennonite culture repulsed and embarrassed me—the closed-minded slavery to rules, the thriftiness, the superior airs, the really bad sense of fashion—but there were also bits that I hoped I still had within me. I admired the ethic of hard work, the ingenuity, and ever-ready generosity towards those in need. I liked the idea of simple living. I was proud of being a "Menno," as we called ourselves. But maybe all those years bouncing around the globe had erased the last vestiges of my Mennonite culture. Being a straight, white, English-speaking male—a sort of baseline of ethnicity and identity in my world—made me a bit shy to talk about these things. How complicated could my identity really be? Still, I had enough questions to set off on a journey in search of it.

I planned to ride south, through the United States and into northern Mexico, where I knew I'd find large numbers of Mennonites. I would go to Belize to visit Mennonites with close ties to my own family, and then zigzag my way through Central America. Then to South America, where I knew I'd have to ride all the way to Bolivia before finding large Mennonite communities. Paraguay, Brazil, and Argentina had all been colonized by Mennonites, and once I'd driven my motorcycle that far, I might as well go to Tierra del Fuego, at the very southern tip of the Americas. My trip planning consisted of identifying the Mennonite communities sprinkled across the Americas and linking them together into a meandering route south. I'd decide which roads to take as my journey unfolded.

A large group of extended family were there to see me off. To wish me luck on a long and dangerous trip. We sat in folding lawn chairs around the fire, which snapped and threw sparks spiralling into the dark sky to join the stars. Our campfire was in a bluff of oak and elm. Hordes of mosquitoes buzzed around our heads.

A pickup truck with its open end-gate laden with coffee and hot chocolate, an auntie's home-baked cookies, made with extra butter and full cream, the Mennonite way. The evening was chilly, even with the fire, and the cold drew our circle tighter. My new Kawasaki KLR650 motorcycle was parked next to the fire. The firelight set its reflectors ablaze. My uncles appraised the bike with practical farmers' eyes.

"With a shiny bike like that you'll have to pay bribes to the Mexican police for sure," one of my uncles said.

"Kawasaki? But that's not from China!" another teased. They found the fact I had lived in Hong Kong both exotic and mystifying.

"Strong and simple," I explained. "It's basically a big dirt bike, so it will be good on all those rough roads down there. Single cylinder with a carburetor. Something I can repair along the way if I have to. Like a good Mennonite farmer."

They laughed. I'd strayed pretty far from my Mennonite-farmer roots, and secretly I shared their doubts that I'd know how to fix the bike if it broke down. But that was my plan.

My aunties plied me with food. Home-baked biscuits and a jar of honey. One of them tucked a few oranges into my pocket, another gave me a bag of freshly toasted *zwieback* that rustled in their paper bag. "Travelling food, just like Johann would have eaten," my auntie said as she hugged me.

Another auntie gave me a small angel pendant. "To keep you safe, because it's a long road you're travelling," she said.

"You think you'll make it?" an uncle asked, his work-heavy wrinkled hand set firmly on my shoulder. "I have a cousin in Belize, on your mother's side," he told me, going into a long description of the bloodlines connecting me to the past.

"Are you going to Paraguay?" another asked. "Which places, do you know? Because in Loma Plata there's a guy that I met here in Canada years ago, he has a big business there now..."

Already, the thousands of kilometres were being stitched together by contacts, stories, relations. Around the fire the conversation skipped between Plautdietsch—for some it was used just for an occasional exclamation or joke, for others it was still a living mother tongue—and English. The younger ones, my nephews and nieces, understood some of the Plautdietsche jokes, the slang and witty responses, but few of them spoke it. In fact, it was kind of uncool to speak it when we grew up. Very few of the people I had grown up with still had a solid grasp of the language. My own Plautdietsch was weak, but I knew it would improve because it was the only language I'd have in common with many of the Mennonites in the south. My uncles spoke it through mouths of sunflower seeds—the Manitoba Mennonite alternative to tobacco—spitting the husks out and chewing the seeds without pausing their stories.

"Our grandparents often told us about Russia, how good it was, and then how terrible it became," said Menno Kroeker, a local historian who had joined us for the evening. He was named after Menno Simons, the founder of our faith. He spoke English with the flat Germanic accent I'd heard all my life, pausing for emphasis, the fire lighting him in orange from underneath. "Our grandparents and great-grandparents fled, a whole exodus. There were some eight thousand Mennonites in all that came here to central Canada, and even more that went to Kansas and Nebraska. When our families came, the province of Manitoba was just a few years old. This was wild land, most of it."

Johann was nine years old when he arrived, although he is listed as younger on some ships' manifests; he must have been short like me and most of the other Duecks that followed him. He was brought to Canada by his thirty-one-year-old father, a labourer, and his twenty-nine-year-old pregnant stepmother—his own mother having died in childbirth. There was also his four-year-old brother Peter and his sickly nine-month-old half-brother, Heinrich. Heinrich died just weeks after they arrived, the first Mennonite to be buried in Manitoba soil. It was one of the few firsts our humble family could claim.

I'd learned about Johann through his diaries, written when he was an adult, then lost in a dusty attic for generations. Eventually they were found, my uncle published them in two volumes, and my father sent me a copies. It sat on my bookshelf, unread, for years.

Most of it was grain prices and notes on church meetings—pretty dry reading. Only when I started planning my journey did I read it, searching for threads of myself in his story. My mother's family came to Canada on the same ship as Johann, but his diaries and my resemblance to him brought his story to life for me. Seeing pictures of Johann as a young man gave me a funny feeling. The feeling you get when you catch a reflection of yourself in a window and you're surprised by what you see. In one picture, showing him with a cane and white beard standing in front of his general store, he could be mistaken for my aged father. Johann, then my grandfather Jacob Dueck, then my father, Leonard Dueck, and then me. All with the same nose. I'd never met my grandfather, he died a few years before I was born. But I'd claimed a grey fedora he'd once owned, and each time the sweat-stained rim touched my head I felt connected to my grandfather and even to Johann himself.

By the time we arrived in Canada Mennonites had already set a precedent of requesting that kings and governments grant them a *Privilegium*—an official document that defined special rights and privileges for the Mennonites, ranging from releasing them from military service and swearing oaths to allowing them to run their own schools in German. They had been granted *Privilegia* by Prussia and Russia, and Canada did the same. Our demands for a *Privilegium* shock me now. Imagine, migrating to another country, but demanding that the host country waive their civic norms to accommodate arriving immigrants. Imagine if today's immigrants asked for that— they're barely allowed in as it is. These demands were a habit of ours that I'd have many more opportunities to wonder about on my journey.

"We came because of the promises that were made," Menno continued. "The government said it would allow us to run our schools in German. The Mennonites would be left alone to their own ways, their schools and churches, inheritance laws and the ways they ran their villages. We were known as good farmers, which was why Canada wanted us."

When Johann arrived, there were already French and Scottish settlers along the riverbank, but inland the Prairies remained unbroken. That's where the Mennonites sank their plows into the earth and planted wheat. My relatives still lived in the villages and towns that were founded when the *International* dropped Johann on this riverbank. We built farms and grew rich and employed non-Mennonites when the work became too much. More and more Mennonites moved to Winnipeg, the provincial capital, less than an hour north of our campfire, now the largest urban concentration of Mennonites in the world. In Winnipeg, being Mennonite is not exotic.

Mennonites prospered, as they had in Russia, but as Canada began to take shape as a nation, so did its laws and national identity, and our *Privilegium* came under scrutiny. That meant the same laws for everyone, no more exceptions for the Mennonites. The government said no more schools in German and insisted on overseeing education. My family adapted—my mother gave all her children very Canadian-sounding Irish and Scottish names—while trying to remain separate from the rest of society. But that kind of Canada wasn't good enough for all Mennonites. Some felt cheated.

"In the 1920s some of our people began to move, about seven thousand of them. They went to Mexico, where they bought lots of land, for a good price," Menno said. "Soon others moved to Paraguay, for the same reasons."

This was the beginning of the story I was setting out to discover for myself, the story about the Latin American colonies of Canadian Mennonites, those who had left to find yet another promised land, a new *Privilegium*. I knew almost nothing about the Mennonites who had left Canada and moved south. There were tens of thousands of them, living in exotic, steamy corners of Latin America. How would they compare with my idea of what it meant to be a Mennonite? What would I have in common with them?

Menno took a swig of coffee and shifted his chair away from the campfire smoke.

"But, of course, Mexico also changed, and there were people with different ideas, Mennonites who wanted change, and those that didn't, and farmers who could no longer afford the land. Compromise of any kind meant giving in to the ways of the world, so the most old-fashioned ones, the most conservative of them, and some who were just interested in fresh land, started looking for a new place."

It happened again and again, creating a trail of colonies and farms cut from virgin forests and dry plains across the Americas. Each one marked a new frontier, a fresh start that ended in disappointment for a stubborn few when the respect shown towards their *Privilegium* was not to their liking. They carried that contrarian spirit to the next plot of fertile soil and planted their wheat in promises that they would be left to their own ways.

"That group that moved to Belize, they weren't from here, were they?" an aunt asked in a gravelly voice from the shadows.

"Well, sure they were," an uncle responded, debating the facts of something long ago but never forgotten. "That group, it included some of our own. Some of them went to Mexico first, and didn't like it, so they moved to Belize. We had cousins that moved with them, no?"

The Mennonites spread across the Americas, planting wheat wherever they went. In dry corners of Mexico, in the lushness of Central America, in the green hell of the Gran Chaco, all the way down to Patagonia, often requesting, and being granted, a *Privilegium*. The seeds of those communities came from here, from this riverbank, from the families that came to Canada from Russia. Mennonites with noses just like mine.

The bonfire popped with an explosion of sparks. Two of my aged uncles dragged more deadfall firewood out of the woods with a great deal of huffing and puffing. Conversation drifted through the historic moves, the names of the countries with the biggest groups, where I might find relatives; which branches, which breakaway church went where and when. The place names, repeated time and again in the countries where Mennonites planted their big dream: Manitoba Colony, Swift Current, Rosenhoff, Menno Colony, Steinbach. The same blood, the same names, the same seeds, again and again.

"*Na yo,*" one of my uncles said, slapping his knee for emphasis. *Na yo.* Meaning, it was done. There was nothing more to say. Let's go, it's getting late. They all stood up, folding their lawn chairs. One by one they hugged me goodbye, climbed into their cars, and drove away.

I crawled into my cold tent and tried to fall asleep, but my mind was kept awake chasing dreams. The restless movement of the Mennonites struck a chord with me. I'd been moving incessantly my entire adult life, but instead of virgin farmland I'd sought out the world's largest cities. I funded my travels with pen and camera, trying to scratch my maddening itch of restlessness. Was that a Mennonite trait? Maybe hearing from those Mennonites who kept searching for their own utopia would give me some answers. Maybe meeting them would make me say, "Ah, that's where that bit of my identity came from!"

Long, complicated, and somewhat dangerous journeys were not a new fascination for me. A childhood preoccupation with adventure had been fuelled by reading books that were far beyond my understanding of the world. Each one I snuck off my older brother's nightstand took me to new worlds. *Papillon* and *Midnight Express* painted vivid images of the swashbuckling escapades and dangers to be had across the seas in foreign lands.

My parents also travelled, but not to resorts and cultural destinations. They went to foreign places to do volunteer missionary work. It was the accepted way for a Mennonite to see the world. When farm work slowed down for the winter they joined church groups and flew off to build schools and radio stations, sew uniforms, and bring financial support to missionaries in Mexico, Paraguay, Brazil, and Haiti. They came home bearing exotic gifts—Dad once brought a suitcase full of switchblades for his boys, unaware that they had a more sinister purpose than whittling sticks—and their stories of adventure spurred on my imagination.

I sailed yachts across oceans, dropping anchor in dodgy foreign ports, finding my way through the ice of Arctic seas, travelling to places where tourists didn't normally go. Then

I discovered motorcycles. The mobility, the hours of constant motion, and the rawness of it. Never mind the wind, rain, and baking sunshine, or the fear of getting hit by a truck. I loved the exposure the motorcycle gave me to a time and place. I could hear the shouts of children playing beside the road. I could smell cooking fires down an alley and feel the change of pace when I pulled into mountain villages. On a motorcycle I was in the centre of it all, totally independent and mobile, and I could travel great distances.

I drifted to sleep following the yellow dotted line of an open highway that led south, connecting people, homes, language, and foods that I hoped would feel familiar to me.

My alarm awoke me at dawn. I remained burrowed in my sleeping bag for a few minutes, savouring the warmth. Then, as the sleep cleared from my mind, I remembered.

"This is it, the start. Day one," I quietly said to myself.

I could feel the presence of the Red River but could hear only the steady hum of traffic on the nearby highway. I crawled out of my tent and pulled on my boots, shrugging into my motorcycle jacket as I skidded down the riverbank on the slippery grass for one last look. The Red flows north, one of the few rivers on the continent to do so. Contrarian, like a Mennonite.

It was a cool, grey morning, and mosquitoes buzzed by in their lazy, weaving hunt. The cackle of familiar laughter had drifted away with the smoke, leaving behind only the smell of the cold campfire. It was just me, my bike, and my maps. And the river, which flowed smooth and steady, moving on to a better place.

I scrambled back up the bank and broke camp. I ate some *zwieback* with honey, had a gulp of water, and saddled up. The rasp of the engine starter shattered the stillness of the campsite. Then I turned onto the highway and opened the throttle, slashing through expansive fields of wheat, following the Mennonites south.

CHAPTER 2

United States

Middle America

I stayed in the fast lane, hunched over my tank, ears plugged against the scream of the engine, visor down to fend off wind and attacking insects, like a warrior on a mission.

In my mind's eye I had a clear geographical picture of this audacious plan to ride across two continents. The Mennonites in Mexico, Belize, Bolivia, and Paraguay formed a chain of islands across the continent, while the bits in between were less clear, linked by roads I had yet to discover. I wanted to get into the centre of that picture in Latin America as fast as possible, and that required crossing the United States. I'd criss-crossed the US on previous road trips and knew the soul-destroying effect of its freeways. They take travellers through endless suburbs without cities and past service centres identical in their blandness. So I sought out the secondary roads, where the curves were tighter and the smells riper. The fragrance of freshly mown hay, a pungent cattle feedlot, the sting of exhaust from an old farm truck, and the rancid waves emanating from a dead dog on the grass verge filled in what the eye didn't see at highway speed.

I stopped to refuel in Ohio, at a station on Highway 224. A red pickup truck with a man and a woman inside growled to a stop at the pump beside me. The driver, wearing his Hawaiian shirt unbuttoned to show a chest of curly white hair, climbed down, stuck the fuel nozzle into his truck, and then sauntered over to my bike.

"Looks like you're travelling a ways," he said, looking at my Manitoba licence plate and heavily loaded bike. "How far ya goin'?"

"Argentina." I thumped the duffle bag slung across my seat for emphasis.

He gave a low, drawn-out whistle. "Great trip. You drive safe now," he said before he returned to his truck.

"Mary, that guy is going all the way to Argentina on that motorcycle," he told his companion as he climbed back into his truck.

"Well, I say!"

"Isn't that something?"

"Sure is."

"Mary, where is Argentina? Is that in Mexico?"

At night I camped in state parks and built crackling fires for company. I studied my map in the firelight and counted the miles done and the ones to come. When I collapsed into my sleeping bag, I could feel my body tingle with echoes of engine vibration. My hands were swollen from gripping the handlebars and my ass was so sore I winced as I remounted the bike each morning.

But my bike and I were becoming one. I soon realized the bike was grossly overladen, so I began jettisoning gear—an extra pair of jeans left here, a spare packet of batteries there. I'd buy what I needed as I travelled. Even with just the "basics" my bike and gear weighed so much I feared I'd never be able to lift it back up if it fell over. Tent, sleeping bag, campstove, camp pots, warm clothes, cool clothes, rain clothes, sunscreen, laptop computer, video camera, regular camera, small camera, second small camera, big camera, toiletries, first-aid kit, spare tire tubes, tire pump, wrenches, screwdrivers, spare spark plugs, spare light bulbs, and a thick stack of maps that told me where to take all this stuff.

Within a few days I was riding through the American Midwest, where our Mennonite cousins lived. Pennsylvania, off to my left, was the Amish heartland. We'd started out in Europe together

nearly five hundred years earlier as Anabaptists—rebaptizers—
rebelling against both the Catholics and the Protestants.
The Anabaptists believed that Christians should be baptized only
when they were old enough to understand their faith, and that
the faith had to be an active, tangible part of their lives. By design
it was a fragmented movement without a clear leadership structure, because it was the power structure of the state churches they
were rebelling against. That didn't go down well with the Catholics
or the Protestants, and the Anabaptists were tortured, drowned,
and burned at the stake. A lot of them.

But the Anabaptists stuck with it and their numbers grew.
Some of them decided to live communally, following the teachings
of a minister named Jakob Hutter. They shared all their possessions
and became the Hutterites that today live on colonies in the Canadian Prairies and the northern United States. A Frisian minister
named Menno Simons led another Anabaptist group, who called
themselves Mennonites. Menno Simons preached pacifism
and a quiet family-focused life, and his followers refused to swear
oaths. They quoted James 5:12: "let your yea be yea; and your
nay, nay," and argued that because all they said should be truthful,
swearing oaths was unnecessary.

But that wasn't hard-core enough for some, so in 1693 a Swiss
Mennonite minister named Jakob Ammann set off to create
his own group. Ammann preached the need for a distinct appearance, from untrimmed beards to uniform dress, and a large group
of Alsatian and Swiss Mennonites left Menno Simon's group
to become the Amish. Early in the eighteenth century the Amish
began to migrate to Pennsylvania, Ohio, and eastern Canada, building pretty farming villages and orderly white fences that marched
across green hills. Today, they famously shun cars and electricity.
Instead, they drive horse-drawn buggies and wear the same style
of clothes they wore when they arrived in America.

The Amish have become minor celebrities, attracting tourists by the busload who stop in Amish communities to buy quilts
and homemade candles. The movie *Witness*, starring Harrison
Ford, helped place them on America's cultural map and contrib-

uted to widely held stereotypes of the Amish.

The reality television show *Breaking Amish* follows Amish and Mennonite youth who have left their communities to live in New York and experience the evil temptations of the world. I've been asked dozens of times if I experienced *rumspringa* as depicted in the reality show—the Amish tradition of allowing teenagers a few years of freedom before they commit to the church and community. No, I didn't.

Neither did most of the Mennonites living in the states off to my right, in Kansas and Nebraska, who came to the Americas from Russia in the same wave as my family. Mennonites are a lot less recognizable than the Amish because Mennonites do not all wear long beards and ride horse-drawn buggies— but some of us do. We're less homogeneous and there's a broader spectrum of conservatism among Mennonites than there is with the Amish, as well as a more varied migration history.

The strictest Mennonite sect is called Old Colony, and they shun technology just like the Amish do. Old Colony refers to Chortitza Colony, the first colony that Mennonites created in Russia when they arrived from West Prussia late in 1789. Old Colony Mennonites were poorer, less educated, and more conservative than the Mennonites who had followed them from Poland to Russia years later. This marked difference in conservatism continued when Chortitza members emigrated to Canada in the same wave as Johann. Many of their social rules were formalized in Canada, creating the blueprint for Old Colony communities across the Americas. Their rules include prohibitions against technology, motor vehicles, and electricity, although some modern farming conveniences are allowed, and the men wear *schlaub'betjse*, which are heavy denim bib overalls.

Other Mennonites, like my family, live pretty average North American lives. Regardless of our degree of conservatism, we share language, foods, and migration stories. Most famous Mennonites don't look different—you'd have to do a Wikipedia search to identify some of the high-profile Mennonites in the world today. There's Floyd Landis, the American road cyclist caught using performance-enhancing drugs. Or James Reimer, the National Hockey League goalie, who grew up in a village not far from my own. Dwight Schrute, a fictional character in the American version of the TV comedy series *The Office*, has Mennonite grandparents and lives on a forty-acre beet farm with his cousin Mose and speaks an old Germanic dialect which I can only guess is similar to Plautdietsch. Dwight D. Eisenhower, the thirty-fourth president of the United States, came from Mennonite roots but was raised as a Jehovah's Witness. Eisenhower's mother objected to his decision to study at West Point and pursue a military career because it conflicted with the pacifist views of her Anabaptist upbringing.

In the US, most Mennonites are Swiss Mennonites, who, like the Amish, remained in Switzerland and Germany until they moved to the New World. Their language and customs are slightly different from those of the Mennonites who migrated via Russia. There are also hundreds of thousands of Mennonites who identify with the evangelical religion but not the culture, attending Mennonite churches in places as far away as India and Africa. They wouldn't know a *zwieback* from a wagon wheel. Their names are not Penner, Plett, Reimer, or Dueck, and they did not come from Russia or Switzerland. They're just attracted to the simple, pacifist beliefs of the Mennonite faith. People like author Malcolm Gladwell, whose British parents joined an Ontario Mennonite community when he was a child, and who still identifies himself with the Mennonite faith. There are more than two million Anabaptists around the world, including Mennonites, Amish, and Hutterites.

But we Russian Mennonites like to think of ourselves as special. While some Mennonites went to America directly from Switzerland and Germany in the 1700s with the Amish, my ancestors immigrated to West Prussia and then to southern Russia, in what is now Ukraine. Our moves were driven by a search for religious freedom and by the attraction of available farmland. Kings and queens promised us peace and plenty in *Privilegia* because they needed passive, self-sustaining farmers to help develop their countries, but those promises always seemed to expire, prompting another move.

It was in West Prussia where the Plautdietsche language, the foods, and the radical isolationism that Russian Mennonites are known for today came together into a cohesive culture. Mennonites who had come from different parts of Europe melded together and the Mennonite culture, the food, and the ways of life, took root.

But it was in our next home, in Russia, where the *Privilegium*, granted largely on religious grounds, came to carry economic and civic meaning. Faith, ethnicity, and civil and economic life were cemented together for all Mennonites protected under the banner of the *Privilegium*. Mennonite leaders held both religious and civil power, creating a theocracy, and if you were not an upstanding member of the church you might be cut out of business deals and your children might be excluded from Mennonite education and subject to Russian military conscription. For Johann, sticking to the Mennonite faith became a form of survival, not just a way of believing.

Johann helped bring that culture and meaning of community to North America, and it was this Russian Mennonite culture, the one that I had come from, that I was seeking out on this journey. Russian Mennonites had a reputation for defiance of authority, with more recent stories of persecution for their beliefs than the Swiss Mennonites or the Amish.

Of the 45,000 Mennonites living in South Russia in the 1870s, about 10,000 left for the United States and 8,000 immigrated to Manitoba in that first wave with Johann. Some were from the Old Colony church, considered the original, most traditional group, others were members of the Kleine Gemeinde, or "small church," which was a newer group that put more emphasis on spirituality. Canada appealed to the more conservative families because it created a Cabinet order extending a *Privilegium* to the Mennonites, while the United States refused to put promises in writing. The Mennonites in Canada had faith that Queen Victoria, a Christian, would keep her promise that they would be allowed to run their own schools in German and be exempt from military service. Canada also allowed Mennonites to create large culturally homogeneous areas where all the land was Mennonite-owned, building the foundation for the same kind of communities they had enjoyed in Russia.

The more liberal Russian Mennonites chose to settle in Kansas and Nebraska, where they gave up their *Privilegium* in exchange for rich arable land in a more developed country swelling with optimism and growth. The Russian Mennonites settled not far from the Swiss Mennonites who had come before them. They'd been victims of the whims of kings and queens for long enough, and this time they'd try a republic. The US Senate rejected their appeal to buy large tracts of land and live in closed communities like they had in Russia. Those Russian Mennonites who had settled in the American Heartland did not maintain the cultural severity of those who went to Canada. Those early concessions proved telling, as my research had already shown me that nearly all of the Mennonite communities I would find in Latin America had Canadian, not American, roots. As well, the US did not receive a fresh wave of Mennonites in the 1920s like the one that had bolstered Canadian Mennonite society. Instead, the stubborn Russian Mennonites went to Canada.

So I rode through the Midwest without stopping to visit the Mennonites who lived there. Besides, I had already met them, years earlier.

A few days after my high school graduation I drove to Kansas to visit a Mennonite girl named Lori. I'd met her the previous summer on a Christian-teen mission trip to Spain, where we spent the summer in work boots, doing volunteer construction at a church camp and singing hymns on the street corners on the weekend. We were all chaste, clean-scrubbed church kids, but I still found the non-Mennonites in the group slightly intimidating, so I was immediately drawn to the pretty blond Mennonite girl from Kansas.

We returned to our respective homes when the summer trip ended and spent the next year scribbling letter after letter to each other—real handwritten letters. Then I acquired my first car, a red Chevy Sprint, and I promised Lori I'd come visit her.

My parents were hesitant, but when they heard she was a Mennonite they relented.

"She's a Claassen?!" my father exclaimed. Whenever I met a Mennonite he didn't know his ears perked up. He was playing the Mennonite Game.

"What's her dad's name?"

"Mr. Claassen, I guess."

"Well, ask her who her grandfather is. If I knew his name I might be able to tell you who she is."

I already had a pretty good idea who Lori was, but you don't really know a Mennonite unless you know their grandparents and which church they attended. Then you can judge them by the sins of their fathers and forefathers and put them in their proper box.

"Did they ever live in Nebraska?" my father asked. "There are people from your Mother's side who live in Nebraska, and some of them might be Claassens. We spelled it with a K, but it could be the same family."

"I have no idea, Dad." I hated the Mennonite Game. I didn't care if he knew her grandfather or great-grandfather. In fact, I hoped he didn't.

Turns out some of Lori's great-great-grandparents came from the same Molochna Colony in southern Russia that Johann came from. Some of her ancestors had lived only a few kilometres from his village of Schoenau. They immigrated to Nebraska the same year Johann came to Manitoba, and several ancestors on my mother's side of the family—Klasssens—also chose Nebraska over Manitoba. My father had good reason to be curious. Johann's and Lori's forefathers probably knew each other, but that had nothing to do with my motives for driving to Kansas.

I set off a few days after my high school graduation, and when I got to Kansas I marvelled at how Mennonites could be so different, so worldly. Lori's family didn't speak Plautdietsch and didn't appear to have the same feeling of being under siege from the rest of the world that we were taught was the way Christians should feel if they were living truly righteous lives. The Mennonites in Kansas moved free and easy among the *weltmensch*—they didn't worry about maintaining a sense of us and them. *Weltmensch*, people of the world, included anyone who wasn't Mennonite. The others. Lori wore a short skirt and was a high school cheerleader—dizzyingly exotic to my sheltered mind—just like a *weltmensch* would do. Her family had the Christian faith, they prayed and went to church and read the Bible. But they were so free! It didn't seem to matter if there was a line around their community or not.

Where I grew up, in a small Mennonite community near Lake Winnipeg, remaining separate wasn't that hard. The nearest store, and our postbox, was twenty kilometres away. We went to town by car once a week to pick up the mail, buy oatmeal and spotty bananas, do the banking, and to catch a glimpse of the *weltmensch* going about their lives. Our only other exposure to *weltmensch* was when insurance salesmen came to the farm or the Watkins dealer arrived with his battered car full of soaps and potions. Strange accents, the fragrance of tobacco smoke, women who wore their hair short, and the glint of jewellery were ample signals that these people were different.

We had no television and little access to popular culture. Our Mennville Evangelical Mennonite Church bought its first piano was when I was in Sunday School—it was thought too worldly to own one until then. Military service and the language of our education had become moot points long ago, but the three-room, church-run Mennville School still refused to fly the Maple Leaf, a small jutting of the jaw towards the government. If we didn't fly the flag we weren't their slaves. The school board had a sudden burst of nostalgia and reintroduced German to our curriculum one year, but it didn't last. There were few, if any, non-Mennonite students and my class totalled three people—Nathan, Joell, and I—all boys, no girls, just our bad luck. Nathan and Joell both played hockey in the nearby non-Mennonite town of Riverton, but my father forbade me to join, because he thought the town boys might be a bad influence on me. Mennonite farmers did not harvest their crops on a Sunday, even if it had rained all week and it was the only dry day in the forecast for the next month.

Business dealings with other Mennonites were still preferable to those with a *weltmensch*, but business was done, either way. Our parents grudgingly sent us to Riverton for the last two years of high school, but by that age they expected us to have perfected the art of holding the world at bay.

As outward appearances became less pronounced, inner rhetoric became more important. Faith, being "born again," living for the Lord, was the steel lightning rod for all else in life. We were different because we said so, and we wore it like a badge of honour. And because we believed we were different and separate, it became so. But moderate Mennonite communities such as Mennville have changed a lot in the past twenty-five years. My generation was the last one to speak Plautdietsch fluently, if at all. Intermarriage with non-Mennonites became the norm. Religious practices and doctrine became indistinguishable from those of other conservative North American evangelical churches. Technology, alcohol, and working on Sunday became common, but Mennonites are still, on average, very bad dancers.

Another thing that didn't change was Mennonite generosity. Mennonite communities are some of the most generous donors of cash, expertise, and volunteer labour across Canada. We took in Southeast Asian refugees in the 1970s and today Mennonites are once again taking on more than their share of refugees from the Middle East, Africa, and elsewhere. Tithing, the giving of 10 percent of your income to the church, is only the starting point for many generous Mennonites.

My summer trip to Kansas didn't bring the wished-for everlasting romance, but it did give me an inkling that the Russian Mennonites who moved to Canada must be especially stubborn. So stubborn that when things changed the most adamant of us felt an irreconcilable sense of umbrage, packed up, and went off seeking new promises in Latin America, always leaving a few Mennonites and kernels of wheat behind.

Much of the wheat I'd seen, driving through the US Midwest, was a variety of hard red winter wheat, which has a similar migration story as Johann and my family. The original strain, called

Turkey red, was bred from a variety of Old World red wheats by the Ottomans, who occupied the land between the Black Sea and the Sea of Azov periodically from the fifteenth to eighteenth centuries. When Russia annexed the Ukrainian steppe in 1783 and moved Mennonites onto the land, the Mennonites grew the wheat that the fleeing Turks had left in the granaries. When Johann and his neighbours migrated to North America in 1874 they brought a few sacks of Turkey red wheat seed with them, ready to start their new farms.

In North America, where the land and climate were very similar to that of the Russia we had just left, the drought-resistant wheat was the first thing the Mennonites planted. The next year, in early summer, they had fresh bread. The high-gluten Turkish wheat was especially good for baking, and it soon gained popularity across the Plains. About a decade after they arrived, a clever Mennonite grainsman imported 10,000 bushels of Turkey red from the Ukraine, and today it is the most common variety of wheat grown in the United States. Turkey red died out as a popular variety in the 1940s, but it is the granddaddy of modern wheat. It has been modified and crossbred to suit modern tastes and production, but the wheat beside the road I was riding on was very likely a distant cousin of a kernel that came to America with the Mennonites.

Hard red winter wheat was so important it had its own futures contract on the Chicago Board of Trade. I knew it well—I'd once been a Chicago-based commodities journalist, writing about pork bellies, beans and wheat and other things we eat. The wheat on either side of my motorcycle told me I knew this place, sliding by, green turning to yellow, as I followed the Mennonites' path south.

Each day of riding began early, at sunrise if possible. I had a book of highway maps and as I drove I tore out the travelled pages and stuffed them into fuel station rubbish bins, leaving miles and maps behind in equal measures.

Old America still lives on its secondary roads, where barking dogs tried to sink their teeth into my tires and people waved from porches as I passed. Sturdy red-brick buildings built close to the road, their lush lawns planted with so many American flags I wondered if they grew wild around these parts. I rode through little towns, with one diner open for lunch and ramshackle fuel stations staffed by pimply-faced teens who ran out to serve me when I drove across a black hose that rang a bell. The trucks on main street came from surrounding farms, with mud on their fenders and a jumble of tools in their boxes.

By the second week my body had become accustomed to life on the road. I no longer noticed the steady, jarring vibration of my bike's knobby tires and single cylinder engine. When I became cramped and stiff, I stood on the foot pegs, bracing myself against the rush of wind to wiggle and stretch in an awkward form of highway calisthenics. Then I'd sit down again and watch the rush of the road for another hour.

I discovered what bikers meant when they talked about brotherhood. In America, motorcyclists greet each other with an upside-down peace sign, flashed low and beside the engine, a wish for safe riding that means "keep two wheels down." I learned to flash the biker salute to every motorcycle I met, but there were also greetings at gas stations, offers of help, and directions to tire shops. I'd never considered myself a biker before. I didn't ride on a daily basis at home, and I didn't even normally own a bike. But now strangers greeted me like they knew me because I was travelling on two wheels.

All my impressions came from the saddle of my motorcycle and the rapid stops to refuel and gobble down greasy diner meals. But I was travelling in the right direction. The Appalachian Mountains led me into the southeast. The dead roadside deer of the north were turning into dead armadillos. Accents were slower and rounder. The dusty smell of ripe wheat turned to loamy, sultry gardens. The road beneath me grew hotter with every hour of driving.

The simplicity of me plus bike plus road equalled pure joy. I stopped when and where I liked and sought out dodgy small-town bars if I was staying in a motel. I sat beside campfires, eating dinner straight from the cooking pot, the golden firelight glinting off my bike. I felt like a cowboy riding the range.

My only steady companion was my motorcycle. I'd chosen it like a lot of Mennonites chose their wife—it was sturdy, simple, and with a long history of reliable performance. The Kawasaki KLR650 model had probably made more trips through the Americas than any other model because of its proven ruggedness. But I was still in a constant state of worry over its well-being.

"The engine seems hot, I wonder if the radiator is working... What's that funny rattle when I brake? Did that oil on the pavement come from my bike?"

My worries were rewarded in Texas, when my progress came to a shuddering halt. It was the day before I was to cross into Mexico. I was riding through Big Bend National Park, where the road went over a long series of small rolling hills between candelabra-shaped saguaro cacti. At the bottom of one hill there was a jolt and a rattle, and the rear of the bike sagged as the suspension gave out.

I gingerly rode to El Paso, three hundred kilometres in the opposite direction from where I wanted to go, and found a motorcycle shop to do the repairs. But it was Friday afternoon, and they said nothing would happen until Monday morning. So I checked into the Coral Motel for the weekend. It was a seedy joint bathed in traffic exhaust, where the grubby curbside pool was now a sandbox. My room was dark, stank of stale cigarette smoke, and the girls staying next door didn't look like the sort you'd bring home to Mother.

My rear tire was bald after 7,000 kilometres, and this was the perfect opportunity to change it for the new one I'd carried strapped to my luggage. As I'd ridden across the country I'd accumulated a tool kit that I thought would cover all my needs, including three small pry bars to use as tire tools. They were not designed as tire tools, but they were lighter and cheaper than the real thing, and I congratulated myself on my cleverness. I'd saved a few dollars like a good Mennonite, who uses every part of the pig but the squeal.

On Saturday morning I stripped the old tire off the rim and then grunted and cursed as I stretched the new one on. My clever, lightweight tools were rubbish. They flexed and slipped off the tire, catapulting across the parking lot with a twang. When the new tire was on the rim, I started inflating it, but my portable pump broke within the first ten strokes. I carried the tire to the gas station across the road and inflated it. By the time I had the tire back on the bike, it was flat again.

The tube showed a dotted line of the nicks that I'd made with my improvised tools, which had viciously sharp corners. I put another new tube into the tire, this time being more careful as I pried the tire back onto the rim. When I tried to inflate it, the air escaped as fast as I could pump it in. I'd nicked another one.

I imagined how this would amuse all the self-reliant Mennonite farmers I'd grown up with. They'd know better than to set off on some soul-searching motorcycle trip to begin with. Where was my Mennonite resourcefulness? It was a trait that was lauded above all else in the story of our immigration, replanting, and restarting. Started with nothing, whole world against us, everything built from the ground up, and now look at our righteous success. Mennonites might preach humility, but when it comes to our own perseverance and resilience, we are wont to boast.

I needed the resourcefulness my father had shown. Dirt poor but eager to work, he and my mother had lived the frontier life in the 1950s, at a time when most young Canadian couples were swing dancing and throwing cocktail parties in their affordable suburban homes. Instead, my parents cut down trees with handsaws and then borrowed bulldozers to rip roots from the soil until there was space to plant a crop, and that's how they built our family farm in the Interlake, between Lake Winnipeg and Lake Manitoba.

Now, when his growing flock of grandchildren and great-grandchildren gathered, the story was retold for the hundredth time. We knew the details better than Dad remembered them.

"Built a fire right under the engine of that old International truck, right, Dad? Truck was frozen solid and that's the only way it would start, eh?" He nodded, his watery eyes coming alive with the memory. "Weren't you worried that the truck would catch fire?"

He shrugged his shoulders and hee'd and hawed.

"It didn't seem that dangerous at the time," he always said. "We were too stupid to know what danger we were in. We had to get the work done."

"All this, the farm, the house, everything, you built it from scratch."

"That's how we did it in those days."

All I had to do was fix a few inner tubes. If I couldn't even change a tire, how would I complete this epic ride I'd dreamed up? When I told my white-collar friends about my ocean-sailing adventures and traversing deserts by motorcycle, they often asked how I'd learned to fix the boat or get the motorcycle running again when it died.

"Well, I'm not a mechanic, but, you know, I grew up on a farm, so…" I'd say with a large dollop of false humility. The fact was, I didn't have a clue how to fix an engine. Or a flat tire, it appeared.

I patched the tubes and walked to the nearest mechanic's shop, the flat tire banging against my leg with each step. One of the workers kindly took time to work the tire back onto the rim, without cursing, breaking a sweat, or dropping a tool in the process.

But when I filled the tire and was checking the pressure, I heard it…the accusing hiss of air. Even my patches weren't working!

I had only one patch left, and I applied it carefully. Then I carried both tire and inner tube back to the shop, where the mechanic had it back on the rim in minutes, tight as a drum. We pumped it up to full pressure—there was no hissing. By that evening the motorcycle shop had replaced my suspension, making my bike as good as new. And then I bought a set of proper tire tools, designed especially for changing motorcycle tires. They cost only US $5 each.

CHAPTER 3

Mexico

A Fight for Water

Directly across the US-Mexico border from El Paso is Ciudad Juárez, one of the most violent cities on earth, rife with drug cartels and thugs. I was terrified at the prospect of riding through this den of transgression. Living in the relatively safe cities of Asia for many years had made me soft.

I'd heard it would be safest to cross early in the day, while the bad guys were still recovering from the night shift, so I was queuing at the border as dawn broke. I'd eaten a big breakfast, my fuel tank was full, and my bladder was empty—there should be no need for me to stop until I'd reached safety. I felt like a weak swimmer setting off across the pool, eyes firmly fixed on the safety of the far side while dog-paddling for all I was worth.

I rode at the speed limit—I'd heard many a story about being stopped by Mexican cops and the bribes that were required. There were also crosses stuck into the sand beside the road to remind me that a lapse in concentration could be fatal. Some were painted white or draped in wreaths of faded plastic flowers. Here and there stood small shrines, painted gay blue and pink and yellow. Lives picked out in flowing script. *José Luis Rodríguez, Jan. 3, 1983–Sept. 4, 2008. Luciana Evelyn López, July 12, 1978–Oct. 12, 2010.*

The most elaborate of them had small glass windows that looked onto photos of those who had lost their lives on this road. Smiles that were innocent of the horrors to come. Eyes wide open were now closed for good, right here, on this patch of sandy roadside. I passed a whole crop of white crosses, a dozen, maybe more, two rows standing at attention in the ditch. A bus crash? A gruesome cartel killing?

I didn't stop until I had reached Cuauhtémoc, named for a sixteenth-century Aztec ruler but now a Mennonite capital about four hundred kilometres south of the border. A shiver went up my spine as I rode through the crowded streets, heard the soft lilt of Spanish, and smelled the tacos cooking in street stalls. Now I felt like I was on a real adventure.

I found a café and waited for Abram Siemens, or Bram, the only person I knew in all of Mexico. Bram was my elementary school teacher and the principal of our three-room Mennville school for several years. Bram was Mennonite, but had grown up in Paraguay, rode a racing bicycle to town on the weekends, and spoke with a distinct German accent. He was a different kind of Mennonite than us. He was strict and his otherness only added to his authority.

I was a troublemaker in grade five. I'd once accepted a dare from the older boys and wrote *Bram is a fag* on the side of the school using ripe dandelion heads as my paintbrush. I wrote the letters as large as my short arms would allow, rubbing the yellow flowers into the white stucco of the school wall. Bram didn't find it funny and the time of reckoning was painful. The sun took a long time to undo my work, and the slur remained for several weeks. I had been nervous to contact him again, but he immediately agreed to meet.

I recognized him as soon as he walked into the café, even though I hadn't seen him in more than twenty years. Now in his mid-fifties, he was thinner of hair and the creases in his face had grown deeper, but he still had the same erect stature, intense eyes, and broad smile. Bram was the publisher of the *Deutsch-Mexikanische Rundschau*, a German newspaper serving the Mexican

Mennonite colonies. He was also the host of a popular radio show that thousands of Mennonites listened to every day. We shared news of our families, and I gave him an abridged version of what I, one of his least-promising students, had done with my life. I told him about the journey I had only just begun.

"You're a Menno on a moto," he said, grinning at me. Menno. It was a self-deprecating term, usually said in jest. "The Mennonites you meet may not always see you as one of them, even though you think there's a connection. But it's worth a try."

"I'm hoping you can help me. For starters, where are the colonies located?"

"Okay, this is where we are, right in the middle of Cuauhtémoc," Bram said as he pushed aside our coffee cups and drew a map on a scrap of paper. "This road here leads to the Corredor Comercial Menonita where most of the big businesses are. This is the heart of the colonies, and here is where the radio station is, and my home is down a road to the right, down here." He drew Xs and circled key intersections, pointing out Mennonite schools, senior citizen homes, supermarkets, and the most popular cafés.

Many Canadian Mennonites still live in tight-knit villages, but few still practise communal land ownership. However, when they came to Mexico the Mennonites bought large plots of land under a single title and created colonies where the infrastructure was owned communally, in a system that mimicked the one used by Mennonites in Russia. They divided the land among the farmers, with plots set aside for a church, a school, and a common grazing pasture. The colonies also export dairy and beef as a community, buy farm supplies in bulk, run their own banks, and build roads and infrastructure when the local governments don't serve them to their satisfaction. There are about thirty colonies fanned out to the north of Cuauhtémoc, reaching almost all the way to the United States border.

"There are about 50,000 Mennonites living around here, and some more down in the south of the country," Bram said. "Here's Manitoba Colony, that's one of the bigger ones, and here's the road north to all the other colonies."

I'd heard about a fight over water that was threatening not only Mennonite farms, but their pacifist ways as well.

"It's an issue affecting all of the colonies," Bram said. "It's what everyone is talking about. It's not a new problem, but it's been dry lately, and now the conflict has become a bit more tense. Here's a number for a guy, John Friesen. He'll show you around."

John was an avuncular retired farmer who drove a white Chevy 4x4 truck that was so new there was still protective plastic on the insides of the doors. John and his wife had lived in Canada for several years, but they had missed their lives in Mexico so much they returned. He took me on a driving tour of the colonies.

"Look, isn't it beautiful?" John pointed at the green fields on either side of the road. "The Mennonites have built all of this, made these farms what they are today."

About 120,000 hectares of land in Chihuahua was converted from lower-impact ranching to crop farming in recent decades. The Mennonites planted wheat, beans, and corn. They also made a popular soft white cheese known as *queso Menonita*. They embraced every technological advance they could lay their hands on to boost crop production, from irrigation and heavy tillage to the most toxic of chemicals and fertilizers. Hurting the earth to make money didn't undermine Mennonite virtue.

"Look at a farm and you can tell it's Mennonite because it's much nicer than the Mexican farms," John said as we drove through the colonies. "The Mexican farmers are often poor around here. They are not very good farmers."

The Mennonite farms had straight rows of corn and tidy houses fringed with flower beds. White fences contained fat, well-bred cattle. Shiny tin buildings stood out crisply against the verdant land. Houses were built of red brick or concrete blocks painted white, with black- or red-trimmed windows, and they were always ringed by planted trees. Women were bent over hoes in their gardens, watering plants and mowing grass in their long skirts. Often, they were barefoot, dirty ankles peeking out from under their dresses. John was right, the Mennonite farms looked prosperous.

"Mennonites, they always try to make the farm look nice. Look at all the flowers you see, the gardens, that's a Mennonite thing," John said as we passed yet another immaculate farm.

But their success came at a cost. John turned down a dirt lane that cut across a farm. We came to a barbed-wire fence, where I hopped out and picked my way through the cow patties to open the gate. I inhaled the fragrance of pasture and manure as I waited for John to drive through. The rutted lane dipped towards a narrow creek, where the peacefulness of the Mennonite farm was interrupted.

The grass had been trampled and torn up by machinery and a herd of cowboy boots. Chunks of concrete littered the banks and a broken dam stood jagged and raw, like the open mouth of a brawler. John jumped on a broken piece of concrete and surveyed the damage, making quiet noises of displeasure. Dark water rushed through the ragged hole, and the pond behind the dam was nearly empty, its banks exposed and naked.

The armed Barzónistas had been here a day or two earlier. They had warned the police to stay clear, and the police listened, standing aside as the Barzónistas put their excavating machine to work breaking the dam. The Mennonites tried to stop them, starting a scuffle. The police, at first too afraid to intervene, finally waded in, firing their guns in the air to break up the melee. But by then it was too late, the water ran free.

The Mennonites were not only competing with the indigenous and Hispanic farms for land, but their intensive industrial farming practices pushed their fragile land to its very limits. The water table under the valley, which was surrounded by distant blue mountains, was running dry. The greed of the Mennonites over the remaining water was offending their neighbours.

"The Barzónistas say they help those that have been treated badly by others," John said. "If they see one person getting very rich, they see to it that he has to share that wealth. And that's what they say is happening here, that we Mennonites are not sharing the water with others. But the Mennonites didn't even build this dam, it was here when the farmer bought this piece of land many years ago."

The Barzónistas were named after the yoke ring to which a rope is attached to pull a plow, a term used in a Mexican revolutionary song about injustices against the farming class. They took up causes such as high electricity prices and indebtedness to banks. They blocked roads, picketed banks, bullied Mennonites, and planted the fear of mass revolt with their protests.

"*Debo, no niego, pago lo justo,*" (I owe, I don't deny it, I'll pay what is fair) they chanted in front of banks.

The socialist in me sympathized with the Barzónistas, and it was hard to ignore the better-than-them attitude of the Mennonites. Recent droughts had only made the disparity worse. The Mennonites had closed a few wells in concession, but they weren't being closed fast enough for the Barzónistas. So far, the Barzónistas had destroyed five dams, with twenty-three—or forty-three, depending on who you spoke to—more on their target list.

"Those dams provide water for a lot of cattle and irrigation, and without them these farms can't exist," John said.

Stories of standoffs between Mennonites and Barzónistas were multiplying by the day. One Barzónista interviewed by a newspaper described the Mennonites as Germans burning up Mexican lands like the Nazis had burned up the Jews. A Barzónista leader and his wife were shot dead, and their bodies turned up in a field near a Mennonite colony, raising suspicion that the Mennonites were involved in their deaths.

"What do the Mennonites in Canada say about this? Do they support us?" John asked. He cared deeply how other Mennonites viewed those in Mexico and asked repeatedly how different aspects of Mexican Mennonite life were perceived in Canada.

I had to confess I didn't know, it wasn't something I'd heard discussed in Canada. I suspected that Mennonite farmers in Canada would take the side of their brethren in Mexico. Their conflict with Mexicans was comparable to the view most Mennonites took of Indigenous people in Canada. Yes, it was too bad, all that poverty and abuse and victimization, but they should fix it themselves, like the Mennonites did. It didn't matter if you didn't have bootstraps to pull yourself up by.

"It's not good, the image that this gives Mennonites here in Mexico," John said. "One farmer, when the Barzónistas came to his farm to tear down his dam, he told them they shouldn't do this, that it was wrong. But they wouldn't listen. So he told them he would cook them a meal, and then after they'd shared a meal maybe they would leave the dam. He kept his word and made them a meal, but they wouldn't eat the food, that was just too much for them, although they did take a drink from him. There were government officials there with the Barzónistas, and the farmer showed the officials that his dam didn't block a river, it just kept water that was already on his land from leaving. The government officials agreed, told the Barzónistas not to destroy the dam, and then left. As soon as they left the Barzónistas knocked the dam down, and the farmer just stood there, there was nothing he could do.

"Giving them a meal doesn't make the problem go away," John said. "But it makes them weak, and it brings the government to our side. If he'd come out there with a rifle, he would not have won the respect that he has won now."

Offering the other cheek, like the character Dirk Willems in *Martyrs Mirror*, a book describing the persecution of the early Anabaptists. Dirk was arrested in Asperen, Holland, in 1569 for being an Anabaptist. He escaped and fled across a frozen lake. His pursuer fell through the ice, and Dirk turned back to save him. That good deed meant he was recaptured and later burned at the stake. Mennonites held up the story of Dirk as the epitome of their pacifism and servitude.

John and his neighbours saw themselves as a hard-working, hard-done-by people, playing an important role in Mexico's agricultural economy with no thanks from the Mexicans. If the Mennonites were breaking laws, it was because that was just the way business was done here. Mennonites like to pretend that we stand apart from the rest of society, that we let others control the levers of power, and therefore can never be sure when the circumstances will turn against us. Never mind that as large-scale landowners and employers of indigenous and economically depressed people we are part of the system, a key part of the power structure. Never mind the *Privilegia* we've been granted.

This was just the latest chapter in the often-repeated narrative of Mennonites as a wandering people continuously unwanted and rejected from their various temporary homes. Mennonites embrace this victimhood. We work so hard, we bring virtue and honesty to these places, but still we are rejected. The forces that push us on to the next country—whether that is Russia, Canada, or Mexico—are always out of our control because we are the outsiders. Mennonites believe that each new slight against us, each forced sale of our recently colonized land, is a test of our faith. It's God's will. He wants to see how loyal and loving we really are. Poor, righteous Mennonites. We're just innocent bystanders, who work so hard but don't fight for our rights. We are the real victims, and because we don't have brown skin that we can show to the government to get handouts and tax breaks, we are the victims. Bullshit.

The extra dollop of whipped cream on this tasty pie of self-serving victimhood is that we still show Christian love for those who wrong us. Like Dirk saving his pursuer and the farmer feeding the Barzónistas. In Russia the Mennonites opened their doors to bandits and treated them well: fed them, and warmed them by their fires, and this dulled their hate and anger. And the Mennonite victims were even more righteous for it.

This was the multi-generational, ocean-crossing story John was telling me as we drove through the colonies. When conversation waned, John would break into song, switching between singing and whistling, all the while pointing out the sights as we drove through the countryside: "He leadeth me, He leadeth me, / By His own hand He leadeth me."

"My wife and I like to sing and play music together in the evenings, and now we have even recorded ourselves. Here, listen to this one." He pushed a home-recorded CD into the player. Soon I could hear his whistling accompanied by a ragged banjo and then a harmonica.

"Oh, it's time for Bram's show," John said as he ejected the CD and turned on the radio.

Bram was starting his daily Dietschet Radio Programme on XEPL, a mix of news and commentary. Every word Bram uttered was dissected and discussed in the colonies. His opinions were more liberal than those of many listeners, but he was aware of where the line of tolerance was, and he toed it carefully.

"Now we get to the matter that everyone here is talking about," Bram said in Plautdietsch. His familiar voice crackled over the airwaves. "This problem with the wells and dams is easy to see from a business point of view. Our farms need that water. But what if we approach it as Christians, what would we do differently then?"

John hmm'd in agreement. "I admit, we're not innocent in this matter," he said as we drove by giant sprinkling systems that marched their way across fields of corn and created rainbows and lush crops in an otherwise parched landscape.

"But still, the Mexicans are taking it too far," he said, an injured tone in his voice. "I think, from our experience with the government, they will give us money to fix the dams."

The Mennonites had a generally warm relationship with the local government because they generated a lot of taxes, provided much of their own social services and infrastructure, and lived peaceful, quiet lives. The government was keen to keep the Mennonites happy.

The Mennonites were accused of—and admitted to—drilling illegal wells for the purpose of irrigating their fields. They had drilled too many wells, bigger wells than their licences allowed, and had drilled the wells too deep or too close together. Sometimes their licences and permits were obtained through bribes paid to government officials. The going price for false papers to drill a well was in the neighbourhood of US $40,000. The wealth and readiness of Mennonites to pay bribes had created a cozy, if complicated, relationship with the officials. The Mennonites shrugged their shoulders and said it was the only way to get things done here in Mexico.

"It's just like in Russia," John continued. "The Mennonites became wealthy and powerful, with big grain farms and businesses. We had our own hospitals, orphanages, and mission organizations. Just like here. And we also didn't fit in there, because we spoke German and didn't want to be Russian."

The Mennonites had made little effort to assimilate in Mexico, and this only magnified the spite of their critics. It wasn't hard to imagine why the Barzónistas might resent that the Mennonites had moved in and bought up the land. The Mennonites were referred to as "Menones," a name that had taken on a derogatory tone. The Mennonites, ignoring the fact that many of them were born in Mexico and carried Mexican passports, referred to the Spanish Mexicans as Mexas and Sponsch, and the names were not spoken in a tone of respect. Caucasians who were not Mennonite were often colloquially referred to as Enjlisch.

I spent hours riding the colony roads, admiring what the Mennonites had created. The soil around the city was a deep red that contrasted with the bright green of the crops and the hazy blue foothills of the Sierra Madre Occidental to the west. Many farmers were still planting in mid-July, and shiny red, green, and yellow tractors crawled across the fields, chased by clouds of red dust.

Riding my motorcycle gave me a lot of time to think. I caught myself thinking in Plautdietsch for the first time in my life. I'd spoken Plautdietsch before English as a child, but as soon as I'd started school it became uncool to speak it. I understood it, and my parents might speak to me in Plautdietsch, but I replied in English. Now I had a terrible accent and limited vocabulary, and my family snickered every time I tried to speak it. When I'd first arrived at the Travellers Inn on Manitoba Colony I had the odd experience of checking into a hotel in my mother tongue for the first time in my life. Check-in...how would I say that in Plautdietsch? At the Los Arcos restaurant next door, I was amused when the waitress greeted and served me in the flat, guttural tones of the language I'd heard since childhood, but rarely used myself. It reminded me of my attempts to speak Chinese—stringing together words to explain something when I knew there must be a single word that would do a better job of it. It didn't help that the Mennonites here were more likely to revert to Spanish than to English, and I didn't speak Spanish.

When I'd finished my lunch, I paused. How to say "Check please"? or "I'd like my bill"?

"*Etj welle nü betohle*," I called out to the waitress as she passed. The look of surprise she gave me told me she'd understood, but that it wasn't how most people asked for the check.

But I liked how Plautdietsch changed my inner dialogue. There was less debate, and it made my thoughts more blunt and rudimentary. Plautdietsch offers very little nuance unless you're describing rainfall or cow manure.

"What if I'd stayed in Manitoba. I wonder how these Mennonites would appear to me then? I'm different too. Or maybe that's just in my head," I thought, hunched over the handlebars.

The constant need of Mennonites to be different, the fear of belonging to something they don't wholly agree with or embrace—I could see that in myself. Was that a remnant of my Mennonite identity? I joked with friends that I was a commitment-phobe, but I wondered if it was just another case of a Mennonite resisting assimilation. I'd always liked that part of being a journalist—being an observer, an outsider to every meeting, plan, or crisis. Like a Mennonite farmer who does all his business and shopping in town, but never says he's from there. He's Mennonite; he can't belong to a town full of *weltmensch*.

The Mennonites in Mexico didn't even get along with their Mexican neighbours well enough to share a bank with them. The Unión de Crédito Agricultores de Cuauhtémoc was in a colonnaded brick building at a key road junction between Cuauhtémoc and the Mennonite colonies to the north. This was where the Mennonites hoarded the rewards of all their hard work taming the land. Within twenty years of its founding it became the third largest credit union in Mexico.

The credit union served the entire spectrum of the Mennonite community. Families from the Old Colony church, with the men in *schlaub'betjse* and their stolid wives in long dark dresses and black head coverings, shushing barefooted children in the waiting area. In the couples from more moderate church groups it was only the women who wore distinctive clothing, a small headscarf or a dress that was unfashionably modest. Then there were the most progressive Mennonite farmers, dressed no differently than the Mexicans, in jeans and scuffed cowboy boots, pale foreheads glowing above sun-raw faces when they took off their tall white cowboy hats. Mennonite churches were divided by arcane differences in biblical interpretation such as what colour of head covering the women wore, whether men wore *schlaub'bet-jse* or regular trousers and whether the children were educated in German or English. But Mennonites of different stripes could peacefully coexist under the same roof when it came to money.

Most local Mennonites didn't have the necessary education to work at the bank. Attempts to train young Mennonites for a career in finance failed because they could earn quicker money in manual labour, farming, and industry. So the Mennonites hired Mexicans to count their money. Nearly every teller was Mexican and the women outnumbered men. The women were dressed in urban office attire, high heels, knee-length skirts, and makeup, while the Mennonite women customers waited in their drab dresses and black kerchiefs. But it was the drab ones who owned the bank. I looked at the drab ones, and then at the coiffed, confident women behind the counter, and I felt no connection to my people.

The credit union lent money exclusively to Mennonites, although a few wealthy Mexican landowners were granted the privilege of depositing their money with the Mennonites so they could enjoy the higher interest rates the credit union offered. The Mennonites were well aware that their isolation benefited them, and they didn't want to erode that advantage by lending money to those untrustworthy Mexas.

I spent several days with John, until we were familiar enough that he invited me to stay in his guest house, built into a corner of his machine shed. It was where he and his wife had lived before they had the money to build the simple house they now lived in.

"This is my *frü*," John said as his wife came to the door.

He did not offer her name. She smiled at me, saying nothing. She wore a plain dark dress, a dark kerchief covering her head.

"He's come from Canada by motorcycle. I told him he was welcome to stay with us. You can set another place for dinner, right?"

She nodded and disappeared into the kitchen; the perfect demure Mennonite wife.

And with the offer of dinner and a bed for the night came an invitation to attend evening service at the Steinreich Conferencia Menonita de Mexico church. The church was next door, across John's lawn and through a row of trees.

Their church was running the traditional, week-long series of evening sermons often called revival meetings. Normally run in spring or early summer just after the seeding season, such services are a tradition of Mennonite community life. The sermons are often delivered by a visiting preacher who attempts to spark spiritual renewal and public professions of faith. I still had strong memories of the revival meetings of my childhood, particularly the foreboding sense of guilt they brought, the tearful confessions and trips to the front of the sanctuary where we would kneel for prayer. "Rededicating" your life was a teenage rite of passage in our church. It meant confessing all the bad things you'd done and promising to try harder in the future, and the exercise won you praise. But capitulating too often wasn't good either, you had to strike a balance. I also remembered the drowsy monotony of the services. My friends and I held vigil over the heads of the tired farmers and mothers, breaking into snickers when their heads would roll and lurch with exhaustion. I told John I'd be thrilled to join him at church.

Like most Mennonite churches, John's church was very plain. The faith and the people made the church, not the building. I liked that aspect of Mennonite churches, and the honesty it suggested. White walls and a tile floor contained rows of straight-backed wooden pews. This was an informal weekday service: the newest jeans, clean of course, cowboy boots, simple dresses. Families sat together, toddlers trampled on laps, some fathers tried to assist mothers with the brood while others were oblivious to the chaos.

Worshippers exchanged subdued greetings, nods and smiles for their neighbours as they filed into the pews. It was very similar to the church I'd grown up in.

The service started with German hymns and choruses accompanied by guitars and a piano. The *Evangeliums—Lieder* hymnals smelled musty with a hint of varnish from the racks on the backs of the pews. Strong baritone and tenor voices filled the church. There was no raising of hands or swaying to the music— that would be too flashy. Just sing with all your heart. Then the children were invited to the front for a Bible story. The herd of children that ran up the aisle was testament to the community's longevity. The entire congregation craned their necks to listen, as well as to see that little Frieda and Henry were behaving themselves. There was laughter at the children's naive responses to the lesson. When it was over, they stampeded back to their pews, but a few stragglers wandered up and down the aisle, fingers stuck in slobbery mouth, eyes wide with alarm as they searched the crowd for their parents.

Then the sermon. The preacher, from a neighbouring church, began with a few anecdotes, a bit of mild humour, delivered with humble candour in Plautdietsch. His slight social distance from the congregation gave him the liberty and authority to chastise them. His message was one of morality and clean living. There were little things in everyone's lives that were sinful and very hard to give up.

"Salt must remain salty," he intoned. "If the salt is no longer salty, it doesn't make your beans taste any better, does it?"

Delivering less than a kilo of beef when you were paid for a full kilo was a sin, just like pride, and lust for money, power, and recognition. He paced back and forth behind the pulpit, occasionally pausing to check his notes on an iPad. He knew his audience, knew their language and their way of thinking, and he was a masterful speaker. He admitted his own failings and weaknesses, beseeching all to work together to live better, holier lives.

"Don't let those things that bring short-term benefits distract you. These things have no place in a Christian's life."

The air was hot and stuffy. Just one fan whirred near the ceiling. Heads began to nod and people fidgeted and shifted in the hard pews. Some people remained alert by following each Bible reference the preacher mentioned, flipping through their Bibles in a whisper of India paper. Then, when the muggy sanctuary was still like a pond, a motorbike passed the church with a Doppler whine. Heads swivelled towards the windows. The bike was gone, but the dust from its passing still hung in the air. Who in the village was not at the service? Who was outside, playing in the dying light and evening coolness, when they should be sitting here, listening to this good sermon? I shared in the curiosity, but I also knew that feeling of tearing past on the road, filled with glee and a tinge of guilt at my escape.

The song leader returned to the front of the church and we sang a closing song that evoked sentiments of hope and humility. The preacher delivered a homily, something familiar and final. Eyes reopened and children ran for the doors.

John introduced me to family and friends on our way out into the cool evening air.

"It was interesting to hear him talk about resisting the vices that come with a life of wealth and power," I said. "But nothing about how to get along with people around you."

John chuckled. "If we can't get along with people we just move somewhere else, and we think there it will work better," John said. "But if we don't solve our problems they'll just follow us to the new place, and we'll be fighting there. But that's how we are taught. Better to go start a farm and dig a well in some other place if there are problems where we are."

Some thought it might be even better to go back to the place they'd come from.

CHAPTER 4

Mexico

A Return to Russia

I was thinking about how Russia had gone from being a utopia to holding a place of horror in our hearts. The Mennonites there went from having everything to losing it all, and then we were driven from the land.

These thoughts distracted me as I rode several hours north of Cuauhtémoc on a two-lane strip of tarmac that passed through the farmland of northern Mexico. I'd been in the colonies for several days, and it felt good to ride the open highway on my bike again, the howl of the engine opening my mind to daydreams. Row upon row of corn and soybeans flashed by with rhythmic conformity. The land had just enough contours to it that approaching cars dipped in and out of view as they crossed the hills. The farms had tin windmills and fences and trees in rigid straight lines against the hazy backdrop of the Sierra Madre Occidental range. We'd had it just as good as this in Russia and look what had happened. Again and again.

First, in the early-to-mid 16th century, we fled the Catholics in the Low Countries and went to West Prussia, where the king and the rich landowners welcomed us to settle in the Vistula delta and gave us a *Privilegium*. We drained the swamps, because we knew how to do that from living in the Low Countries, and built farms. It was during our more than two centuries in West Prussia that speaking Plautdietsch and eating *zwieback* and *foarmaworscht* and living on colonies became the Mennonite way of life.

But then there was a war, and King Frederick William II of Prussia needed soldiers. He didn't respect the *Privilegium*, and he didn't give the Mennonites special treatment like previous kings had. Soon families were saving money to buy their sons out of the military. And we needed more land, so we started looking for a new place.

The Mennonites sent scouts to southern Russia, where Catherine the Great had issued a manifesto inviting European colonists. She welcomed the Mennonites, promising land for every family, and plenty of wood, fish, and hay. She would give the Mennonites credit to build farms, and the best part of all: they would not have to join the army. Another *Privilegium*. They accepted Catherine's offer and became rich, buying more land and building bigger barns and houses. Soon the Russians were working for the Mennonites, and they learned to speak Plautdietsch if they wanted to eat.

But in the 1870s the rules in Russia changed, which is when Johann packed his bags for Canada. The wealthiest Mennonites— the ones who couldn't bear to lose what they'd earned through such hard work—chose to stay in Russia. Those who remained in Russia suffered horrible indignities during the Bolshevik Revolution and the World Wars, and we were taught to be thankful that our forefathers left when they did. Those of us that moved first had put value in our religious principles above our riches, and that had saved us.

Those Mennonites who remained in Russia soon lost their autonomy and property. The Red and White Armies took turns pillaging food and livestock from the Mennonites, and Mennonite industries were seized by the military. Anarchists attacked the wealthy farmers, and the Mennonites' Germanic background bred suspicion among the Russians. Mennonites were murdered, robbed, raped, and imprisoned. Religious freedoms were restricted, and churches were monitored by the government. Many of the remaining Mennonites fled Russia in the 1920s, with more following after World War II.

So, in Mennonite minds, Russia was a place of tragic failure and broken trust, of bad things done to decent people. Whenever Russia was mentioned the elders shook their heads with sadness. The name *Stalin* and the word *communist* sent shivers down our backs as children. If something was bad, hopeless, and cold, my father would compare it to godless Russia. For us, the fear of Russian invasion went far deeper than Cold War nuclear threats. Russia was the ultimate bogeyman, representing the evil in all our bad dreams. When, as children, we were caught tormenting each other, my grandmother scolded us for acting "like communists."

The biggest threat of Russia's communism was the godlessness of it. During the Cold War and the threat of Soviet invasion we asked ourselves, How would we live under such *gottloos mensch*? If those godless people torture me, will I still be brave enough to say I love Jesus? What would come first, the rapture or the Russians, and which would be scarier? As a child, I thought if the communists came to Canada and forced me to decry Jesus, I'd go to hell. That was a real enough fear to warrant fervent prayers, said in my pajamas, kneeling beside my bed.

I was jolted from my thoughts by a major highway intersection, the one I had been told would appear after the place I was looking for. *After*—so I'd driven too far. I wheeled my bike around and spotted my destination, Gas K-19, on my return. Steel tanks, rust peeking through their paint, sheds, and bits of machinery filled the yard. A small office building with a front porch. The rotten-egg stench of propane filled the air. I splashed through a large puddle in the middle of the yard and found a firm patch of ground that would support the kickstand of my motorcycle.

I knocked the mud off my boots on the porch of Gas K-19, which took some time given the rain, and walked into the office. Through a back door of the office I could see the *schmiede* (metal workshop), and hear the sizzle of a welder, the clang and rattle of metal and machinery.

"Hallo," said the burly blond machinist with a grime-streaked face. He was standing behind a high counter.

"How can I help you?" he asked in Plautdietsch. The height of the counter combined with the shortness of my legs made me uncomfortable, and I took a step back.

"Sounds like you're busy today," I said, peering over the counter and around his shoulder at the work going on in the *schmiede* behind him.

He nodded. Too busy to make conversation.

"Is Hein Voth in?" I said. His full name was Enrique Voth Penner, but I had been told to just ask for Hein Voth.

The worker gave me a look that suggested he'd been asked this before. Hein had people talking.

Hein appeared, giving me a curious look over the counter. I introduced myself, then stumbled as I tried to explain why I'd come looking for him.

"People told me you're the guy who knows something about this Russia thing. I don't know…do you have a few minutes to talk?"

A pained look crossed Hein's face. He looked at his watch, then led me down the hallway to his office.

"Ya, a few minutes, sure."

Hein was tall, with trim grey hair and wire-rim glasses. He wore cowboy boots and jeans held up by a silver-trimmed belt. The pocket of his blue long-sleeved shirt bulged with pens and a box cutter. He carried himself with energy and confidence: a modest Mennonite businessman.

Hein was Sommerfeld, a branch of the Mennonite community that embraces social conservatism while adopting any technological advances available in their farms and businesses. His people had fled from Russia to Canada in the same wave as my great-grandfather Johann, and then some of them came to Mexico. Sommerfeld women dressed conservatively, with small head coverings, but they drove cars and trucks and knew the value of computers when it came to marketing their crops and managing their businesses.

The shelves in Hein's office were cluttered with miniature mustang horses and Mustang cars. A bull's head hung on the wall and a brown leather saddle was slung across a frame. These were the icons of Mexican *gaucho* lifestyle, a pop culture familiar to the Mennonites and their relationship with the land, even though it was the folklore and spirit of another people. From a Mennonite point of view it was a safe form of pop culture.

"You like horses a lot. Or is it the car you like most?" I said, pointing at the red model sports car.

"All of it. I like that kind of stuff," Hein said, adding a nervous laugh.

"You drive a Mustang?"

"No," he said, waving at the air as if that was a ridiculous suggestion. "Nice cars, but no."

"Horses? You ride horses?"

"A bit, sure. But I just like the…" Hein waved at the paraphernalia.

When Mennonites move across oceans, into deserts and the deep forest, they often say they are doing so to escape from the influences of the world, in order to live separate. But it never works. They always absorb their surroundings and the cultures they imagine themselves isolated from, like islands. They can't stop the sea from lapping at their shores. I thought of the Mennonite restaurants that dotted the colonies, serving a mix of Mexican and Mennonite staples. *Caldo de res* and *chile rellenos* next to *foarmaworscht* and *koomst borscht*. The *borscht* was adopted on the steppes of southern Russia, the *caldo* here on the dry plains of northern Mexico, and they'd both become staples of Mennonite cuisine. So much for being pure Mennonite.

"So I wanted to hear more about this move to Russia," I said. Move to Russia. Just saying that was enough to startle me. Mennonites were not meant to move back to Russia.

Hein winced, pursing his lips.

"I'm a bit worried over what people will say if they know," he said. "It's not a good time, with what is happening between Mennonites and the Mexicans. Everyone is upset, who knows what could happen if they know we want to leave. What are you writing for? A newspaper? I don't want to have my name in a newspaper about this now."

I assured him that I wasn't writing for a newspaper. No one in Mexico would be reading what I was writing for a long time.

"It's for a book."

Hein nodded, satisfied.

"The issue is that there is not enough land," Hein said as he settled into a chair behind his desk. "If we had ten times more land, I think we could have that in crops right away, it would not be enough. Also, there's not enough water here. We need water and we need more land for the poor Mennonites. How can we make this work for the poor, so that they can benefit?"

One hundred and forty years ago the Mennonites' search for a new home away from Russia was driven by faith and culture and the belief that to assimilate was to lose it all. At least that's what we were always told it was about. In reality, two-thirds of the families in Johann's Molochna Colony were landless, and the lure of land certainly made the move easier. But this time land was the sole motive. The same methods could serve different purposes.

The 7,000 Mennonites who moved to Chihuahua in the 1920s had multiplied nearly tenfold in population but they weren't able to add land at the same rate that they had children. Now, with droughts year after year, each hectare felt smaller than ever. Land prices had soared beyond the reach of small farmers, with irrigated land near the colonies selling for prices similar to those recorded in the US Midwest.

In 1983 some of Mexico's Mennonites moved farther south to Campeche state, where land was more affordable. Fifty years later they had once again outgrown their land, and one of the Campeche colonies purchased a 15,700-hectare plot of land in the neighbouring state, where they were starting a new colony, creating more space for expansion. Others moved to Belize, Bolivia, and Paraguay, and soon I would see for myself the colonies they had created in these places. Some even moved north to Texas, but no one had considered moving back to Russia. Until now.

"We'll have to negotiate our own deals with the sellers," Hein said. "The government won't set up the deal for us. But they said the land there can be bought for a tenth of what it costs here."

Hein's eyes shone as he said this. The promise was just so great. What a sucker, I thought.

When Joseluis Gomez-Rodriguez, a Canadian-educated Mexican businessman living in Russia, came knocking on Mennonite doors he found willing listeners. Joseluis acted as a land agent and invited the Mennonites to visit the Russian Republic of Tatarstan, which is rich in oil, natural gas, and farmland and nestled between the Volga River and the Ural Mountains. Land was plentiful and affordable and tax breaks and freedom were there for the taking.

Not exactly a *Privilegium*, but many of the same commitments as those made when Johann made the journey from Russia. When Johann was planning his escape from Russia there were agents, unseen men working from the world's greatest cities. Their names—Hespeler, Jansen, Shantz—became bywords of hope and opportunity to the immigrants. These contacts offered help: they would find financing, they had spoken to the men in power and would have everything ready for their arrival. Now Hein and his neighbours were putting that same trust in Joseluis.

"He said that there are some Muslims there," Hein said, referring to Joseluis's description of the Tatars, a Turkic minority. "But there are still five million hectares of land available if we want it, and they will give us some tax breaks."

Joseluis's promises sounded like a familiar refrain, sung by a new agent every time the Mennonites prospected for new homeland. But there was also another repetitive factor at play.

Mennonites such as Hein could negotiate with officials from a vastly different culture, build and run a successful business, and invent and then manufacture clever, well-built products that no one else had thought of. They could create a community, learn new languages and adapt to foreign lands, and become rich within a generation of landing on foreign soil. They could do all those things to survive. They could learn whatever was needed to make the farm work, to build up the business, to ensure Mennonite prosperity. It was in their DNA, it was what Mennonites did.

What Mennonites didn't do, and what their village schools

didn't teach, was to think beyond the physical, practical matters of building farms and feeding families, unless it involved memorizing the biblical truths. To weigh up the political, the abstract, or the historical context, was trying to measure those forces best left to the Lord's control.

"What do you think of Putin?" I asked. Hein looked at me, questioning.

"I don't know much about that," he said.

"Well, he's very nationalistic, for the old Russian motherland," I explained. "Russification is a big thing now, the same as when we left Russia, and they don't always welcome foreigners."

Hein shrugged in dismissal and indifference. Russian politics were of little interest to him.

"We want them to guarantee our freedom. We want them to commit to us that we won't have to serve in the military, that we can have our own schools," he said. "They have already promised us this, on a provisional basis, but not officially."

Freedom, *independence,* and *opportunity* were not the words that came to my mind when I thought of Putin's Russia. Hein used these words with naive hope, praying them into truth so that the Mennonites could take advantage of this golden opportunity. Russia's iron-fisted control of its people, churches, and media weren't factors in his consideration. Those were faraway problems, far from the pressing need for land and a fresh start.

"So Tatarstan. Where exactly is that in Russia?" I asked, turning to more practical matters.

"It's somewhere in the northeast, I think," Hein said. He made a round globe with his hands, looking at me questioningly. "But of course once you're there...well, the world is round, it will be...where? Which side of the country?"

We turned to the computer on his desk, and he seemed as interested as I to see where Tatarstan was located, about eight hundred kilometres east of Moscow. Not in the northeast, but in the southwest of the country.

Many of the farmers sizing up a move to Russia were struggling to match the economic growth they saw some of their wealthier neighbours enjoying. They looked at Russia as a second chance to build financial security. This was also in keeping with tradition. Many of the first Mennonites who left Manitoba for Mexico in the 1920s were struggling farmers rather than successful ones, just as many of the first ones to leave Russia for North America were landless.

I don't know what our family's financial situation was in Russia, but I did learn that Johann's father, my great-great-grandfather, was an occasional farmer who also worked as a teacher. At small Mennonite schools there a long tradition of male teachers being the ones who were bad at farming, or seen as weak or frail, forced into a last-resort type of job. The female teachers were spinsters, the women who couldn't get married and have their own children. My great-grandfather Johann became a teacher like his father, so I come from a family of bad farmers. Being a writer has similarities to teaching, and I'm a bad farmer, so I see the family resemblance. Knowing they were teachers also makes me feel safe in concluding that our flight to the New World was at least partially driven by economic factors. The wealthy always remained, hoping that conditions would improve and allow them to keep their well-established farms.

"Maybe Russia can be a new start for the poor," Hein said. "Mennonites, we need to own something, to have our own business, our own thing. We don't like to work for others on an hourly wage. That's not our way."

I took in his shop, employees, and tanks full of fuel with a sweep of my arm. "Your business here looks successful. You'd be willing to sell it and move to Russia?" I asked.

Hein looked uncertain. "Well, who knows. We have to see first. I might not even move there myself. But I can still help the others that are sure they want to move."

The wealth divide among Mennonites was growing wider, and it was often viewed in terms of land, rather than of the truck they drove, the house they built, or the vacations they took. It was still seen as distasteful, sinful even, some might say, to flash your cash. My father intentionally bought used cars instead of new fancy models, even though he could afford better.

"I'd feel funny driving a fancy new car when others can't afford one," he'd say.

Some Mennonites took it even further, prying chrome off the fenders of newly purchased cars in order to make them look more humble. Having a big farm was more acceptable, though it didn't stop people from talking. How many hectares is that family farming? That son will inherit it all! The poor muttered that the avarice of the rich stood between them and God, while the rich were content knowing that their wealth gave them power and position in the community, which was almost as good as genuine probity anyway.

Land within the boundaries of the Mennonite colony in Mexico was much more expensive than "Mexican" land because it included the roads and irrigation systems built by the Mennonites, and it was closer to their slaughterhouses and cheese factories.

"We don't know how long we will be able to stand it here, doors are closing for us. People with money can still buy land, but the poor cannot. The fat, they can feast, and the poor, they get skinnier," Hein complained bitterly. "The poor have no say, no power. The rich here don't let the poor starve by a long shot. They give money, but not enough for the poor to get their own land. When the rich man and the poor man are fishing side by side, it is the rich man who is catching fish and the poor man who remains hungry."

Land, and the gulf between have and have-not Mennonites, gave Hein and his group a sense of urgency. But the bickering over water supplies and the growing friction between Mennonites and Mexicans also set the stage for a well-rehearsed grouse among the Mennonites.

"We can see that here the Mexican people are no longer on our side, they don't like us anymore," Hein told me with a glum face.

Mennonites appeared affronted that some of the Mexicans didn't want them as neighbours. They were hard-working and clean-living, and their businesses provided jobs for Mennonites and Mexicans alike. Their infringements—buying up land, farming it intensively, and sucking up all available water supplies, refusing assimilation and fostering a righteous superiority over their neighbours—struck them as too nuanced to be taken so seriously. Once again, Mennonites were the nationless martyrs and victims.

"The Mennonite people have no fatherland," Hein said. "We are strangers in this land. If it were our land, we'd set things up and fix these matters so that we could be successful, but we can't, it's not within our power to do so. Now our freedom to grow is gone, so we have to go where we can grow. That is how it has always been. We will never find a fatherland, it will always be like this. The Bible says that we Christians will always be moving, that we will never be at rest. That is God's plan. I feel that doing this is part of God's plan."

"Your own family was forced to flee Russia, and now you want to go back," I said. "The story of how Russia treated us has been a big part of our culture for 150 years. Do you ever think of that history when you make these plans?"

Hein twisted his mouth in the shape of dismissal before speaking. "If we are Christly people God will carry us. I know that Christianity is not strong in Russia. We think the Russian people are good people now, but yes, it could happen again, those terrible things that happened, and we'd have to leave again. Many people here are against the idea, they still have bad feelings for Russia. One preacher said to me, 'That what happened may be over, but I still don't like the Russians.'"

The moves to Prussia, then Russia, Canada, and Mexico, and now back to Russia were all based on promises that the Mennonites would have their home, would be left alone to farm and raise their families. In reality, each king, queen, and government making those commitments also needed the Mennonites to feed and build their growing nations. And, if the plan worked, the nation would reach a level of sophistication, density and modernity that would be unacceptable to the Mennonites.

So Hein was right—the Mennonites who refused to integrate and adapt were damned to an endless wandering, arriving in underdeveloped, impoverished nations and then choosing to leave once that nation was on its feet. The offers always sounded tempting when heard from halfway around the world, when the Mennonites were once again coming to the end of one of their cycles.

Those Mennonites content to remain in Mexico viewed Hein and his group curiously, even expectantly. What would they find in Russia? Some hoped for reports of a new promised land. History had shown that if the first group was able to establish a beachhead more would follow.

But, like in previous migrations, there was also a feeling among the broader community that it wasn't quite that bad where they were, that Hein was overreacting a bit. The fact that it was often the poor who moved first was fodder for snide comments long after they left. The Mennonites who remained in Russia in Johann's time surely mocked the poor, hope-filled farmers who had left, just as those of us who remained in Canada disparaged the Mennonites who moved south. Now it was the Mexican Mennonites who looked askance at those considering a move to Russia.

But they did hope that, now that Russia was no longer communist, their neighbours would once again be successful colonialists. Russia had cost Mennonites much pain and blood, but most of that was directly blamed on communism. That word, *communism*, had become so loaded with mistrust and misconceptions that its removal left only a plot of virgin fertile land in people's minds.

Hein and his group were still a long way away from selling their homes and moving to Russia. First, they needed to go on a scouting trip, and Hein was anxious with travel arrangements. A group of eleven men, those who were known for their business acumen and eye for land, collected US $55,000 from potential immigrants to pay for a reconnaissance tour of western Russia.

Russian farmers in the region had experienced their own droughts in recent years, but the dark soil still looked fertile in comparison to that of northern Mexico. The conditions in Russia were closer to those of their old homes in the Canadian Prairies than their Mexican home. Winters in Tatarstan are cold, summers mild, perfect for growing wheat, sugar beets, and potatoes.

"We are a bit nervous about it all, but we are going now to look, not to buy," Hein said. "I've been amazed at how many people came and asked about this. We do not have any fixed numbers on how many will go right now, if it were to happen, but many come to me and say, 'If this happens, I want to come along.'"

"We think that if we do have to move, then this opportunity in Russia could be an open door for us given the situation here. Mennonites did very well in Russia, and we were good, peaceful people. Maybe the Russians remember that."

"*Na yo*," Hein said as escorted me to the door. He stood on the porch and watched me put my helmet and jacket on. It was still wet outside. Not raining, but a shower had just passed, or another was about to start.

"If it keeps raining like this maybe you won't need to go to Russia," I said, shouting to be heard through my helmet. "There will be enough water for everyone."

Hein gave me a faint smile and raised his eyebrows to acknowledge my comment. Clearly, a little rain wasn't going to put him off his plan.

CHAPTER 5

Mexico

Manitoba Colony

Manitoba Colony was still with afternoon heat. It was Sunday, a week after I had arrived, and the tractors were parked. The pickup trucks drove right past the farm-supply stores on the Mennonite Corridor and instead stopped at the ice cream parlours. A fresh breeze ruffled the fields of lush corn that continued on with their work while the masters rested. Families were at home or visiting neighbours and relatives. They could *spezear*—casually banter about local news, farming plans, and church gossip—for hours on end, interrupted only by *meddach'schlop*. The weekly afternoon nap was dear to the hearts of hard-working Mennonite farmers and remained central to the Sunday schedule.

It was a stillness that I remembered well from growing up, when only the essential farm work was done—collecting eggs, milking cows, and feeding livestock—but field work was forbidden. Everyone went to church in the morning and then, usually with guests or extended family, ate a large lunch. In the afternoon the farmers lolled on couches or in the shade of their backyards, *spezearing* and retelling stories we'd all heard a hundred times, told through mouths full of sunflower seeds. Pure laziness reigned, on Sundays and Sundays only. As the afternoon shadows grew longer guests would shift to a different home, like a game of musical chairs. We would arrive at our neighbour's or a relative's home unannounced, and it was expected that they would serve *faspa*, a light meal of *zwieback*, the white rolls made on Saturday for Sunday consumption, cheddar cheese, cold meats, pickles, and pastries, and *plümemoos*, a cold, milky plum pudding, all washed down with gallons of coffee. *Faspa* was eaten only on Sundays and holidays. In summer it often ended with watermelon served with *roll'kuake*, lightly salted deep-fried dough dipped in Rogers Golden Syrup.

The indolence was stifling for us children. Not that we were eager for more farmwork, but the stillness of a Sunday afternoon, when adults were hard to rouse into action, was the opposite extreme. We rode our bicycles and wound down country roads on dirt bikes and three-wheelers, trailing plumes of dust. But all the roving across our Mennonite community could not hide the fact that nothing much would happen on this day.

I was staying in Bram's newspaper and radio offices in the heart of Manitoba Colony. The reporters were gone for the weekend, leaving me space to write and do laundry. But the Sunday-afternoon stillness brought back that old restlessness, so I hopped onto my bike and drove aimlessly through the colony, feeling fourteen again.

Young Mennonites roved the colony in groups. They parked their cars and trucks in small clusters on the roads and leaned on fenders, *spezearing*, free from the withering gaze of elders. Rock and Mexican pop music spilled from open doors. Some boys were red-faced and drunk, teetering in their tall-heeled cowboy boots, plaid shirts open a daring button or two lower than during the week, their tall white hats pushed back on sweaty foreheads. The girls with them, still wearing their long dresses but with their hair hanging free, flirted with the boys, running across the fields with a squeal when the boys gave chase.

Drinking is forbidden in most Mennonite communities. When I was a teen we drank secretly in rock quarries and around campfires, and if our parents caught us we were in big trouble. I was nervous when, already an adult, I had a glass of wine with a meal in the presence of my father. I still felt like I should hide the glass under the table.

Paradoxically, some of the most conservative Mennonite sects are also the most tolerant of drinking among youth—a less formalized or mythologized form of the *rumspringa* that the Amish practice. The partying is tolerated as long as teens don't mingle with *weltmensch* too much. Once they are baptized and have become members of the community they are expected to give up this behaviour. Baptism, which takes place in one's late teens or as a young adult, officially makes you a voting member of the church, and also the colony. Youthful misbehaviour is forgotten if the person makes a change in lifestyle, if they "grow up" and take on adult responsibilities in the family and community.

I stopped at a farm where a car and a pickup truck were parked side by side in the front yard, some of the young men sitting on the truck box while others lounged in the shade of a nearby tree. They were a mix of Old Colony and Kleine Gemeinde Mennonites, differentiated by their dress but united in their boredom. The Old Colony boys wore the bibbed overalls called *schlaub'betjse*, the Kleine Gemeinde wore plaid western shirts and jeans, dressed like cowboys. Some swigged cheap local mescal mixed with sports drink, others favoured whisky and cola. Conversation dropped to a murmur when I turned off my bike engine and greeted them in Plautdietsch. I introduced myself and they only nodded. Despite their outward bravado not one of them would look me in the eye, and the girls, even the one lying across a boy's lap in the back seat of a car, refused to acknowledge me or look in my direction.

"Good day to be lazy," I said in Plautdietsch.

There was a long silence before one of the boys answered. "Ya."

"So which of you lives here, on this farm?" I asked. I tried to turn it into a joke. "Who's the boss?"

They didn't find me funny. The same boy, shooting me a sidelong glance, answered: "We don't live here." Then he muttered something I couldn't hear, and his friends laughed.

I hung my helmet, which had a camera mounted on top, from the mirror of my motorcycle. I was adjusting the camera, hoping to capture the scene, when the talkative one sauntered towards me, a cigarette dangling from his lips. The mud on his trousers hinted that his legs had been unsteady for a few hours already. There was a puddle between us, and as he crossed it, he gave the water a kick, spraying me and a few of his friends with mud. He cackled with laughter while I tried to smile as I wiped the muddy water from my face, unsure if he was trying to be funny or intimidating.

"Is that thing on?" he asked, and pointed at the camera.

"No, it's not," I reassured him.

"Good. If you take pictures, I'll beat you up. We don't like to have our picture taken." He was close enough for me to smell his boozy breath as he rocked back and forth on the heels of his cowboy boots. He squinted at me, sizing me up. I smiled, doing my best to appear benign, unsure if he was about to take a swing at me. His friends were enjoying the suspense more than I was.

"Why is that?" I asked. "You seem to be pretty open-minded Mennonites. You're drinking and listening to music. Why no pictures? Where I grew up, in Canada, we could take pictures, but we weren't allowed to drink or smoke cigarettes."

He snorted and took a swig from the bottle dangling from his hand, and then recited the rules he was living by, in perfect cadence and rhyme.

"Ya, wie tjenne drintje, schmeatje enn fleatje, oba bild aufnehme doohne nijch." (Ya, we can drink, smoke, and swear, but we do not take pictures.)

A school bus pulled into the drive and disgorged a load of drunken, hyper Mennonite teens. The boys stumbled towards the low concrete wall and lined up to relieve themselves. The girls made a show of averting their eyes and screamed with laughter, their faces red from drinking and excitement. When the boys were done, they zipped up and stood about, swigging from bottles. They acknowledged but did not socialize with those who were there first. I asked one of the new arrivals where they had come from and who had organized the bus. Was this some kind of Mennonite pub crawl? There was a sullen, mumbled answer and another young man chimed in to claim they were part of a church group. That elicited a collective guffaw from the group. Soon the new arrivals piled back into the bus, and it lurched down the road with its drunken payload, a long toot of its horn saying goodbye to those who had never left their spot under the tree, where they swatted at flies and stared out into the empty, sunbaked yard.

"Do you ever go into Cuauhtémoc to drink in the bars and clubs rather than here?" I asked one of the boys under the tree. "It might be more fun than this."

He shook his head.

"They're full of Mexa," he said, shaking his head. "We're German, that's why we wouldn't drink with them. The Mexa shoot each other. It's too dangerous to go there."

Instead they opted to play out their frustrated boredom in the safety of their own community, a strategy I knew well from my own secretive rebellion in Mennville. There was a callowness to our teenage partying. Sheltered from pop culture and generally forbidden to associate with non-Mennonite teenagers, our curiosity and recalcitrance were expressed by building Saturday-night bonfires in the stone quarries, drinking ourselves silly on beer and vodka, and then making colossal efforts to appear in church the next morning. For all our attempts to reach beyond our village, we knew that we were just rowdy country bumpkins. Urban nightclubs filled with *weltmensch* were more intimidating than appealing. The swagger of an *off ya fallja* Mennonite, those who have "fallen away" from the church, is for the benefit of other Mennonites, not for outsiders.

Often the term *off ya fallja* was used with a smirk. It was reserved for those who had burst out of their repressed former lives with an embarrassingly energetic embrace of all things worldly, all things sinful. The more repressed they had been, the more pronounced the change when they became *off ya fallja*. Sometimes young men who came to Canada from the southern colonies became *off ya fallja*. They were excited by the freedom they discovered but they were still painfully unfashionable and intimidated by the outside world. Their idea of cool was often decades behind the current trends. They bought loud cars, listened to louder music, swilled cheap booze, wore sunglasses—forbidden by some sects—

and bragged about it all in stumbling flat-toned English that gave away their Mennonite roots no matter how hard they tried to bury them. The *off ya fallja* girls—always fewer than the boys—wore the tightest jeans they could find and applied makeup until it was impossible to tell if they were pretty or not.

These teens were curious about me, casting sidelong glances at me and whispering among themselves. One of the boys worked up the courage to ask me where I'd come from. How come I spoke Plautdietsch? I explained that I'd grown up in Canada, a place they were all familiar with because most of their families had come from Canada one or two generations earlier. I told them I now lived in Hong Kong, where I was a writer. They looked at me blankly.

"China," I said. Then they understood, vaguely. Successful Mennonite businessmen were known to travel to China in search of wholesale farm chemicals, machinery, and household goods.

"I'm riding to Bolivia, Paraguay, and Argentina," I said, knowing that many of them had relatives in those countries. They examined my motorcycle more carefully.

"It must go very fast, that bike. The trip won't take long," one of them said.

"Can I drive it?" the drunk one with the muddy trousers asked, grasping the handlebar and making a move to push me away from the bike.

I laughed nervously, and managed to convince him that it was a bad idea, given his state. "If you see me when you're sober, I'll let you take it for a ride," I said, hoping that would never happen.

Conversation had worn thin. The teens had lost interest in me but were not comfortable returning to their party with me nearby. A few of them wandered off behind the farmhouse. One of the girls suggested a new location, and they prepared to leave.

"*Na yo,*" I said. I had pulled on my helmet and started my motorcycle when the same belligerent boy came running from behind the house with a bucket of water in his hand, chasing a screeching girl across the yard.

When he saw me, he changed targets and veered towards me with stumbling steps. When he encountered the puddle in the middle of the yard he slipped and fell. His friends broke into laughter, and the girl he had been chasing bent over to catch her breath, laughing nervously, wary of the boy. His face, already red with drink, now turned dark with anger as he picked himself up, mud dripping from his clothes, to face me. I was astride my idling bike several metres away, but I needed to drive past him to exit the walled yard. I started off, weaving wide around him and the puddle. As I passed him, he made a lunge for me, missed, and then pitched the empty bucket at me. He missed again. And then again when he yelled an unintelligible insult at my back. I pulled onto the road, my revving engine failing to drown out the taunting shouts of his drunken friends.

I felt sorry for them. The elders said they were rebelling against God, against the faith itself, but it was more complicated than that. I knew this myself, from my own experience. Their embittered rebellion was against the Mennonite leaders and the control of the community, against the very separation that made them who they were. Against being told that if you wanted to be part of the safe, wealthy, and comfortable community, you had to live a certain way, in a certain place, play a role even when it didn't feel right. I knew their feeling of being caged, frustrated, and bored, but scared of the outside world and of the reaction of their family if they were to try a different way of life. If they were unsure if the Mennonite way of life was right for them, they lacked opportunities to find out what the options were. Some would be happy and content with that life, some would always feel like misfits in their community. Some would leave, as I had done. But for now they were just *off ya fallja*, embracing the things they were told to shun, because it was the only way they could push back.

The threats to the Mennonite way of life did not all come from outside. The simple lifestyle and honourable name the Mennonites enjoyed had inspired a dark business. When the Mennonites spoke about "the drug problem" they weren't speaking about drug use, but rather the business of being drug mules and laundering money.

The Mennonites, with their piousness and separateness, were perfectly positioned to be used by the drug trade.

Mennonite communities across the Americas remain strongly connected, with constant travel between Mexico, Belize, Bolivia, Canada, and the United States, and there is a reticence among Mennonites to turn their relatives or neighbours over to the police.

Many of them hold Canadian citizenship through their parents and grandparents, even if they were not born in Canada themselves. At one point the Canadian government required overseas Canadians with citizenship obtained through their parents and grandparents to spend one year in Canada before their twenty-eighth birthday. This spawned a steady trickle of young Mexican and Bolivian Mennonites coming north for a year's work in the agricultural and manufacturing industries of southern Manitoba and Ontario. Then they went back...and forth and back again.

Many Mennonites drive rather than fly on their regular trips between Canada and Mexico or Central America. Whether it's because their large numbers of children make flying too expensive or because driving makes them feel more independent, Mennonites make a lot of trans-America road trips. US and Canadian border guards are well accustomed to seeing heavily loaded vehicles carrying Mennonites coming north to work a seasonal fruit harvest or to spend a year working in an uncle's *schmiede*. Some are simply visiting far-flung relatives. Mennonites might overstay a visa or try crossing a border without the correct documents, but for a long time no one suspected them of smuggling.

The cartels began to recruit Mennonite drug mules in the 1990s, and soon there were plenty of stories about Mennonites busted for drug smuggling. The stories all had familiar components. Mennonite men, who had grown up moving between Canada and Mexico, were recruited by the cartels to drive trucks packed with marijuana and cocaine north across the border into the United States and Canada.

They were helped by the fact that business conducted on the colonies produced significant flows of hard cash, often in foreign currency. One popular ruse had Mennonites buying used agricultural machinery in the United States with the money they had earned running drugs north. The machinery was moved into Mexico, where it was sold and the cash was put to work on the colony. Some of it appeared in new houses, shiny trucks and business start-ups that were mysteriously well funded. Drug smuggling had become an accepted fact of life on the colony.

I was in a bookstore on Manitoba Colony, when the shopkeeper began lamenting the social damage caused by the smuggling.

"It's rotting the community from the inside. They see the new trucks and the cash, and the young guys want to get into smuggling too."

Just as he was taking a breath to pitch into another tirade, the bell above the door chimed and in walked a skinny, frightened-looking man.

"Here, talk to this guy, he knows everything there is to know about drugs!" shouted the shopkeeper, pointing at the man. The man did not look comfortable having his expertise being so loudly advertised.

"We were just talking about the drug problem around here," I said.

"I see. And your name?" he asked.

I introduced myself. His name was Jacob Harms.

"You should sit down and have a good visit with this man. He has stories to tell," the shopkeeper interjected.

It was hard to resist the pressure, so Jacob and I made plans to meet at his house later in the afternoon. I scribbled the directions to his place onto a scrap of paper and left Jacob at the mercy of the shopkeeper.

A few hours later I stopped my bike on his driveway and he came out to shake my hand. Jacob was around forty, with a hesitant laugh and twitchy manner. His tired, sad eyes peered from underneath a red baseball cap. His jeans and yellow polo shirt were baggy on his thin frame. Jacob lived near the centre of Manitoba Colony in a comfortable home next to a new steel shed, where he ran a small business making picture frames and dried flower arrangements.

Jacob led me to his office, a small room off an attached garage that was cluttered with dried-flower arrangements, stacks of paper, and pictures of his family. He had taught himself how to make architectural blueprints for houses and he hoped to create an architecture and home design business, although he had no formal training in either.

"Down here they like some of those designs of the houses they see in the States, and I know a bit about computers, so I learned how to use this program to make drawings for the houses. Here in Mexico they're not so particular if you have the license or not," he said as he turned on his computer to show me plans for a large suburban-style home.

Most of Jacob's time was spent trying to move on from his past. I prompted him several times, asking how he had become involved in the drug trade, but Jacob waved my questions off. He rocked back in a leather office chair, arms crossed behind his head, and tried to return the conversation to more mundane matters.

"So, you said you were from Manitoba? I have a brother there, a welder in Rosenort," he said.

"Really? So do I."

We had brothers working in the same manufacturing plant. Jacob flashed a wide, toothy smile, which appeared and disappeared so fast I doubted I'd seen it at all.

"Ya, we probably know lots of the same people," Jacob said, warming up to the Mennonite Game. "I know lots of Mexican Mennonites who have moved to Manitoba."

"Oh, I probably don't know them. I've been away for a long time."

In Canada, the Mennonites from down south were a subject of ridicule. It was always the most conservative, radical groups that moved ever farther from civilization, whether to Mexico, Belize, or Bolivia. Then they'd come back to Canada wearing outmoded clothing, either too skinny or too fat, with bad teeth and greasy hair. They also had too many children. Whole swarms of little Mennonites would pour from the back of their battered Econoline vans and covered pickup trucks when they arrived in Canada. Invariably they were road weary and broke when they showed up at the door of an unsuspecting distant relative who felt obligated to find them shelter. It didn't help that they came north for the simple jobs, taking unskilled factory jobs, butchering chickens and picking eggs, scraping together enough hourly wage between father and grown sons and daughters to pay the bills. They were smart—not book smart, but learn-the-job-and-work-your-ass-off smart—and those who stayed in Canada soon pulled themselves out of poverty and opened their own small welding shops and farms.

But they were coarse. We called them Mexa, the same derogatory term that they themselves used to describe Spanish Mexicans. It seemed more often than not that when they arrived the wife needed cancer treatments and a sick child needed to go to the hospital. It was wrong to fly the Maple Leaf, but it was okay to return to the den of sin to collect on some state-supplied medical treatment. They'd collect the monthly child support payments without a thank-you, cashing in on that Canadian passport in their pocket. We resented them.

In the 1980s and '90s Mennonites who had lived in Mexico and Bolivia for a generation or more began returning to Canada in large groups. Mexican violence was becoming too great a threat, and some felt the Mennonite communities had become too modern and integrated with broader society. They moved to remote communities in Alberta and Saskatchewan, as well as to provinces in the east. That gave their young men another reason to travel, often returning to colonies in the south to find a bride.

Jacob, like many of the smugglers, had grown up as an Old Colony Mennonite in Mexico. In his early twenties he left the ultra-conservative community and was working on a farm in Kansas. He enjoyed his freedom and adventure away from the colony, but he was lonely, as there were few other Mennonites in his area. So he returned to Mexico in hope of finding a Mennonite wife.

But his experience of living in the United States had put a bit of swagger in his step that was hard to maintain back on the colony, and he soon fell in with the wrong crowd in Mexico. His new friends had connections with the drug cartels, and he joined them in driving vehicles full of marijuana across the border into the US. He was paid US $6,000 per trip.

"I took six loads and each time there were different amounts of drugs in different hiding spots in the car, and I did not know exactly where the drugs were. We could carry about a hundred pounds in the gas tank and about forty pounds in a tire. If you hide it in a side panel of the car the weight can vary a lot."

"I wasn't used to having money. The first time I had even $1,000 in my hand, I didn't know what to do with it. I went and bought nice clothes and shoes, no more cheap stuff. All the money I earned with marijuana I spent very fast, and then I generated debt on top of it. It caused me a lot of problems."

In 1997 Jacob was caught at the border, his first offence. His partners bailed him out, the charges didn't stick, and he walked free. But the experience scared him straight. He found a wife on the colony and planned a move back to Kansas, where his old employer offered him a job. But Jacob was too cash-strapped to make the move.

His old smuggling friends suggested he take one more run north. His cash problems would be solved, and he'd be in the United States, ready to start his new job and married life. Jacob agreed, and he and his wife made it across the border at Juárez before making a brief stop in El Paso to change a flat tire.

"I said nothing, but I felt relief. We'd made it through, I thought."

Then they came to another highway checkpoint several miles inside Texas. The border guards asked Jacob to take off his dark sunglasses and his nervous eyes gave him away.

"They bored into the side of the car with a drill, and when the bit came out there was weed on it. My wife knew nothing, I hadn't told her anything. I just told her we were moving to Kansas."

"The people who hired me said they'd put a hundred pounds in the car, but the DEA recorded, for the court, that there was seventy-four pounds. So someone stole about twenty-five pounds of it for himself. But I kept quiet, because if they hadn't stolen some they would have found a larger amount and I'd have been. locked up for even longer."

Jacob expected his partners to show up and somehow solve this problem. They had promised to bail him out, back him up, and support his wife of four months, who was pregnant with their first child, if he was caught. But he heard nothing, so he resigned himself to prison life, where he felt intimidated by the mostly black and Hispanic prisoners.

"They called me white bread, but they didn't know I understood Spanish. 'What's this white bread doing in here?' they would joke. I didn't say anything for a long time, even though they kept teasing me. And then one day I said, 'I came here to find out what the toasted bread was up to.' The whole place got quiet then they all bust out laughing."

He kept to himself and stayed out of trouble, earning a reduction on his sentence for good behaviour. He walked free after eleven months.

"When I got out, they deported me to Mexico. I've never gone back to the US. I would like to go back, because I have relatives in Kansas. I wanted to be rich and have nice things like the other smugglers. That didn't work out."

When he got out of prison, he knocked on the doors of the men who had hired him to carry their drugs.

"They had told me they would give me money if I didn't give up their names. So when I was out I went to them and asked for my money, but they said they didn't have any money," Jacob said, the disappointment still visible in his face. "They said they would give me work here in Mexico, carrying marijuana to Juárez. I said no. I had some land and cattle, and I wanted to farm. I just needed the money they'd promised me to get started. They said no."

Jacob went into construction, where he got his idea to start drawing up housing blueprints. But the bitterness of his experience, and knowing which of his neighbours had been, or still were in the trade, gnawed at him.

"There are a lot of Old Colony people around who I know were doing it, but also from other Mennonite groups. I can go to a church now and see many people who I know used to smuggle but who were never caught, so they never paid for it."

He fell silent, staring at his sneakered foot, tapping at thin air with a steady vengeance. His mouth tightened and puckered sour, his eyes narrowed. His neighbours knew that he knew which ones had done what and got away with it. They were able to hold their heads high in church because they got away with it, but he had to hang his head in shame because he got caught. Those Mennonite neighbours had come to visit him once, spinning circles on his yard with a pickup truck to intimidate him before telling him to keep his mouth shut. He showed me photographs of the tire marks on his yard, his hands shaking as he held them out to me. I felt sorry for him. The fear and capitulation came off him like the stench of sweat.

"I just want to be left alone now. If they leave me alone, I'll leave them alone," he said. I asked if he could point out the homes of the smugglers.

"Sure," he said with a dry laugh. "But I won't. They're here, close by, just down the road, some of them. Just look for the nice houses, and then you'll know. In the last while there have been fewer smugglers from around here. It's become a bit more dangerous, there's a lot of shootings here, and a lot of Mennonites are getting scared of it," he said. "There were a lot of people who got out of the business and left the country because they knew if they stayed here, they wouldn't be able to get away from it."

There were too many stories of pickup trucks abandoned beside an empty highway, bodies strewn on the road, bloody and bullet-holed. Others had seen and heard the shootings, by masked men with guns. So far the shootouts hadn't involved Mennonites, but it was just a matter of time. The drug cartels treated everyone the same, Mennonite or *weltmensch*, and sooner or later things would go wrong and the guns would be aimed at the Mennonites.

"Around here each person would say the marijuana trade is wrong, that we shouldn't do it. But the money covers it up and makes it okay. The money; there's so much, it's so comfortable, so it's easy to get into it again. A lot of people here know what's going on, maybe not the exact details, but it's easy to fib a bit. The money says a lot. If I wanted to buy farm machinery in the States the smugglers would say, 'Oh, if you're buying a tractor there, I'll pay for it with cash in the US, and you can pay me back in Mexico. That way you don't need to send money to US to pay for it.' That's how they launder the money, and that still happens."

Jacob was teaching his children English in the hope that the whole family would move to Canada someday, but he didn't know if or when that would happen with his criminal record.

"I have brothers and sisters in Canada. They warned me not to get involved in it, and now I know they're right."

I could hear Jacob's family in the house; the shout of a child, the thump of furniture being moved across a floor.

"How much do they know about all of this?" I asked, nodding towards the sounds. I hadn't met Jacob's wife, and he hadn't offered to introduce her. In the framed photos in his office, and the screensaver on his computer, she looked like a good Mennonite wife. Demure and honest-faced, hair pulled back from her face and tucked into a small head covering.

"Ya, she knows it all. I'm very lucky she took me back and forgave me. I thank God for that, and for her, every day. The kids…" He was silent. "I told them that Daddy did some bad things, and that he was in jail. They know that much. But I didn't tell them more. I told them that was the old Daddy, that he doesn't do that anymore."

Jacob had had a religious conversion while in prison, though he'd gone back to drinking for several years after his release before sobering up for good. Now, he said, his heart and soul were committed to helping others. He hoped others could learn from him.

"I go sing in the jail now, with people from church, and I'm still a bit…" Jacob theatrically peered over his shoulder, widening his eyes in mock fear. "Even though I know I can get out again."

CHAPTER 6

Belize
Pacifists

Belize is an odd stepchild in the Central American family. There is an absence of the Spanish Catholicism that so defines the rest of the region, and Belize does not share its neighbours' history of grinding guerrilla warfare.

Instead, it has a distinctly British colonial air—it used to be called the British Honduras—and is still the only country in Central America whose official language is English. It is far less densely populated than most of its neighbours and is generous with parks and reserves. Most visitors come for diving and beaches—it is the home of the Great Blue Hole.

I entered the country at its northern border with Mexico, and immediately noticed that Belize also felt poorer, more ramshackle and disorganized than Mexico. Every fuel station I stopped at had broken pumps, so I filled my motorcycle from plastic cans sold beside the road. Houses standing on tall spindly legs to protect them from floods and bugs were clad in rusting tin and scraps of wood. Men, women, and children lounged on front stoops, watching the world go by. Everyone appeared to be waiting for something, and it looked as though they'd already waited for a long time.

Belize consistently has one of the top ten national homicide rates in the world, and as I rode through the country it was on track to set a new record for murders in one year, at 145. That in a country with a population of only 335,000.

I rode south through flat countryside, past shaggy banana fields. The roads were empty save for the occasional battered car that limped along like a crooked dog. Fly-covered donkeys pulled rickety carts in the heat. I passed the turnoff for Belize City, which was on the coast to my left, and instead turned west, towards the Guatemalan border.

Nearly every person I've met that has visited Belize remembers the same incongruous feature about the country.

"We were on a tour bus, they had the reggae music cranked, and then we stopped and picked up these people dressed in old-fashioned clothes. The men had long beards."

"I was going to a rainforest hike and we passed this village full of rich white people. Are those the Mennonites?"

Yes, they are. The colony of Spanish Lookout, the largest of numerous colonies in Belize, is nestled in the hills right on the Guatemalan border. As I approached the colony the road became smoother and the fields on either side of it were covered in richer, greener crops and hay than elsewhere. The farms, when they appeared over a small rise, were orderly. Tall palm trees shaded the yards, and shiny red and yellow farm implements were parked in neat lines.

It was early afternoon as I rode into the heart of Spanish Lookout and drove down Center Road, past construction businesses, small factories producing farm machinery, an insurance office. The Farmers Trading Center housed a bank and the colony's largest store and its parking lot was full of late-model pickup trucks. I parked my bike and entered the Golden Corral, a rustic family diner, where a blond waitress greeted me in Plautdietsch. I ordered *glomms veranke* and *foarmaworscht*, everything fried, like my mom used to make. The tangy cottage cheese inside the doughy *veranke* contrasted with the salty smokiness of the sausage so well that for a few moments I was carried away to our family dining table decades past. I only looked up once I had wiped the last of the gravy from the plate with a slice of bread. A ruddy-faced man at the next table was watching me. I introduced myself, making an extra wipe at my mouth in case any gravy had escaped.

"I'm looking for a guy named Klaas Friesen," I said. "My uncle in Canada gave me his name. Do you know where he lives?"

My Plautdietsch, although marginally improved after a few weeks in the Mexican colonies, still contained a distinct accent that didn't belong here. It didn't belong anywhere, really.

"I sure do!" he said, laughing. "That's my dad."

A few minutes later I pulled up to a farmhouse, where, on a shady porch, Klaas and his wife Greta sat chatting with a few others.

"I have a Mennonite from Canada here," their son said in a booming voice as he led me to the porch.

"You have to tell me your pa's name, then we will really know who you are," Klaas prodded as I settled into a seat.

I told him.

"Ahh, Leonard and Linda Dueck, we know them well."

I instantly felt at home, here in the sticky Belizean heat, two months' journey from where I'd grown up.

Greta was a large woman who moved with difficulty. She wore a blue flowered dress, thick glasses, her long grey hair pulled back into a ponytail. She had a wide toothy smile and she cackled with delighted laughter. Klaas was tall, lean, and loose jointed, wearing a floppy sun hat. He reminded me of my long-gone Grandpa Friesen, with a quick grin and a constant stream of corny jokes. Like Grandpa, he was painfully honest and sincere, which could come across as crudeness but was driven by a kind heart.

"Well, that was before my experience," Klaas was saying.

"Before what?" I asked.

"I had an experience once, it was hard, but I became a new man. I thought I was dead, but Jesus brought me back to life."

Klaas could see he had me hooked.

"Ya, life has never been the same," Greta added.

Klaas had fallen silent. He was staring at his shoe.

"I'll tell you about it another day," he said. "I'll take you to where it happened."

Now I had to stay.

"Is there a hotel or guest house nearby where I could get a room?" I asked. I hoped that they would offer me a bed in their own home instead.

"Well, that's not necessary," Greta said. "You can stay here. And eat with us."

"Those Mennonites in Manitoba, and those that came here to Belize, that's all one big nest," Klaas said. "Sometimes you know people without knowing them directly. We know a lot of the same people or we've heard about them, and I'm sure I've met your pa, so you and I know each other."

Greta led me to their summer house. It was weathered and rickety, but in a pleasant camp-like way. It had two single beds covered in colourful quilts, a wooden rocking chair, and a small desk built into the wall under the window. There was a raw, dusty smell to it. The creaky floor was uneven under the linoleum, and holes in the walls and window screens let bugs in. It was perfect.

The next day I told Klaas that I would be happy to work for my keep. The words were barely out of my mouth before he had me stationed in a musty corner of his barn to clean beans. The ragged tin roof and plank walls let in shafts of light that pierced the dusty air like lances. There was a constant brown blur pouring from the bottom of the noisy screening machine, an endless stream of beans and tiny lumps of dirt nearly the same size and colour, but one was good and one was bad. My job was to pick out the bad as fast as my fingers could move, tossing them on the ground and reaching for more. Again and again I fell behind, scrambling after the conveyor belt. I was a lousy farmer, through and through.

In the mornings I sat and wrote at my desk in the summer house. I could hear Greta and her teenage daughters, Kenia and Evelin, and the clang of pots and pans through the open kitchen window, just a few metres from where I sat.

The girls had been orphaned when their El Salvadoran mother died, so Klaas and Greta adopted them, in addition to the eight children they already had. The girls screamed and laughed, Greta tutted and scolded in Plautdietsch.

Fritz, the family's German shepherd, sat on the porch of the summer house and stared at me, his pink tongue lolling. Beyond the porch, which was missing a few floorboards, was a backyard of deep grass, a shade tree, and a chicken coop. The sour stench of chicken manure mixed with the sweet loamy smell of cows and took flight on the morning breeze. In the distance, muffled but unmistakable, was the sound of Klaas cajoling his cows into their milking stalls. He was impossible to ignore. His booming laughter and voice filled the house and revealed his location no matter what far corner of the farm he was working in.

Every morning: "The Lord has given you another day, so that's something to be thankful for, right?" Klaas's face beamed as he said it.

But then I heard him speak to one of the farm workers.

"Ya mon," he said, arms akimbo, floppy sun hat failing to keep his large nose from turning red. "Dat's de way we gonna do it mon, you got dat right." He slipped into the Belizean patois whenever he spoke to non-Mennonites. At first I found it offensive, thinking it was condescending mimicry, but as he told me more of his story, I could see there wasn't a lofty bone in his body. He just wanted to be understood.

"My papa, he had an influence on me, and one thing he held very important is that he should never treat an *een-heimisch*—a native—like the Mennonites treated the Russians in Russia," Klaas told me. "He was always very conscientious about treating the Belizean people fair."

Klaas and Greta had both moved to Belize from the colonies in northern Mexico as children in 1958, part of the first group of Mennonites to settle on Spanish Lookout. Their families were in search of more land after repeated droughts in Mexico. In Belize, they bought wild land that had only a few logging trails cut into thick jungle.

But the Mennonites were quick to build up wealth, and their pacifist beliefs meant that they didn't carry guns, making them vulnerable in a country as violent as Belize. Guatemalan guerrillas and bandits were known to cross the border into Belize to carry out raids, posing an additional threat, and it had become more difficult for Mennonites to remain pacifist.

Ordained Mennonite pacifism can be seen especially in the Münster Rebellion, in the German city of the same name, in 1534. A diverse group of Anabaptists seized power of the city in an attempt to establish a theocracy. They held it for nearly one and a half years, during which time Münster became increasingly militarized, with citizens arming themselves and church steeples repurposed as cannon batteries. The daily lives of residents were strictly controlled, and they were required to wear simple clothing to erase social distinctions. The Catholics wrested it back in 1535 and the captured Anabaptists had their heads chopped off and placed on spikes for display, their genitals nailed to the city gate, and their corpses stuffed into steel cages and hung from the steeple of St. Lambert's Church.

The Anabaptists regrouped after the siege to try to restore their unity, but all they could agree on was that they would remain pacifist in the future, that they would not fight back with violence as they had during the siege. Münster became a turning point for the Anabaptist movement, as they never again became a cohesive political force, and their future growth would be fragmented, creating the Amish, Hutterites, and Mennonites. But everyone agreed to shun violence.

Mennonite pacifism in Russia was tested after World War I, when the Russian government had collapsed and the Red and White Armies, along with anarchists, roved the land. The Mennonites were targeted for being rich and Germanic, and were robbed, jailed, beaten, raped, and murdered in large numbers. It was too much for some Mennonites, who abandoned pacifism, armed themselves, and created militias. It didn't go well, and the violence against them only worsened, creating a handy lesson for later generations. What happened to the militant Mennonites in Russia showed that peace and non-resistance was the only way.

Pacifism meant a lot of things to me where I grew up in Canada.

It meant I mustn't join the military, or even the police, because they have to carry guns. By some fluke my childhood toy box contained several two-inch-tall plastic toy soldiers. Perhaps they came from the charity shop, or some *weltmensch* dropped them along the way, but there's no way my parents bought me those toy soldiers. They were already in the toy box, and throwing them away would have been wasteful, so, to remain true to his pacifist beliefs, my father cut the tiny barrels off the tiny guns using a hot knife. No more war, now they were just helmeted men wearing backpacks and holding odd-looking clubs.

A few days after my arrival in Belize I reminded Klaas that he had his own story about pacifism, which I wanted to hear.

"Let's go," Klaas said. He stood up and grabbed his truck keys. "I have time this afternoon, I'll show you the place."

His daughter Kenia begged to join us, and we set off.

Outside of town, about five miles from the Guatemalan border, with Mexico not far to the north, there were newly broken fields still ringed by piles of tree branches and roots, pushed aside by heavy machinery to make room for crops. This was the edge of Mennonite territory. The fields were interrupted by the occasional bluff of untouched jungle, reminding farmers that the wild was always waiting to return. Klaas slowed to a crawl and inspected a bluff of untouched jungle more carefully. He looked in his mirrors, trying to gauge the distance we'd driven.

"This is the road we were travelling on when it happened," Klaas said. His laughter became shorter, his smile more strained as we drove. Now there was a tightness to his voice. "Here's the corner where we stopped, right here."

A wall of sultry air hit us as we climbed from the truck. The still engine ticked with escaping heat. From the towering trees on either side of the road came the undulating screech of insects. The white gravel road glared under the bright sunshine, but in the distance the sky had curdled into dark clouds that were rapidly churning towards us.

On the morning of May 8, 1991, a Wednesday, a group of Spanish Lookout farmers made a reconnaissance trip to inspect this land, a new purchase. Forty-two people on two trailers, pulled by tractors, out on a fun day trip, chatting and dreaming the dreams of colonialists. Klaus was riding on the front trailer.

"Before we knew it, there were four people with rifles coming out of the jungle over there, and two from there," Klaas said, as he pointed into the woods. "And back there were another two people with rifles. And they shot over our heads…pow pow." He extended his arm like he was holding a starter pistol.

"Behind me, people were lying on the floor of the trailer. I thought they'd been shot dead, but they'd just thrown themselves down. I stood up from my seat and went and asked the man, 'Hey, do you have a problem? What can we do for you?' God already had a grip on me, and I had no fear. It was as if Jesus was carrying me.

"They told me to lie down on the ground, and I said I would not lie down on the ground for no man. I first wanted to see what they could do. So they said okay, then you come into the jungle with us.

"They started dragging me into the jungle, and I said, 'I'm not going into the jungle.' But they were screaming at me, and I thought they might shoot me dead, so I went with them."

The armed men dragged Klaas and five other men into the jungle while the remaining Mennonites fled back to the colony in terror.

"It's a long time ago, but I can still feel it here," Klaas said, patting his chest. He fell silent and stared into the jungle. His floppy grey hat with its red band sagged over his face and dark circles of sweat had appeared on his shirt. The constant toothy smile was still in place under his large nose, but now it looked more like a grimace.

"They took all the money we had in our wallets, as well as my friend's watch," Klaas said, pulling his wallet out and opening it to demonstrate. "And then they just guarded us. We had some food and water. If I wanted to go to the toilet they'd follow me, with the gun. And then I started to pray.

"On the first day I stared one of them in the eye so long he started looking away. By lunchtime on the first day he was so scared of my eyes that when I looked at him he'd look the other way.

"In the evening, when everybody went to sleep, I remained awake. I thought, I'm going to scare these people. I took a stone and I threw it into the underbrush, and it made a rustling sound. The guys jumped up with their guns and looked with their flashlights. Which of us had escaped? Half an hour later, once they were all settled again, I took another big stone and threw it into the trees. They jumped up to go take a look. I did that all night, and towards morning they shone a flashlight into my face, to see if it was me doing it. Just then I did like this," Klaas said, feigning sleep where he stood in the middle of the road, complete with a throaty snore. "They said, in Spanish to each other, 'There must be monkeys somewhere.' They searched the trees above, to see if monkeys were throwing stones down. There were no monkeys."

The next morning, two of the Mennonites were sent back to the colony with instructions to return with money if they wanted those left behind to live.

"That afternoon, at four o'clock, the money was supposed to come. That was the longest day of my life. At two o'clock the Holy Spirit said to me, there will be no money coming, you have to prepare yourself for death. And so we prepared to die. At four o'clock the people with the rifles came to us, angry. They said, 'We told you if you didn't bring money, we'd shoot you dead.'

"They tied us to a tree. I thought our lives were over. My partners were crying out loud. All of a sudden, the Holy Spirit told me to speak to these people. And that's what I did. I said, 'I love you, you are my friend, and Jesus loves you.' And they could not shoot. That's what the love of Jesus Christ can do, it can tie the hands of people, and they could not shoot us. That's why I'm alive, because I knew the name of Jesus.

"They wanted B $100,000 [US $50,000], and they said they would give us one more chance. If they didn't get the money this time, they would shoot us dead. So we went through the test another time."

Klaas paused. He gestured at the jungle with a wide sweep of his arm, the truck keys in his hand jingling as his arm swung in an arc. He swallowed. Kenia stood nearby, saying nothing. She had watched spellbound as he told his story. Now, seeing her father shaken, she stared down at the ground, a toe tracing designs in the dust.

"Ya," Klaas said, blinking, as if he'd forgotten the rest of the story. He took a deep breath and remembered.

"Saturday morning, I spoke to Jesus, and I said, 'If you are a living Jesus, send some live monkeys through here, to show me you are alive. Before there were no monkeys, but you have made the world, you have made me, you are all powerful, I believe in you.' Fifteen minutes later a monkey came by, and I could barely believe it. I asked Jesus, 'Is this true?' I saw, high in a tree, a big monkey. Then Jesus came to me in a bright light, and he asked, 'Do you want to work on this earth for me longer?' And I said, 'Yes, I do.' And then he asked again, 'Do you want to work for me?' Four times he asked me, and I said, 'Whenever, whomever, wherever, I will always work for you. My life is your life.' That's why I'm still on this earth.

"As I'd finished saying that, I could hear those people running up again, with their rifles, and they said, 'There is no money!' They were angry. And one of them said, 'We don't have time to talk! Let's run to Mexico.' I said, 'No, I'm not running to Mexico, I'm going home.' I don't know what my face looked like, but those people could no longer look me in the eye. They were looking down like this." Klaas bent over to look at his feet in exaggerated submission.

"And the guard, his rifle was like this." Klaas pointed at the ground. "Five minutes later he said, with a friendly look on his face, 'You can go home.' And that's what I did, with my three partners."

There were tears and shouts of joy, prayers of thanks and wonder at the protection of God when they walked into the colony on Saturday evening, four days after they were kidnapped. But the kidnappers planted an extra seed of fear in their heads before releasing them, threatening to come to Spanish Lookout and grab them from their beds at night if they didn't deliver the promised cash. The threat gnawed at them when darkness fell, and every shadow became a Guatemalan guerrilla coming for his due.

"When I came home, I saw scared people. The Mennonites were completely unaware of what to do. They were in shock."

The former captives asked the community to help them pay the ransom. Some of them threatened to flee to Canada if the ransom wasn't paid, they feared the kidnappers so much. The police advised them not to pay, but they took up a collection anyway. Not as much money as the kidnappers had demanded, but hopefully enough to appease them.

"One guy said he was single, he had no wife or children, so it didn't matter if he was dead, so he went," Klaas said. "We were terribly afraid. In hindsight I think maybe we shouldn't have given them the money, but at the time I was very happy that they were doing it."

The Mennonites tucked a Bible into the bag of money, so that this encounter should not be in vain.

"He said, 'We brought you the money, now please give me back my wristwatch,' and he got his watch back. So they departed with a handshake and peace. And I was so happy, so joyful. I felt peace."

Klaas clapped his hands with finality, beaming at me. But he also seemed eager to leave the scene, and we hurriedly climbed into his truck. He was not the first, nor the last, to be kidnapped. Menno Penner, a citrus farmer and small business owner in the nearby city of Belmopan, was kidnapped on his farm on March 17, 1999. Men dressed like soldiers came out of the jungle and took him away in his own pickup truck. Five days later his family received a ransom note demanding US $1 million, threatening that they would never see their husband and father again if they did not receive the money. The family refused to pay, and Menno was never seen again.

"The kidnappers are just like corn farmers," Klaas said. "If you get a big corn crop you plant corn again. If they get easy money, they do it again. But now the possibility of making money is too small, the Belize Defence Force (BDF) is alert now."

The Mennonites suspected that their farm workers were passing inside information to the kidnappers and helping them carry out the attacks. It was an unsettling thought.

"We were strongly encouraged to make parties and invite the neighbouring villages. To create some connections and help them build roads, schools. And that is what we have done," Klaas said. "The more people we have in favour of us, the harder it is for the kidnappers to get away."

Klaas's confidence returned with each kilometre he put between us and the kidnapping site. We drove to Aguacate Lagoon park, which had been built by the colony. It was near the border, where the kidnappers were thought to have come from. Empty picnic tables dotted the trim lawns and a lonely-looking dock jutted out into the lake. There was no one else there.

Five years earlier two Mennonite men had been kidnapped and brought to this park. They were tied to trees and the kidnappers stole their pickup truck. The kidnappers drove to the colony store, which also contained the colony bank, to carry out a heist. Inside, they stumbled into police who were shopping on their lunch hour. The police gave chase, but the suspects escaped across the border into Guatemala, leaving the two Mennonites tied to the trees until the police found them.

"Before all this happened the park was busy all the time," Klaas said as we drove down leafy, winding roads. "You can use it for free, and stay here for the night if you like, but I wouldn't recommend it."

Klaas refused to pick up hitchhikers unless he knew them, and when he slowed at the ubiquitous speed bumps placed along Belize's highways, he made sure his doors were locked and windows closed. Most of the colony stores closed before sunset, before trouble could get a start. Greta cautioned me against leaving my laptop computer near the windows of the house, which was separated from the road by an expansive lawn and a grove of trees.

"It's too easy to see the computer if they walk by, and then they have an excuse to break in," she said.

Mennonites were pacifist and weren't supposed to carry guns, or even hire people to carry them on their behalf, but Belize's culture of violence was just too much. The colony hired armed police to patrol its streets, and many of the large businesses also had armed guards at night. One of the guards was shot dead in an attempted robbery in 2010. Once again, taking up arms in defence had only made things more complicated, just like in Russia.

Klaas's kidnapping caused him to have a mental breakdown, so he moved to Canada for a year of treatment—that's when he met my parents. When he returned to Belize, he remembered the commitments he'd made in the jungle.

"In those four days I was in the jungle I learned two things. That is to pray to God, and believe he hears it, and to like all people, Mennonite or not. I am *non*-racist," he said, wagging his index finger.

We were back at the house, sitting on the front porch. Greta watched her husband, nodding and occasionally interrupting to corroborate him.

"The first thing he said to me when he came home was, 'I like all people', and I thought that was a bit weird to say after what had happened," she said, tucking her chin in and furrowing her brow as if she was once again hearing it for the first time. "But, it's true, it's the way it should be."

"There's a lot of racism with the Mennonites. We are better than the other people, or else we wouldn't be right," Greta said, laughing and slapping her rounded knee at her own joke.

Klaas's renewed charismatic faith ran against the grain of the subdued, quiet form of religion that Mennonites traditionally practise. He lost his role as a church leader, and the rejection hurt.

"That experience opened my eyes. I was very closed-minded, so dumb with religion, handcuffed by it. Jesus wanted me to be rid of that. God made it very clear to me while I was captive. People are all the same. It doesn't matter if they are Chinese, Creoles, Garifuna, Indians, Mennonites; I've learned to love them all."

CHAPTER 7

Belize

Spanish Lookout

It was easy to be unique in a place like Spanish Lookout. It helped if you weren't afraid of being different, or even relished it a little bit.

I rode along with Klaas as he drove his red pickup truck from store to bank to mechanic. At each stop he put a sparkle in people's eyes, a look of expectation for a joke or a story. And there was also something deeper, something mildly condescending. A sense of amusement at the expense of others. In Plautdietsch we call it *spotte*.

"Hallo!" Klaas hollered when we walked into the Farmers Trading Center. "The Lord has given us another great day!"

The demure Mennonite women at the checkout counter blushed with uncertainty over how to reply. They snickered at his jokes, and then smiled at each other knowingly when Klaas moved on.

When we arrived at the mechanic's shop to pick up a machinery part an amused smile appeared on the owner's face as soon as he saw Klaas.

"Hallo. So how is the world?" the mechanic asked, a comic prodding lilt to his voice.

When I told people on the colony where I was staying, the response was often the same.

"Ah, I see. At Klaas and Greta's?" they'd ask with a smirk.
"What's that like?"

Klaas and Greta were beloved in the community—they
did far too much good for there to be any animosity—but they
stood out for being different. It wasn't just because they had adopted
Kenia and Evelin when they were young El Salvadoran orphans.
What set their family apart was that they were vocal and fervent
promoters of education and assimilation.

"We're a bit *Oot bunt*," Greta said, a hint of pride in her voice.
She meant contrasting or clashing with the pattern of a quilt.
"All of our children finished high school and went to university
or college."

Neither Klaas nor Greta were educated beyond the usual colony
school, which put little emphasis on the sciences and did not include
high school.

"At fifteen, I can remember sitting in a tree, crying that
I couldn't continue school," Klaas said. "I promised myself that
I wouldn't stay dumb. Each person I meet can teach me something.

"The first one has to build the bridge, and then the next
drives the train over. We're building the bridge," he said, leaning forward in his chair, as he grew more earnest. "The educated
are thought to be too proud. Most Mennonites believe that
you have learned enough if you can read the Bible and know
not to steal. Then you should quit school and go to work. Two plus
two is four. If you have two and take one away, you only have
one left. If you have learned that, it's all you need."

We were sitting on the front porch again. The porch was where
everyone gathered for a break in the shade, and as the day grew
hotter more people appeared and the breaks grew longer. We drank
iced tea, and when our glasses ran dry Greta would call out to Kenia
or Evelin to bring refills. Klaas was growing animated, nearly
upsetting his tea as he gesticulated with both hands.

"The Mennonites have gone through a sieve. Those Mennonites that wanted to remain dumb fell through and moved
away. Those that had learned too much to believe in the non-
sense of moving away have stayed where they were. All those

ignorant enough allow themselves to be swayed by the preachers who say if you follow me, you'll be able to go to heaven,
and you don't need further education. That's religion. All those
Mennonites that moved from Canada moved because of religious
matters, and education was one of those matters. They wanted
to remain dumb and thought it would be easier to get into heaven
if they were dumb than if they were smart."

A lean-to attached to the house was cluttered with wooden
benches and tables, glistening with fresh varnish. Klaas had built
the furniture for a school their family had started twelve years earlier. It was steadily expanding with his daughter Tina as principal.

"You should go see it," Greta said, giving me directions
to the school. "There's still time before dinner."

Jireh Fundamental Education was on the farm one of
Tina's grandfathers, Greta's father, had built when he moved to
Belize fifty years earlier. Mature trees shaded the aging outbuildings. A two-storey farmhouse, its wooden siding peeling
and pockmarked, was the main schoolhouse. With ninety children
enrolled for the upcoming school year, they were rushing to build
an additional classroom beside the house.

The school operated on a tiny budget, but it was earning
a reputation for its academic standards. At first, the community had viewed the school with suspicion, but as it proved itself,
it had gained support.

"When I started teaching here, they said if the building
is too ugly the students won't learn," Tina said, her laugh echoing
in the empty classroom as she gave me a tour. "I proved them
wrong. Everything is old, and they still learned a lot!"

Tina was about forty, with clear blue eyes and light brown
hair pulled back into a ponytail. She giggled like a schoolgirl
as she showed me around her all-consuming passion.

The school bell consisted of a steel disc from a farm implement,
rung with a hammer. Bedrooms and dining room were converted into
classrooms. Kitchen cupboards held basic science equipment, an old
linen closet now held pencils and chalk. One classroom contained
an antique clothes wringer, which was now being used as bookshelf.

"My grandma used it when she was washing sheets and work shirts," Tina said as she gave the handle a crank, turning the drums with a rusty squeak.

"When we first started, I thought about it a lot, that this was my grandparents' house, and it was very special to me. But everything we've lived through here is more real and bigger than the fact that this used to be my grandparents' bedroom."

Classrooms were being cleaned, books sorted, and computers repaired for the upcoming school year. It was one of the few Mennonite schools in the area offering high school diplomas, and enrolment was soaring. The teachers were busy evaluating new students, who were transferring in from other schools.

"Many of the new students test much lower than I'd hoped they would, because the standards of the schools around here are way beneath what we expect. When we bring new students in it's very disappointing for them and their parents," Tina said. "They come and say they've done grade eight, but academically they're maybe up to grade four or five. It's because they have shorter school years and they do not emphasize things like homework and pushing through the curriculum."

Although English is Belize's official language and most Mennonites in the area had Canadian roots, the level of spoken and written English was poor.

"Our idea was to have a school where children would learn English to a good level," Tina said, herself at times struggling to express ideas in English. "No one speaks proper English at home, it's either Creole, Spanish, or German."

The poor education was not due to a lack of resources or because the children were impaired by malnutrition and domestic strife. Instead, it was, as Klaas had said, due to a deep-seated cultural aversion to education among Russian Mennonites. School, for most families, was seen as a temporary holding place for children, not a potential stepping stone to something greater. The less a child learned, the fewer questions they asked and the easier it was to ensure they followed tradition. Institutions of higher learning would invariably plant strange, dangerous ideas in a student's head. There's an old Mennonite saying for that: *Dee meea jeleaht, dee meea ve'tjead.* (The more you learn, the farther astray you go.)

That was the approach my parents took as well. They encouraged us to complete high school, but my siblings and I did not go to university, as Dad made it clear he would not be paying for it if we did. If we chose to go to a Bible college—small residential schools similar to liberal arts colleges but teaching scripture, church singing, and missionary work instead of art—he would pay all the bills and give us a car to drive. That was a pretty good deal, so I went to Bible college. It was wholesome and fun and not particularly challenging. It wasn't like I'd miss out on a sought-after internship or career opportunity if my grades were poor. We lived on campus, played sports against other Bible colleges, dated mostly other Bible college students, and learned how to proselytize and be church leaders. My college offered diplomas for music, counselling, and aviation—those missionaries need a way to get to the deep dark jungles filled with sin. I wrote for the school paper and enjoyed badgering college leadership, but after one year of studies, I'd had enough Bible college.

Bible colleges are a popular form of finishing school in Mennonite society, giving students a taste of further education and student life without them having to face the full brunt of interacting with *weltmensch*. They are also referred to as bridal colleges, as they're the first opportunity most good Mennonite farm boys and girls get to find a mate from outside their village. Sending your children to Bible college increases the chances that they will return to Mennonite life, perhaps with ideas on how to freshen up the Sunday congregational singing, but back in the fold all the same.

Using a lack of education to limit choice contradicts the emphasis Mennonites put on adult baptism. Anabaptists believe that baptism is valid only when the candidate confesses his or her faith in Christ and truly *wants* to be baptized. It is meant to show a conscious decision to follow Jesus's teachings, in contrast to the involuntary act of infant baptism. I was in my late teens when I chose to be baptized. That difference—that we were making an intentional choice—was emphasized to us by preachers and parents alike. *Our* baptism had greater meaning than that of the Catholics because we chose ours, it wasn't simply a rite of passage. But conscious choice didn't appear to be as important when it came to educating children so they could choose between a life on the colony or a life outside.

Education was also seen as frivolous by many Mennonites.

"My grandmother taught us to always look out for things that were unnecessary. She called it *oneidijch*, and it was sin to spend time on those things," Tina said. "Going to school for a long time would be *oneidijch*. You should be doing more worthwhile things like working with your hands, helping other people."

Tina, her voice full of admiration, said that despite their upbringing her parents had poured whatever resources they had into their children's education, even when the money wasn't there. Even when other families thought spending money on books and tutoring was *oneidijch*, her parents always somehow found money to pay for education.

"My mother has lamented her lack of education all her life," Tina said. "She always said if she was better educated, she could better express her feelings, teach others, and explain things better. She feels locked up, she can't express what's inside, and she always blames it on her lack of education."

But Greta didn't let her lack of vocabulary keep her from speaking her mind on more practical matters, and when Tina was growing up she heard whispers that her mother was too bossy and outspoken. The community's objection to an outspoken woman told Tina her role was to keep quiet and in the background.

"Today, if people say I'm bossy I say, 'So what?'" Tina said, laughing. "Over the years my beliefs about Mennonite women have changed. At first, I wasn't comfortable with leadership because I was taught that was wrong, that women should be behind the scenes and nobody should know that I was involved. When I changed those ideas, things became a lot more enjoyable."

Tina was married to a Guatemalan refugee, and most of her other siblings had also married Spanish or Creole Central

Americans. A cross-cultural marriage didn't exclude you from the community, but it meant you were different, even among the most moderate of Mennonites. It didn't have to mean something, but it sure could if you wanted it to. The differences were further complicated by living on a colony.

"People don't want to let Spanish people into their churches, because then they will intermarry, and if they intermarry, then the good pure Mennonite faith will be lost," Tina said, laughing out loud at the idea. "As soon as their minds are broadened to understand the world is bigger than just this community, then they will start to notice everyone is human and that there is not such a big difference."

Tina was in her late teens before she had any interaction with non-Mennonites, and she was still torn over whether her life within the comfortable bubble of Spanish Lookout was dulling her sense of place in the world.

"It doesn't seem so important what is going on in Belize City, although it should because it is my country. But life is peaceful here. People take care of each other. It seems so otherworldly out there," she mused.

It was the same growing up in Mennville, where my elementary school was about the same size as Tina's. My father occasionally listened to the news on the radio, but world events were never discussed around the dinner table. We did not subscribe to many newspapers or magazines, except for those focused on religion and farming. Politics were of no concern to us. Wars, assassinations, cultural icons created or killed—none of it ever found its way to us. We lived in a very comfortable and safe bubble.

Spanish Lookout colony collected its own taxes and built and operated highways, a bank, stores, and a local police force. The colony's population of 2,000 doubled during the day, when the mostly Hispanic neighbours came to work. It felt, and to a large extent operated, like any other busy farming town. But it was different from other small towns in one important way: only ethnic Mennonites were allowed to become full community members.

Tina's husband was baptized in their church and he had

adopted their Mennonite lifestyle. He even spoke a bit of Plautdietsch. But he was not ethnically Mennonite, instead he was brown, and that meant he could not borrow money at the bank or use the colony's coupon system. Like many Mennonite colonies, Spanish Lookout used a coupon system for local transactions. Residents and businesses all used the same bank in the Farmers Trading Center. Instead of exchanging cash they wrote each other cheques that were only valid on the colony and could not be redeemed through the national banking system. Every month the accounts were balanced, and the bank transferred money accordingly. But the system was restricted to ethnic Mennonites.

Non-Mennonites, even if they had married into a Mennonite family, were also not allowed to own colony land. Much like the banking system, colonies operate a shadow land-title system. Legally, the colony owns all the land, but it's divided into individual plots for colony members.

Just as was so often predicted, accepting non-Mennonites into their schools or taking them as marriage partners and business associates created a new set of challenges. There were many people who wanted to join Spanish Lookout. If they were to take applicants there would be lines outside the colony office. But the Mennonites were afraid of losing the advantage they had created for themselves. They had worked hard for all of this, why should they let others reap the benefits without putting in the same work?

Tina's brother Martin was about thirty years old and slight of build with light brown hair. He had his father's sense of humour and an impish smile; his conversation was sprinkled with puns and gentle barbs. Martin worked at Universal Hardware, which was Mennonite owned and one of the largest hardware stores in the region.

Martin and his wife, Felicia, were both computer engineers. One day they invited me to their home for lunch. They lived in a small house that was temporarily set up on the edge of the family farm. A well-trodden path through the orchard connected their house and the family home. Setting up a small house on a parent's property, affordable and near family support, was an age-old tradition among rural Mennonite newlyweds.

"This is it. Welcome!" Martin said, standing in the middle of the one-room house with his arms outstretched.

A kitchen counter ran along one side, opposite to a bed covered in a colourful quilt, while a small dining table took up the middle of the room. A lean-to bathroom had been added to the porch.

"We get snakes in there sometimes," Martin said, laughing while Felicia shuddered. "Sometimes, when you go to the toilet at night you get a bit of a surprise."

The house would soon be replaced by a larger one they had bought in an auction. One with a bedroom and a real bathroom.

Martin and Felicia met at the University of Belize in Belmopan. Felicia's father was Creole and her mother Mestizo, giving her golden-brown skin and curly hair that she wore pulled back from her face. She and Martin spoke to each other in a mix of English and Spanish, and their house felt more like a university apartment than a Mennonite home.

They had the giddy excitement of newlyweds, brimming with plans for the future. They were more concerned with their careers, buying a larger home, and making bus trips across Central America than with having children, for the moment. And Felicia was still coming to grips with her role on the colony.

"People are always surprised when I tell them I am a Belizean, because my skin is light. Some people think I might be American, but for sure *not* a Mennonite! The darker the skin colour, the harsher the criticism," Felicia said.

She was part of the church, had married into a Mennonite family, and lived on the colony, but her ethnicity meant she was excluded from many of the rights that ethnically Mennonite community members enjoyed.

"Everyone is very nice to me, but the community has to figure out how to deal with the changes this brings," Felicia said. "I can't really be a full part of the community if I can't sign cheques or coupons at the bank or use the bank to borrow money. The truth is, there may be other things I will be excluded from that we aren't aware of because we haven't encountered them yet."

Some of the barriers were less concrete and more common to any tightly knit ethnic community. Felicia did not speak Plautdietsch, although she was learning.

"The old aunties like it when I say some things in German. It brings their guard down and they seem to be less critical."

Martin and Felicia craved a more cosmopolitan and stimulating social scene where men and women are free to interact at social gatherings.

"When we're with our friends I find the separate women and men circles challenging." She meant that men and women literally sat and socialized in different groups, or even in different rooms. "It makes it difficult to have a social life. I am expected to be in the women's circle where I have nothing to say and have to work hard to process the German conversation. Martin has to be in the men's circle, and he gets bored talking about corn prices for more than five minutes. So we just stay at home."

But they remained on the colony, where pay was higher, and life was safer and more comfortable than elsewhere in Belize. Mennonite businesses were successful and growing, sometimes even offering the chance for international business travel. Remaining on the colony was a smart career choice in a country where job prospects were otherwise dim, especially for outsiders. Martin was Mennonite enough for both of them to have a better life on the colony than they'd have among the *weltmensch*.

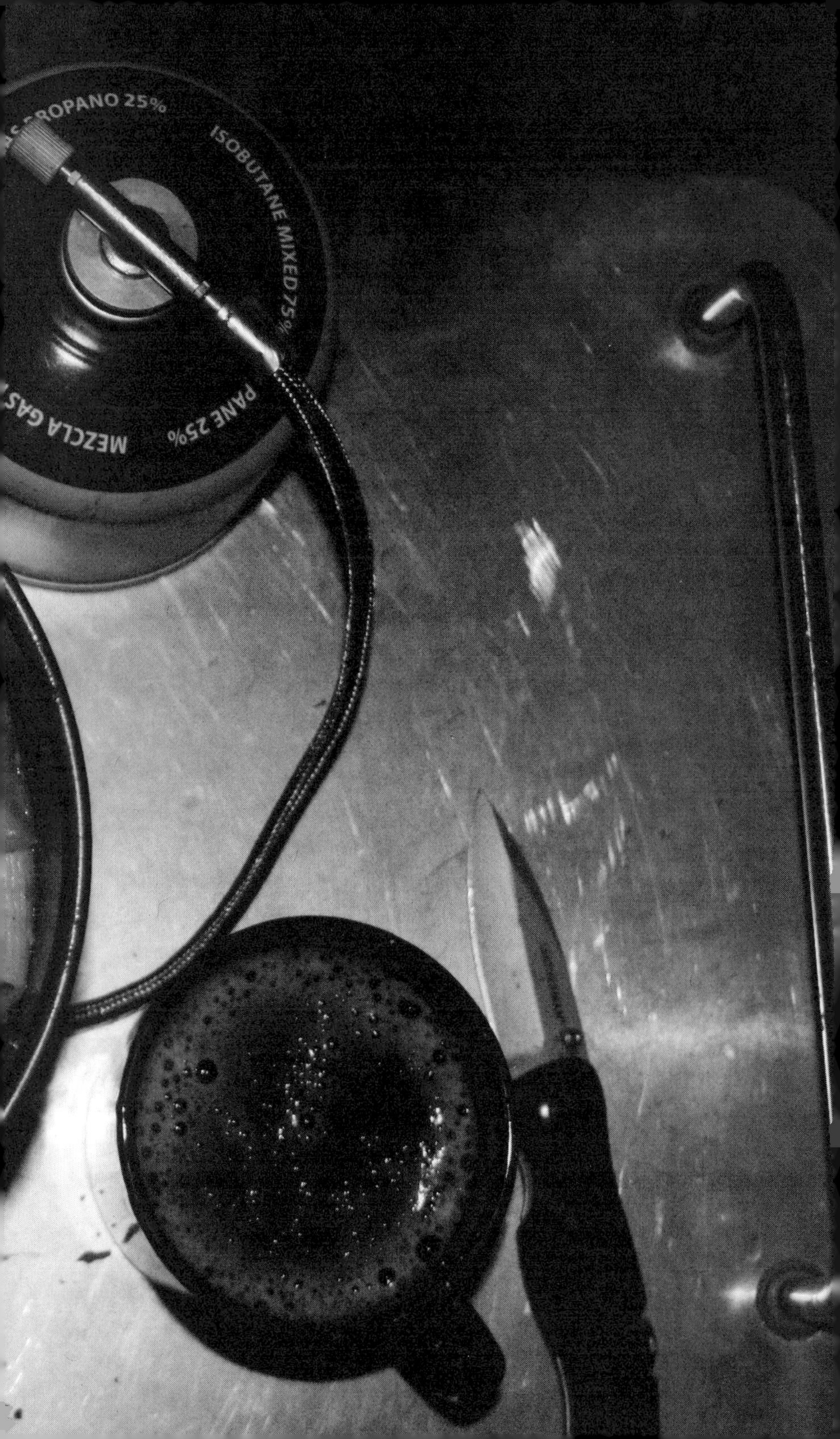
ISOBUTANE MIXED75%

CHAPTER 8

Belize

My Own Piece of Land

"When I'm walking and I see a puddle, I go like this," Klaas said, drawing his boot across the floor, as if digging a tiny ditch. "There, now that water can run away.

"The greatest joy in life is to make the ditches and lead water off the land," he said, his large bony hands tracing the imaginary contours of the land as his voice rose with excitement. "A Mennonite drains land if it's in Canada, Paraguay, or Belize. Every Mennonite likes to drain land."

Klaas was right. Mennonites are good at turning marginal land into productive fields, dominating nature to serve our needs. Perhaps it's our roots in the Low Countries, where holding water at bay was a matter of survival. Maybe it's thriftiness; Mennonites don't like spending their money. They like to buy cheap. Swampy land that needs draining can be had for cheap, and all it takes is hard work to make it profitable. Or maybe Mennonites just like the challenge of it, the satisfying result when waterlogged land is made productive.

I had planned this journey from an apartment in the urban chaos of Hong Kong, far from the Low Countries or the pioneering spirit of draining land, but envisoning my overland trip across two continents had given me an appreciation for topography. I hung large maps of the Americas on my wall to help me visualise my route. I circled the places where I knew Mennonites lived. The circles created a vague zigzagging chain that led from high on the wall, so high I had to stand on a stool to reach the locations, all the way south, near the floor, where I'd drop to my hands and knees, pencil clenched between my teeth as I tried to assess the challenges ahead. I'd stand back, admiring the maps, imagining the road that would take me across borders and mountain ranges, skirting coastlines and deserts.

Then I looked closer and traced the chain of circles with my finger. My maps were topographical, with grey marking the mountain highs, browns and light greens shading the foothills and plains, and deep green in the areas with the lowest elevation. The route I'd marked through southern Mexico, Belize, and down into Paraguay and Bolivia showed that the Mennonite settlements I'd marked were more often than not located on, or at least bordering, marginal land. Deep-green territory, where the land dipped and water gathered, areas that cartographers had marked with cross-hatchings. When the Mennonites had arrived, the land was swampy and wet, often covered in wild forest and jungle, but within a few years it was producing crops. Drainage was, as Klaas said, in our blood.

We'd earned a reputation for draining land, starting in the Low Countries and northern Germany, then on the Vistula delta, on the shores of the Baltic Sea, where we dug ditches and built dikes, turning the region into a rich green haven. We'd brought our skills to the Canadian Prairies, where we farmed wheat on the flood plains of the Red River, which regularly breaks free of its banks when it's overfilled with spring melt. Rosenort, the village that was home to both my parents, is ringed by a high dike to fight the spring tides. Farmhouses are built on man-made hills to keep clear of the annual floods. Each spring the farmers hold their breath, watching the river rise, waiting for it to break its banks. They rejoice when it doesn't and are resigned when it does. Time is measured in floods.

"Ya, that was the winter after the 1950 flood, so I would have been twenty-one years old…that means your mother was only nineteen then. So no, I don't think it was Mary who you're think-ing of…" say my elderly relatives when they reminisce, patching together a history measured in plantings, births, and floods.

My father left the Red River Valley at twenty-two to break virgin peat land on the boggy shores of Lake Winnipeg, in Man-itoba's Interlake region. He bought half a section, a 320-acre plot we always called Section 10, its designation according to the Dominion Land Survey in the 1800s. It was old-growth tamarack and spruce and luxuriant moss. It was home to bears and bobcats, wolves and wilderness that would take years conquer. There were no proper roads leading to it, and just beyond it lay mile after thousands of miles of wilderness. We were on the edge of nowhere. The land was cheap because it was beyond the fringe of civilization, part of a new agricultural frontier in the Interlake. The government offered my father favourable financing terms because he was a young man eager to help build Canada's agricul-tural industry, to tame the nation's vast expanse.

Grainy black-and-white photos in our family album show him and my mother, fresh-faced and smiling as they began carv-ing a farm out of the forest in the early 1950s. They were in their early twenties, poor but filled with the thrill of their prospects. It was a grand adventure to them. One picture shows them resting in waist-deep snow while cutting down the pine forest to make room for their first crops, another has my father on a borrowed bulldozer, pushing brush into long windrows for burning. Then there's the photo of him standing in his first crop of barley, which grew as high as his chest but couldn't hide his beaming smile.

But even with drainage ditches, the soil was often too wet to work. For Dad, digging drainage ditches became as much a part of farming as planting and harvesting. Ditching often took place in the autumn, after the crops were harvested. Sometimes it was just a simple deepening of ditches already dug with the tractor, other times my father would hire heavy machinery to transform the land-scape, thumbing his nose at nature.

But the tractors and harvesters still became stuck. My earliest memories of farming are being mired axle-deep in fragrant peat,

tire tracks filled with seepage. My father put rice tires on the harvester—although there was no rice being grown—hoping to better
churn his way across his swampy fields. To no avail. Instead,
he slapped at the hordes of mosquitoes and once again hooked
a logging chain to the harvester and instructed me to pull it taut
with the tractor. Sometimes the tractor's spinning wheels would
dig giant holes in the quagmire, pulling the machine deeper
and deeper with every revolution.

"No, no! Stop! You're just spinning, it's not doing any good!"
he'd shout over the throb of diesel engines.

I cursed and complained, an ornery teenager. "Why are we farming here? This is the worst place in the world to farm."

"It's good soil, we just need to drain it better. I'll put another
drainage ditch through here and then next year it will be dry,"
he said. But it was never dry. Some years we had to wait for
frost to firm up the waterlogged fields before the crops could
be harvested.

He didn't think about the historical significance, the places
where Mennonites been before, when he bought the land for cheap,
dug ditches, and won. He was young and poor and wanted land,
so sawing down virgin forest and leading the water away before
planting his first crops was the natural thing to do. But it didn't feel
natural to me as a child.

"I'm never gonna be a farmer," I told him more than once
as we stood knee-deep in bog, working to free the machinery.

Then, years after I'd left and my father had long ago accepted
that I wasn't the farmer he'd hoped I'd become, on a trip back
to Manitoba to visit my family, I told him I had some money
I wanted to invest. His eyes lit up and he leaned forward in his chair.

"Hey, there's some land for sale near here," he told me. "It may
not go up in value as fast as those stock markets do, but it will
always be there. They're not making more land."

The language of land—drainage, fences, good soil, stony
or not—was one I'd never learned to speak. But the idea
of owning land, my very own land, still appealed to the Mennonite in me. I'd thought the Mennonite in me had faded, replaced

by urbane tastes and an international lifestyle, so I was surprised at how his suggestion struck a chord in me. Drifting through the world's capitals earning a living with my pen was good fun, but owning land, now that was permanence. That was long-term planning, building something for the future. Owning land means you don't owe nothing to nobody. It means you're your own man.

There was an eighty-acre field a few miles from our own farm, but on higher ground, and for sale. It was cleared of trees, already tamed, and well drained. No digging of ditches needed. It wasn't boggy, I made sure of that.

So I bought the land with a loan from the hometown credit union, a small place where my family had banked for so long the manager still recognized my voice on the telephone. It was with great satisfaction that I took the *For Sale* sign off the gate and walked into the field for the first time.

I kicked a clod of soil and thought, That's mine. I eyed the slope towards the lake, pretending, for a moment, that I knew something about land. I had friends and family who owned thousands of acres, so there was a tinge of city-boy sheepishness to my pride in owning this modest plot. I knew I was reaching back to something that wasn't me anymore, that I had skipped some important steps. I hadn't broken my own land, planted it with crops, let the land tether me to a place, a community, church and family that consumed me all day every day for my entire life. It wasn't the same as what Section 10 had done for my family. This land had not been watered by sweat from my father's brow. It did not come with stories of hardship, work and progress. And I'd never be a real farmer like my father. But I did have a piece of my own land. Solid, well-drained land.

The topic of land—not enough, too expensive, where more could be found, which soil was good and which was bad—was discussed every day, with nearly every man I met on Mennonite colonies. On Spanish Lookout it wasn't just idle speculation. The colony was closing a deal to buy 29,000 acres of unbroken land, adjacent to the 55,000 acres they already owned. The leaders of the colony had called a meeting to discuss how the land would be divided among the eager farmers. The colony would hold the title to the land, and then lease it out to the farmers.

Martin was keen to put his name down on some of the land.

"I'm not sure I want to farm right now, but it would be nice to own some farmland. Later, I might like to farm," he said. "I don't want to be a wage earner all my life."

Being a wage earner and not a business owner or farmer was a big deal on the colonies. Mennonites—men, mostly—with a bit of money and entrepreneurial spirit found quick success on the colonies, leveraging the cheap labour, affordable land, and market opportunities around them. Most of the countries the Mennonites had settled in had underdeveloped markets, poor transport systems, and relatively porous tax and regulatory schemes. That created opportunities to build something from the ground up, and when the Mennonites did so they almost always made money. Being a colony member also made you a part of a country's business elite, with access to funding and advice.

Mennonite wage earners, on the other hand, had to compete with the low-paid local indigenous populations, and there were few protections offered to workers. While some colonies offered employee insurance and other basic benefits, that wasn't common. Working for an hourly wage was seen mainly as a stepping stone for young men before they began their own businesses, and as something young women did until they were married and had children.

So Martin, Klaas, and I went to the land meeting, which was held in an old clapboard church that had been converted into a community hall. The parking lot was nearly full of pickup trucks and motorbikes when I arrived. A steady stream of men entered the hall, exchanging muted greetings and handshakes. There were no women. An urn of weak coffee was drained into Styrofoam cups, slurped by men who stood in circles speculating on the sale.

Next to the coffee were four boxes of soil. Bright red, brown, black, and a sticky dark grey clay, numbered and cross-referenced on a map on the wall. The farmers crowded around the boxes, feeling the soil with their hands. Everyone was too engrossed in the boxes of soil to take any notice of me.

"Ya, this is the good red soil that we know, like on that field I have nearby," said one farmer, wearing a long-sleeved plaid shirt and jeans, a cap in his hand. His feet, calloused and stained with dirt, poked out of leather sandals. He nodded appreciatively as he plunged his hand into first one box, then the next.

I watched a younger farmer, thin, with a fair complexion and wispy blond hair. The man next to him appeared to be his father, slightly thicker than the young man, with a balding head of reddish-blond hair. They were conferring in low tones.

"Well, the land with this red soil will be expensive, we know that. Everyone wants more of that land. But maybe this blacker land, maybe that would be more affordable for you," the father said. "With those acres of the good stuff we have, it wouldn't be so bad if we had some of this blacker soil. Even if we just turned it into hay land."

The son's eyes shone with excitement as they turned to find seats. The room was almost full, and they stood at the back, rising on their tiptoes in the search for empty spots. They spotted two off to the side, and made a beeline for them.

The meeting was called to order, with 150 men turning their attention to the front where their leaders offered up a prayer of blessing. Every Mennonite meeting began with a prayer, so the business of taming the earth and making money was blessed by God. Conversations were hushed, hats were doffed, and heads bowed as the room fell silent.

"Lord, we thank you for bringing us together like this," said Clarence Dueck, one of the colony's three mayors. "We thank you for this opportunity before us, and for the work the men have already done. We ask you that you will guide us in our decisions, that we will do all of this in your name and for your glory. We ask that you be with us here tonight, Amen."

The Yalbac Land Purchase, consisting of two separate plots, lay just northeast of the existing colony. It bordered Labouring Creek, near the Green Hills land that the colony had bought in 1989, where Klass had been kidnapped. The new plot of land was wild and unbroken, with only a few rough roads and outbuildings installed by the previous owner.

Aerial photos and Google Maps images showed the different grades of soil. Some areas were suitable for raising cattle, in others the soil was marginal, but it could be used for certain crops, and then there were the spots with the good soil. Those were like veins of gold and they caused as much excitement.

"The average price is $1,200 an acre, some will go for $2,200 an acre, some as cheap as $750, we think," said Norman Reimer, another of the colony's elected leaders, facing the audience with his hands in his jean pockets. "For anyone bidding on the land, a 20 percent deposit is due in about two months.

"But there are a lot of things we have to decide first, a lot of things left to do. I can't emphasize that enough," Norman warned.

Work-thickened hands rose into the air, followed by deep voices asking questions about the quality of the trees on the land. Would they produce lumber? The hilly areas, where did they drain to? That area there, it looked rocky. Was it as bad as it looked from the air?

"It will pay to log the land first, but it won't be a logger's dream," Norman said, and the men nodded their heads in understanding. He flicked through photos until he found one showing a flattened forest of trees.

"This bit here was knocked down by the hurricane a few years ago, and then burned," he said. "But these are Cohune palm trees, and that's normally a sign of good land."

"And that red soil," another voice asked, from near the back of the room. "Is that the red soil we have on some of our other fields, that really good stuff?"

"Ya, we think so. We think the red areas will be very good cropland. This area is very flat and it will need to have some drainage put in," Norman said, pointing to the map.

It was hot in the hall, and I could feel sweat trickling down my back. There was a ripe smell rising from the men around me. They leaned forward in their chairs, conferred with one another in hushed tones, pointing at the map at the front. As Norman looked out over the crowd, waiting for comments or questions, the noise level from the small discussions rose, octave by octave, until the hall was a babble of voices.

Norman cleared his throat, but no one paid any attention. He tapped his microphone. The men ended their conversations in gruff whispers and turned back to the front.

"Are there any more questions?" Norman prompted.

"I think we all agree that this looks good," a grey-headed farmer in the middle of the room said. Necks craned to see who was speaking. He must have been a respected elder, as heads nodded and men smiled when they saw who was speaking. "The land looks good and I think there is plenty of demand here for it. So what is next? When can we start working on the land, get our machines in there and have it surveyed?"

"We have carried out the initial survey you asked us to do, and now we await further instructions from you," Norman said. "We'd like you to come to us and suggest what you think should be done next."

The leaders struck me as humble, obedient servants as they surveyed the room, inviting more questions. Norman pointed to a hundred-acre lake on the map, surrounded by bush.

"One suggestion we as a committee have is that we save this area. We could still use it for irrigation, but with half a mile of bush around it the lake would make a very nice wildlife reserve," Norman said.

The reserve was a generous gesture, but no one asked about the wildlife that inhabited the land, or what the environmental impact of clearing 29,000 acres of wild forest might be. Belize is home to jaguars, endangered Yucatán black howler monkeys, Baird's tapirs, peccaries, and green iguanas as well as a myriad of birds such as osprey, scarlet macaws, jabiru storks, and the national bird: the keel-billed toucan. They, however, were not present at the meeting.

Seeing how Costa Rica had turned its natural environment into a tourist bonanza had spurred Belize to pay more attention to preserving its own forests, but the government was also desperate for development. When it came to clearing land to create productive farmland there were still few safeguards in place. Deforestation was happening at an alarmingly fast pace, and Mennonites were at the centre of it. There were about 11,000 Mennonites in Belize, less than 4 percent of the population, but they were pro-creating faster than nearly every other ethnic group in the country, and that meant a constant need for more land. Despite the valid concerns of conservationists there were no environmental studies required before 29,000 acres of virgin forest would be cut down in one fell swoop.

The land purchase meeting was dragging on into its second hour. There were more questions: about payments, how the bidding process would work, and how the land would be divided.

"Okay, I think we've talked enough," Norman said. "It's time to hand in your requests, and then we'll go forward from there."

Everyone was given a small slip of paper printed with the different grades of land available, with space to write down their name and the number of acres they wanted of each category of land. Farmers passed the completed forms to ushers at the ends of the rows—just like passing their weekly offerings to the ends of the pews on Sunday mornings.

The men filed out of the hall, breathing in the fresh night air. They stood outside chatting in small groups, voices softened by the darkness. They slapped at insects, speculated, and dreamed about the opportunities the new land would bring.

"So, are you going to get some?" I asked Martin.

"That's our plan. These chances don't come often. My dad would like to see me take advantage of it too. Maybe he can help me break it."

The farmers climbed into pickup trucks and drove off, one by one. Martin and I, each on our own motorbike, followed them, choking on the dust that rose from the dark road. It was still early, but the colony was asleep, the place dark save for a few streetlights. Restaurants were shuttered, the gas station was closed, and the parking lot of the ice cream parlour was empty. Early to bed, for tomorrow was another day of work.

CHAPTER 9

Belize

Lower Barton Creek

The road slithered through mud holes and across the slippery exposed bedrock in the hills of western Belize. It was muggy, the morning rain having just ended. Someone had recently mowed the lush roadside grass, and the clippings were still scattered across the road. A wire fence, weaving and stumbling like a drunk, separated the mown verge and the fields beyond.

I came to a low sign that had been painted white at some point in the distant past. *Lower Barton Creek*, it said in clumsy hand-painted letters. Sleek, fat cattle stood under broad trees, pausing their grazing to watch me pass. More fences, still leaning tiredly, nearly home. The centre strip of the road, between the two tire tracks, was stamped with hoof prints and an occasional feculent offering.

Then, across a small valley, I could see tin roofs among the trees on a small hill, held up by unpainted concrete blocks. Ahead, I saw men mowing the grass. They were all dressed in the same blue or grey shirts, dark trousers with suspenders, and straw hats with black bands shading their faces. They wore long, untrimmed beards. Some wore rubber boots, others had muddy bare feet in sandals. Every one of them stopped their work as I approached and stared at me, open-mouthed. As I drew abreast of them they waved, machetes, scythes, and shovels in their hands, still staring.

Martin and Klaas had given me directions for how to get here, along with their version of Lower Barton Creek's origins. Life on the Spanish Lookout colony was good—sometimes so good that the most pious, including one of Klaas's brothers, split away from the church because they were afraid the comfort would lead them to hell. They created Lower Barton Creek to save themselves from hell.

"If you want to know how to live life the right way, the way God intended, just go visit my brother Walter," Klaas said, the sharp taste of sarcasm lacing his voice. "I believe that we must be in the world, telling people about Jesus and helping them and living with them. Walter believes that he must build a wall between himself and the world."

Klaas and Walter barely spoke to each other now, because they had differing views on church rules. Mennonites are not only better than *weltmensch*, but also better than each other. Disagreements on doctrine and lifestyle regularly sunder Mennonite communities. Mode of baptism is a popular point of dissent—some believe that a person must be immersed in water for the baptism to be effective, while others think simply sprinkling water on the believer's head is the best way. The churches that practise full immersion are seen as more charismatic, and many take such a hard line on the topic that they demand a sprinkled person be rebaptized if they want to change churches. I, for the record, was sprinkled.

Other splits happen because of choice of dress—white or black head coverings for the women, necktie or a plain shirt buttoned to the top for men. Someone is always taking umbrage with their preacher or fellow worshippers over their dress. They find a few others who agree with them and they start a new congregation that sets a new standard of Godly living and unity—until someone leaves.

Church splits often cut through families, and one side has to go to hell because the other side is right. Cousins become distant and unfamiliar because their father didn't join a splinter group with the rest of the family decades ago. Klaas and Walter were like that. Life on Spanish Lookout wasn't godly enough for Walter, so he helped create Lower Barton Creek, an atavistic colony far at the conservative end of the Mennonite spectrum.

The community, located only a short drive away from Spanish Lookout, was established in 1969 by families that came from Belize and North America. They used no electricity or engines, not even for farming—a concession even the ultra-conservative Old Colony Mennonites made. They grew everything they ate and took pains to limit their interaction with the outside world. Education was restricted to basic elementary school and the leaders decided what books and printed materials were allowed into the community.

I followed the tracks up a small hill until I saw Walter, an elderly man with a short stout body and long white beard. He opened his wide farm gate, greeted me, asked my name and where I was from, all in a brisk manner with little pause to hear my replies.

"You're a Dueck. Hmm. Let me think a bit," he said, turning towards the house and beckoning for me to follow. Walter wore the same blue shirt, dark trousers, and suspenders as the men I'd seen working beside the road.

I told him I was staying with his brother Klaas, and that Klaas had sent greetings. Walter grunted and nodded.

His farm consisted of a house, milking shed, hip-roof barn and a small chicken coop. The buildings were all unpainted and the windows had no glass, only screens and adjustable wooden louvres. The yard was verdant and shaded by towering trees. There were no engines to be heard, no whirring fans to worry the ear. Just peaceful silence.

Walter led me onto the veranda. Benches, a hammock, and a small table were set in the cool shade. His wife came out of the house and cleared a spot for me to sit. She wore a heavy black dress that reached her ankles and a severe black kerchief framed her broad face. She didn't say a word but stared at me as Walter filled the silence.

He repeated all of my details to his wife in a loud voice, a chippy lilt to his recitation. She nodded and returned to the kitchen.

Walter turned back to me and continued firing questions at me, as if playing a game. Family connections, community names, trying to place me in his mental map of the Mennonite diaspora. After five minutes of trying he gave up.

"I was only three when I left Canada, so there are many families that I haven't kept up with," he said.

Walter spoke English with a familiar accent that reminded me of my uncles in Manitoba, and just like them he sometimes switched to Plautdietsch for a punch line or even an entire thought. His family came from the same region as mine and the accent had stuck.

The idea to found Lower Barton Creek had been hatched by a group of families from various places and communities. While they were all running away from different problems, they shared a dream to escape modern society as fully as they could.

"We were Kleine Gemeinde but thought that the life was going too high," Walter said. "We didn't like the use of cars, the clothes were getting tight, and the young people were out of control."

"How do you know that you were living too high? What do you mean by that?" I asked.

"Well, we made too much money," he said.

The first big church split came in 1812, when southern Russia was already the cultural epicentre. The Kleine Gemeinde had already met separately from the main congregation in Molochna for several years because they felt spiritual life in the main church was suffering. They thought the majority of Mennonites were displaying poor ethics and morality, particularly those who were providing tacit support to the Russian military by paying fees to exempt them from service. Eventually the split became formal, and although Kleine Gemeinde was a derisive name, the breakaway church accepted it and used it themselves. Johann was Kleine Gemeinde. In the 1870s, almost the entire church community moved to my home province of Manitoba or the state of Nebraska. Splitting from the main church wasn't enough, they needed to leave Russia entirely if they wanted to live godly lives.

In Russia the Kleine Gemeinde were among the most conservative of Mennonite sects, but in Canada the Kleine Gemeinde became more moderate. And more wealthy. Those who disagreed with that change started colonies in Belize, where the little church maintained conservative social rules while allowing modern equipment for farming and transport. If you disagreed with colony life you could revolt and be damned to hell by joining the moderates and *weltmensch* in their sin, or you could rise up the ladder of piousness and go even simpler, even further back in time. Walter chose the latter.

"We tried to live our own way right where we were. But it didn't work well, we were too few, and in the midst of others. So we asked some of the Old Colony if they would join us, and we moved here. They gave up smoking and drinking, and we combined some things, like how we conduct the church services."

The colony, which had begun with twelve families, had gone through difficult early years, and some of its members moved to the US in the 1980s. Now, thanks to their large families, there were about fifty households for a total population of more than three hundred people, and they had spawned numerous daughter colonies in Belize as well as in Bolivia.

"It's still hard sometimes, but I hope that it remains alive. I have twelve children, ten boys and two girls, and seventy grandchildren. I've expressed my wish that they all continue to live like this, and they do," Walter said, leaning back in his seat, arms outstretched on the backrest.

I reminded him that I was staying with his brother Klaas. "Do you see him often?" I asked, knowing the answer.

"We would never go see our brothers and sisters in other communities," Walter said. "I don't like being around those people who believe and live differently. That could affect us and we might lose our faith. And I don't want to support their way, their pursuit of money. It's better if we just stay here."

Walter and Klaas might not have been on speaking terms, but they still shared a similar chummy confidence and outspokenness. They were both characters, not afraid of being different.

Oot bunt. But taking offence with his brother's sinful concessions to modernity gave Walter, the shorter of the two, a sort of pious high ground.

Walter paused, noticing the red blinking light of the camera mounted on the top of my helmet. I'd set the camera on the bench beside me, aimed at Walter.

"What is that?" he asked, pointing at the camera. The jocular tone was gone. "We don't allow any cameras, and we don't take any pictures."

"And if others have cameras?"

"We prefer that they don't take pictures of us," he said.

Martin had warned me that I would not be allowed to take photos on the colony, and I felt a bit ashamed for having tried. I turned it off with an apology.

"So what other rules do you have here?" I asked. "Why are all the clothes the same colour?"

"Well, they're not rules, we all choose to live this way," Walter said. "The colour of the clothes is not so important. We would buy cloth in other colours if these ones were not available. But the clothes should not be too tight, they should not reveal the human form. And we think it's better to have long sleeves."

Sewing their own clothes was another mark of virtue. Besides, anything adhering to their sartorial tastes was hard to find in shops.

"We still have to buy our shoes and our hats. It would be better if we didn't have to," Walter said.

"God meant for men to have beards, so why cut them? And the Bible says the man's hair on his head should be short. So we live just like that, so that you can see the difference between the men and the women. Though I also know of two sisters, Reimer girls, many years ago, who had full beards of thick hair. They had to shave." Walter chortled at the memory. It was a joke I could imagine Klaas sharing as well.

Children entered school at approximately seven years of age and completed their education by the age of twelve or thirteen. The government did not interfere with their curriculum, which consisted of memorizing the Bible, singing hymns, and learning basic arithmetic, reading, and writing.

"We don't learn why or how it rains. I don't know that stuff. We just burn off the forest, dig a hole, and plant our corn, and then we hope and pray that it rains. And if it rains, good, then the corn will grow better. If not, God will take care of us," Walter said. He was boasting, not apologizing.

Their farms used only animal and human power, producing cash crops such as potatoes and watermelons while also growing much of their own feed corn, pork, beef, and other food. Church leaders were currently debating whether harnessing a nearby stream for hydro-mechanical power was a sin or not. Some saw it as a natural way to power their flour mill, others disagreed.

"I don't like the idea because it's no different from using electricity, and we don't allow that," Walter said. "It means we're no longer earning everything with our hands. Maybe it will cause a split in the community."

Another split. Some brothers would be right and some wrong. Some on their likely way to hell, others maintaining the path of righteousness. The break would invariably separate brothers and sisters.

Interpretations of what was and wasn't a sin could be absurd. Even though they themselves were not allowed to own cars, they accepted rides in the vehicles owned by *weltmensch* when medical treatment or business necessitated long-distance travel.

"The *weltmensch* don't know any better," Walter explained.

However, they refused to accept a ride from more moderate Mennonites living on nearby Spanish Lookout, as that would be a sin. A Mennonite should know better than to drive a car, so accepting a ride from him was condoning his sin.

Martin had described the rule to me, chuckling the whole time.

"Mennonite guys from Spanish Lookout will stop and pick up people on the road who come from Barton Creek because they don't recognize the vehicles. So the driver speaks Spanish the whole time, and the guy he picked up thinks he's a *weltmensch*, and then as soon as they're doing a hundred kilometres an hour the driver starts speaking Plautdietsch, and the Barton Creeker thinks he's caused a sin," Martin said, giggling at the prank. "They beg them to stop the car so they can get out."

Someone on the colony was responsible for buying medical supplies and vitamins and distributing them, but not for profit, as earning commission was a sin. Walter's contribution to the community, besides his many offspring, was building wooden tables and chairs for anyone that needed them. The furniture on the veranda was painted a dull brown, but the house had no paint.

"Painting a house is just vanity," Walter said. "Paint costs money, and we don't think it makes that big of a difference in preserving the wood. Therefore, it's just about making the house look pretty, so we instead save that money, so we need to earn less.

"The downfall of many people will be their love for money, the constant need to make more money. But those people can eat no more lettuce or beans than I can," he said. "I could sell things for more money than I buy them for and tell people, 'Here, buy it, it's a great deal.' But I'd rather live off the land, although sometimes I'm concerned that we charge too much for our produce, which is also not right."

There was an old Mennonite saying, attributed to one of the earliest preachers, that emphasized the race for humility: When our hearts were golden our houses were wooden, when our houses became golden our hearts became wooden. While simple living and humility were preached in all Mennonite communities, most Mennonites also worked hard to grow their farms and businesses. Economic expansion and growth were seen as the positive fruits of their labour and honest living, as long as it didn't become all-consuming. There was no better way to gain the respect of the community than to have money and not show it. Buying a new car meant that someone had money, buying a fancy new car showed they were too proud. Where that line between success and humility lay was open for constant judgment.

"I've travelled through Mexico and into the US and Canada and I've visited many Mennonite communities and churches there," Walter said. "I think that most of them are living too high of a life. They have big farms, they bring these big trucks on the yard and load them with so many cattle to sell for money.

"Anything that is not necessary we try not to use. We need clothes, some food, a dry place to sleep. That's all we need in life."

However, it appeared that Mennonites couldn't help but generate wealth. Thanks to hard work and prudent farming Lower Barton Creek had literally generated a pile of cash, a fact that Mennonites on Spanish Lookout again shared with a snide snicker. The community had, for a long time, hidden their money in a hole in the ground rather than deposit it in a bank, as using a bank would represent reliance on modern society. But someone had shared the location of the colony's secret cache, and in the dead of night robbers had made off with the colony's savings. Now the colony had a single bank account. Within the colony, and with trusted nearby merchants, they still transacted with coupons in order to maintain better control of funds and ensure that people did not spend sinfully.

I thought about life in Hong Kong, where acquiring more, bigger, and better was the driving force for most lives. The more contemporary Mennonite colonies were little different from the rest of North America in their embrace of consumerism. Here, the attempt at living free and easy, surrounded by a close community of family and friends, was something any urban hipster would dream of. These Mennonites had removed themselves from many of the petty concerns of the rest of the world, focusing instead on what they believed to be most important, which was God and family. It wasn't that they thought technology or other modern conveniences were inherently evil. Rather, they simply saw that these things distracted them from their real goals.

The pastoral stillness of the farm was appealing. The beards and homegrown food, the suspenders and self-righteousness—hipsters would love all of that. But no books! No carving a guitar and starting a bluegrass band, no brewing craft beer, no riding of fixed-wheel bicycles or...none of that. Just work, family, and church. That's where the hipster dream ended for me. Perhaps there was too much work for boredom to be a threat. Or maybe that was why they all stared so much; they were bored but work kept them from doing anything about it. Maybe the boredom accounted for the big families.

Walter's holier-than-thou attitude, his sapient airs, also undermined it for me. They'd taken the self-righteousness of Mennonite separatism to a new level, and they wore it like a badge. It was an arrogance that was only possible when combined with a large dose of ignorance.

"I wouldn't say we've got it all right just yet. We still have to work against sin in our midst," Walter said. "I think we're very happy people here, some of the happiest in the world. Happiness makes you strong but crying makes you weak."

Walter's wife appeared in the doorway and beckoned us inside for lunch. The house was well-built and clean but gloomy without lights. Kerosene lamps stood ready for the night. There were a few small side cupboards, a daybed in the main room, and a small bedroom with a double bed and a colourful quilt visible through an open door. The quilts were the only colours I'd seen since entering the community, other than the bright blue of people's eyes. The floors were raw wood, and the walls were unadorned.

"You don't like people taking your picture, but does that mean you're not supposed to show any pictures in your house as well?" I asked.

"Yes. We burned all of our photos when we came here. Photos just make you proud. What do you do before taking a photo? You comb your hair and put on nice clothes. So now we don't need to worry about that anymore."

Walter was in the midst of a building project, adding a guest room to the house, as well as a skylight above the wood-burning kitchen stove at the request of his wife.

"She needs some light, so she doesn't over-pepper the eggs," he joked.

Walter directed me to a small washroom containing a bucket of water and homemade soap. They used river water for washing and rainwater for drinking.

We sat at a wooden table set by the window overlooking the pasture. Walter bowed his head to pray silently. The lunch was silent as well, our heads bent over tin plates with boiled potatoes and red beans, pickled cauliflower, bread and butter. Walter shooed the occasional fly off the food, but there was little else to be heard. No engines, no music, just the insects in the deep grass that grew around the house.

His wife, still quiet, served *plumma moos*, a creamy cold fruit pudding, and coffee for dessert.

"We don't always have food like this at lunch, with sweets, but we have a guest, so it's special," Walter said, winking at me.

When his coffee cup was empty Walter cleared his throat, looked at me to make sure I was following his example, and then bowed his head in pious prayer again. The others raised their heads and stood up from the table in one motion.

"*Na yo.* I guess I'll ride back to Klaas's place," I said. "I'll tell him you said hello."

Walter smiled as if that was a kind but unnecessary offer.

I could hear Klaas's voice and booming laughter spilling through the screened windows as soon as I turned off the motorcycle engine in front of his house. I sat on my bike, listening to the babble of voices from inside. Their uninhibited laughter was such a relief after the severity of Lower Barton Creek.

I'd become comfortable with the family, and I no longer waited for invitations to sit down. So I went inside and pulled a chair up to the table. I enjoyed their simple home with its panelled walls covered in multi-generational, multi-ethnic family photos and the dining table that hosted simple but filling meals.

"Your brother Walter mentioned something interesting when I visited him," I said to Klaas, hesitating for just a bit, wondering if I should ask about this. "Something about how you and Greta grew up together."

They both burst out laughing, Greta's face reddening, while Klaas slapped his knee in glee.

"What?! What's so funny?" Kenia asked, entering the kitchen.

"Well, Greta, why don't you explain it," Klaas said, a teasing tone to his voice. He had a twinkle in his eye, and his clumsy but good-natured ribbing and his love of laughter had made me expect a story every time he opened his mouth. Again, just like my own grandpa, his stories more often than not included a starring role for himself, which was more palatable given his humble demeanour.

"Well, ya. For five and a half years Klaas and I were relatives," she said. "My mom and his dad got married, that made us relatives."

"Oh, that story," Kenia said as she turned back to the kitchen.

"It was no big deal," Klaas said, waving his hand dismissively.

"When we moved from Canada to Mexico, we were both babies and our families were on the same train," Greta explained. "And in Mexico we were always in the same village and the same school, and he was my brother's best friend. Then we moved to Belize in the same big group, and we went to school together in the same village."

When Greta and Klaas were seventeen and eighteen respectively, they both lost a parent. Greta's mother and Klaas's father passed away, both leaving behind large families. Every family needed a woman to run the home, clothe and feed the family, and a man to work the farm, which provided for the whole household. It didn't take long for their widowed parents to marry each other, bringing the families together under one roof. Klaas and Walter and all their siblings moved into Greta's house, the building that had become Tina's school.

"I used my wits," Klaas said, grinning. We were still sitting at the dining room table. Greta, Kenia, and Evelin were in the kitchen, stopping their work to come listen or add their voice at critical points of the story.

"I liked her very much, but I knew that if she got to know me as her brother, we'd lose what is needed to get married, so I kept my distance. I was very shy. I always sat at the other end of the table and I was very careful to keep my manners so that she shouldn't lose interest in me.

"In my heart there was an immediate spark, but I hid it. I kept it closed," Klaas said as he put one of his large hands against his chest. "It took two or three years. I gave her an orange or two now and then, little gifts to keep her positive. I was very well-behaved."

Their parents were first cousins, making Klaas and Greta second cousins, but, as they both emphasized, they were not brother and sister by blood, and their family situation was out of their control.

"I read the Bible and it said Sarah and Abraham were relatives and they got married and so I thought I could too," Klaas said.

They chuckled, exchanging glances, ignoring the clamour coming from Kenia and Evelin, who were demanding details even though they'd heard the story many times before. Greta was still playing the innocent one, maintaining she was blind to it all.

"I thought we were just friends," she said, bending her head low over the stove.

They both fell silent when I asked what their parents had thought of it. Klaas cleared his throat.

"They were happy. Especially her dad was very happy. They had concerns, but..." He shook his head and then broke into laughter. "I was kind of a gentleman back then."

"It was hard," Greta says. "But we didn't know that adults could move out on their own. It wasn't done. If you weren't married, you belonged in the home."

Klaas nodded, staring at the floor. "If I saw that happening now, I'd say 'Boy, build yourself a small house at that end of the village and you live there, and your girlfriend lives here, and you come visit when you want to, and when you don't want to you walk on by.'"

Theirs was anything but a normal dating life, even by the modest and chaste Mennonite standards of the day. They lived under one roof as brother and sister for five years before getting married.

"I never had that excitement of the boy coming over to visit me, or asking me out on a date," Greta said.

"Klaas would get up early to do the milking, and I got up early to work in the kitchen as the housemaid, because we had a big family. Everyone else was still asleep at that hour, so we could talk a bit. We'd meet on the porch every morning and that was our date. Very little beside that. There were a few evenings, dates, where we'd really talk. Everyone was teasing us. The little brothers were curious, they'd watch everything we'd do."

Looking outside the Mennonite circle for love was strictly forbidden so they weren't the only ones to find partners close to home.

"Ben, he was seven years younger than Klaas, and he married
my sister's daughter," Greta said. "And then Kerneels came along,
another younger brother, and he married my brother's daughter.
And then the baby girl came along, and she married my cousin.
These marriages weren't any closer relations than anyone else,
but they'd just come to know each other as family, so it felt a bit different sometimes."

Marriages between distant cousins are still common today.
When romantic sparks fly, calculations are made, family trees
consulted. People who share grandparents are first cousins, while
sharing great-grandparents makes you second cousins, at which
point most cultures view marriage as acceptable.

"Sometimes we'd be happy when someone would move
to Canada, so that there wouldn't always be all this intermarriage,"
Greta says. "They moved to Arborg [an area with several Mennonite communities in Manitoba, Canada] and found second cousins
there to marry. At least it was a bit farther away."

And what if it were to happen in their own home, now? What
if one of their sons had taken a fancy to one of their adopted sisters—Kenia, eighteen, or Evelin, fourteen, and proposed marriage?

"Well, what would we be able to do? Is it wrong?" Klaas asked.

"This is different. We were adults when we became part
of the same family, and then got married," Greta said. "These
girls have lived with us since they were young children, they grew
up with our sons."

"It would be far better to marry someone from far away, from
Hong Kong," Klaas said, winking at me.

"Who might also be a second cousin!" Greta exclaimed, chor-
tling at my discomfort.

CHAPTER 10

Belize

Blue Creek Colony

The garden swing creaked softly, its movement hidden by the falling darkness. Ed's voice caught in his throat. He gave a wet sniff and paused to regain his composure.

"He was a special guy. Just the way people were drawn to him, the way the younger kids looked up to him. He was unique, no doubt about that, and we were lucky to have him for as long as we did," he said.

We were sitting on the concrete veranda of Ed Reimer's home on Blue Creek Colony. I was tired. I'd ridden several hundred sun-baked kilometres from Spanish Lookout, north towards the Mexican border, the last forty kilometres on a rutted dirt road with wallowing mud holes, to get here.

Near the door grew a field of workboots and sports shoes, all of them large, dusty, and scuffed. The covered carport was cluttered with a jumble of 4x4 pickup trucks, ATVs, motorbikes, and sporting gear. The land sloped away from the house, trees casting the lawn in deep shadow at the bottom of the hill. As the cooling air sank to the ground it dispersed the smell of earth, woody bark, and grass. A cicada trilled from high in a tree, echoed by a cricket hidden somewhere in the lawn, giving rhythm to the silence.

I couldn't remember having met Ed before, although he had

come to our farm when I was a child. He was a tall, athletic man in his mid-fifties with greying wavy hair and a tanned face. He spoke English with a familiar Canadian Mennonite accent. We had exchanged a few emails as I'd tried to predict the timing of my arrival, but I knew nothing about him until a few months before I had departed on this trip.

Ed's father and my father were friends, farming next to each other in Manitoba's Interlake region in the 1960s. Ed and Leroy, my second-oldest brother, attended the three-room Mennville Mennonite School together, decades before I started classes. They formed a deep friendship, dreaming that someday they would have neighbouring farms, just like their fathers. However, Ed's family moved to Belize when he was a teen, and here on Blue Creek Colony was where he'd become a man, working on his father's successful construction and farming business.

In 1978 my brother Leroy was twenty-one and engaged to be married. He was driving his new Mustang Cobra sports car down the highway on a windy autumn afternoon when he collided with an oncoming car. He and two people in the other car were killed. My family was reeling with grief when a letter of condolence arrived from Belize. Thirty-five years later, while sorting through my mother's papers after her death, I found the letter written by Ed in a bundle of condolence cards she had saved all these years.

> *I am certain that the loss of one of my dearest friends, the destruction of the dreams we had and the sorrow and regret that it brings, are minute compared to the anguish you as his family must have suffered, and continue to bear... As friends seldom are, we were closer than brothers, knowing each other's mind in all the things we did in those early years. I only hope and pray that we meet again in Glory.*

Shortly after, when Ed was back in Canada on a cross-country honeymoon trip with his bride, Carolyn, they stopped at our farm to comfort my parents. It was a gesture of kindness my father would never forget but that I could not remember.

I was only four years old when Leroy was killed. I remember the accident and the following days in short, faded scenes. The cry of my mother when my father came in from the fields and broke the news to the family, his face still blackened with dust. My mother throwing herself across the bed with a scream of anguish. The texture of the bed covering, small furry bumps in patterns I could feel on my cheek as I lay beside her, crying like everyone else but not understanding. The busyness of the house as relatives and friends gathered to offer support. Being held in my father's arms so I could look into Leroy's casket, reaching out to touch his cold hand. The blueness of Leroy's funeral suit. And then years of sorrow. With my older siblings at school or working on the farm I was left alone in the house with my mother, watching her cry, hunched in front of her sewing machine.

The loss of a child was a gulf my parents would spend the rest of their lives trying to bridge. The sadness was always there, just under the surface, brought back by the mention of Leroy's name, by an object he had once held in his hands, one of his doodles found inside an old book, the mention of his unrealized dreams. We had a place at the back of our farm, a clearing in the woods, that was a special place for Leroy. With time it became a refuge for the entire family, and especially for my brothers and me. We set up a simple cabin and firepit and it became the place where we gathered. His spirit still lived in the spruce and birch trees, in the sunshine that filled this spot where he had once been. Leroy's name was not always mentioned when we went there, but we went, in part, because we knew that there our family could be whole again.

Ed went on to live the life Leroy had lost. He did well in Belize, building upon what his father had started. Blue Creek Colony was about seventy kilometres north of Spanish Lookout by air, but several hundred kilometres by road. It was just across the Hondo River from La Unión, Mexico, and the Guatemalan border was just to the south. The porous borders were a part of daily life; smuggling was common, with beef, corn, and rice finding its way into Guatemala and Mexico, while goods such as fuel came into Belize.

Blue Creek had operated its school in English, Belize's official language, for twenty years, and many of its young people went on to university—a point of pride with Ed. The community reminded me of Mennonites in Southern Manitoba. Hard-working, churchgoing, successful farm folk.

Ed and Carolyn raised five sons, naming their first-born Leroy in honour of my brother. Now young men, Ed's boys were maintaining the family ties to Canada through education, summer work trips, and marriage. His son Leroy was in Canada, preparing a home with plans for his pregnant wife to join him shortly.

Then, almost thirty-four years after my brother's death and just months before I was to depart on my motorcycle journey, my family received the terrible news. Twenty-two-year-old Christopher, the third of Ed's five sons, was killed in a micro-light aircraft accident at an airport near their farm.

Chris had loved flying his micro-light, a passion he'd learned from his father and his uncle Albert, who both flew their own light aircraft. He was out early on a Sunday morning, making the most of the still air. A brother and a friend were there, watching from the end of the runway. He steered the aircraft into a turn in preparation to land when, at around five hundred feet, the wing crumpled, and he plummeted to the ground. He was pronounced dead at the colony hospital. The brothers insisted that Chris be buried on the family farm. His grave was almost in sight of the house, in a small meadow, in the shade of a towering tree with branches that spread broad and strong.

"He loved to do things, whether it was on his bike, his quad, his hang-glider. He loved his work. He loved to swim and he just loved life. He loved the people and it's so unfortunate that he fell from the sky that day. We are forced to mourn but we are not mourning without hope," Ed told the local newspaper after the accident. "We know that Chris fell from the sky because his man-made wings failed him but God picked him up and gave him the wings of angels."

My aged father heard the news through the Mennonite grapevine; the news struck a raw chord with him. He told me about it as I prepared my motorcycle for my journey. "Ach, it's terrible," he said, tears coming to his eyes. "I know how he feels, to lose a young son like that. It's something you can't imagine if it hasn't happened to you." The years and distance meant they hadn't kept in close contact, but the ties were still there, part of a diaspora that stretched up and down the Americas, linked by letters, churches, prayers, and intermarriage.

"You should go there, to Ed's place," my father said. "Tell him we heard about the accident, that we're sorry it happened, that we're praying for him and his family."

I was honoured to do so, but I also had my own reasons for wanting to meet Ed. As I grew into a teen in the years after Leroy died, I took on a stronger and stronger physical resemblance to him. People commented on it. The same colour of hair, similar eyes, my nose was a bit smaller, but the rest of my face was very similar. There were exclamations from friends of his when they'd see me. Tears came to the eyes of the woman he was to wed each time we met, even after I'd lived far beyond the age Leroy had reached. There was a look I'd sometimes see in my parents' eyes, a bittersweet mix of remembrance and hope. My father's emotional warning when I was a teenage driver: "I've already lost one son to the road—be careful." Sometimes it made me proud, that I was like my big brother, but as I grew older it became constrictive, an identity that I didn't want to own, or be beholden to. It was the identity of someone I mostly knew through the stories of others, stories that became family legends, the facts of which were often massaged in order to keep alive the good memories. Now I'd have a chance to meet someone else who had known Leroy as a child, but from outside the family. Someone whose stories of him—I hoped—would be different from all those I'd already heard.

But on that first night on Blue Creek we sat on the darkened veranda and I instead listened as a grieving father searched for comfort in stories about his own dead son. The stories were all interrupted by the inelegant, desperately restrained sobs of a grown man. Ed's stories wound in circles between anecdotes of him revelling in the wildness of the Belizean outdoors and boasts of Chris racing his ATV.

"The rest of the guys, well, there were some serious racers in it. From all over the area. Chris, he was just having fun," Ed said, a smile in his voice. "Carolyn and I, we were standing beside the track watching, before the race, and the mother of one of the top guys, she was next to us. She told us about all the races her son had won, and we thought, Oh man, Chris won't have a chance.

"Chris had problems with his four-wheeler. He had to make some repairs at the last minute, so we thought, well, there goes his chance. And the rest of the guys were all far more experienced." Laughter crept into Ed's voice. "So he was out there, and he beat them! He won! And he was just there for fun, just riding hard, but he was fast."

Ed's large rice farm and processing plant created jobs for his sons, and their social circle was mostly other young Mennonites from the region. They drove motorbikes and ATVs, boats, 4x4 pickups. They hunted wild game and swam in the rivers. Chris was sometimes the odd one out among his brothers, less aggressive, more creative and introspective. But the brothers had always backed one another, always acted as a unit, constantly together, with shared circles of friends.

"Chris loved going barefoot. Whenever he could, he'd leave his shoes at home. After the accident, some of the young people from the church went barefoot. They said it was to honour him…"

The story trailed off into hard swallows and choked sobs as he was overwhelmed by the memory. In my head the stories and memories of Chris and Leroy mirrored each other, became each other. More than three decades and thousands of miles apart, different countries and families, but the story was the same, and I couldn't help but wonder.

"Has all of this, the accident, Chris's death, has it reminded you of Leroy at all? 'Cause it sure brought up a lot of memories for us," I said.

"A bit, sure. When you contacted me and said you'd like

to come visit, sure I thought of it."

I waited. Hungry for a story, something about Leroy. A memory, an image, a morsel of Leroy's character. But Ed said nothing more, and I didn't want to prod a grieving man.

We were sitting enjoying the quiet of the night when Carolyn opened the door, padded barefoot across the cool concrete, and put a hand on Ed's shoulder. Carolyn was friendly but quiet, offering up a cautious smile. She was a pretty blond woman, but she looked tired, her eyes wounded with grief.

"Are you hungry?" she asked Ed softly, and then looked at me. "Have you eaten?"

They soon settled on taking me to a local restaurant. "Are you going to stay the night with us? You're very welcome to," Ed said.

"Yes, I'd like that. I'm not sure what my plans are for the next few days, to be honest."

Ed picked up one of my bags and turned to carry it inside, waving off my explanation with his free hand. "It doesn't matter. Stay as long as you like."

When I awoke the next morning Ed and his sons were already out of the house, working on the farm. I felt a tinge of embarrassment as I realized I was the last out of bed, by a long shot. I found Carolyn in the kitchen, softly singing along to the radio as she did the dishes.

"You must have been tired," she said as she poured me coffee.

My sleep had been filled with dreams. Sentimental dreams, faces I recognized but didn't know, tragedies that I felt but couldn't quite understand. Stories that didn't have endings, ones that I wasn't sure were false or true.

I felt raw and hesitant as I nursed my coffee and watched Carolyn work. The kitchen and the dining area were full of good smells and tidiness, a refuge of femininity in a house otherwise filled with masculinity. Just outside her range of influence lay a rifle, on a shelf above the stairs. Tools and random spare machinery parts were scattered around the entrance.

"It's an all-boys house," I said.

She laughed. A light, girlish laugh. "Ya, I guess it is. That's why I'm so excited when the boys get married, because I get a daughter out of the deal."

I spent the morning at the table with my laptop, catching up on emails and writing as Carolyn moved around the kitchen, humming, clattering pots and pans. The peace was broken when Ed and two of his sons returned for lunch, filling the house with heavy footsteps and loud voices once again.

After lunch we relaxed around the table and laughed as Ed teased a parrot they had taught how to speak.

"Hello, hello," the parrot squawked, gnawing on Ed's fingers as he playfully batted it on the beak.

"I need to go check on a few things out on my fields," Ed said, pushing his chair away from the table and returning the parrot to its cage. "Why don't you come along and I'll give you a bit of a tour."

We took a brown extended-cab Chevrolet 4x4 truck that Chris had converted to run on natural gas rather than gasoline or diesel. It ran loud, and with Ed at the wheel, it ran fast. There was little traffic on the road, and he made use of the space, lunging the truck through washed-out holes on the back-country roads.

"This truck was his pride and joy," Ed said, one arm dangling out the window, the other hand whirling the wheel back and forth as we hammered down the road. "It's a good truck, and I didn't want to sell it, so now I drive it. Reminds me of him all the time I'm in it."

The hills here were a bit steeper and more tightly wound than on Spanish Lookout. Blue Creek colony was also much smaller, with only about eight hundred people. But still, the farms stood out from the surrounding area, with rutted Belizean roads improving to hardtop as soon as you crossed onto colony land.

Ed raised cattle in addition to rice, although he had recently sold a large number of cattle when prices had spiked. We stopped at the corral, where he found one of his favourite horses standing under a tree, its tail swishing to and fro in a battle with the flies. Ed climbed over the fence and slapped its neck to say hello. The corral was part of a larger ranch station, with outbuildings and equipment, as well as a small house.

"I like coming out here for a week at a time," he said. It wasn't far from home, but staying at the house allowed them long days of working the cattle and a sense of escape.

He drove the 4x4 truck across the wet pasture, tires spinning on the turf, in search of his hired cowboy. We crested a small hill and found him riding the fence by horseback. A sun-blackened Belizean about Ed's age murmured quiet answers to Ed's questions in Spanish. He'd worked for the family a long time, a trusted employee, and their exchange was relaxed and friendly. Ed hung out the truck window, swatting at the occasional fly, while the cowboy stayed on his horse, surrounded by grazing cattle.

At the back of the pasture was a large pond full of stagnant water and a tangle of wire-mesh cages, the remnants of Ed's foray into fish farming. He had also tried growing oranges, which hadn't paid off. But what Ed really wanted to show me was the creek at the far end of his property, with gnarled mahogany and Santa Maria trees casting the creek in deep shade. He pointed to a rope that dangled above the sluggish green water, smiling to himself.

"The boys have had a lot of fun here. We'll come as a family and camp out for a few days once it cools down a bit," he said. There was a tiredness in Ed's voice even as he described the good times they'd had there, the boys swimming in the creek, the meals cooked over the fire, the neighbours who came to join them. A weather-beaten picnic table, the steel-tube frame of a large tent, and a firepit awaited the next camping trip. Ed kicked at a clod of grass clippings. "We brought the mower in here to get things ready for this year's campout."

"We also have a place like this on our farm, a clearing in the bush with an old cabin," I said. "Leroy used to enjoy spending time in those woods, so the place became more special after he was gone."

Ed didn't respond. He was lost in his own thoughts, looking up at the treetops.

"What do you remember of him? What was he like when you knew him?"

"Hmm." Ed narrowed his eyes. "Man, it's a long time ago. I just remember we were good friends. Like brothers. He was funny, I think. Funny and he liked adventure."

Ed had known Leroy only as a young boy, but I'd still hoped for more. Funny and liked adventure. That could have been any boy, anytime, anywhere. I was disappointed.

"What did you guys do? What kinds of trouble did you get up to together?"

"I guess we must have rode our bikes around. Played in the bush. I don't really remember." Ed shrugged. Forty years of time, five sons of his own who were funny and liked adventure and the blinding slash of Chris's death had pushed memories of Leroy far away. I was grasping for a cord connecting me to a bittersweet past and it wasn't there.

We wound our way back into the heart of the colony with Ed pointing out the churches, school, and clinic. He stopped at the local airport, the one where Chris had crashed his micro-light, to show me his Cessna. Flying and owning small planes was popular on many colonies due to the expanse of the land and the state of the roads. Ed's airplane was a small red-and-white four-seater that he flew to business meetings around the country when the rough roads were too slow. We walked around the small plane, Ed describing some of the flights he'd made in it. He opened the logbook and thumbed through its pages.

"Somehow my interest in these sorts of things has disappeared a bit," he said.

We stood outside the hangar, chatting with his pilot friends for a few moments. As Ed and I had criss-crossed the colony, stopping at the store and pulling to the side of the road to exchange hellos with neighbours, I'd noticed a steady, quiet support. It was only a few months since Chris had died, there was still a softening of the eye when farmers met Ed, a casual hand on his shoulder, a lingering handshake of sympathy. The families on the colony had borne Chris's death like it was one of their own children, and while life had to go on, they hadn't forgotten.

But the airport was making Ed restless. His eyes roved

the airfield, his answers to my questions grew absent-minded and detached. We climbed back into Chris's pickup truck and continued driving.

Blue Creek was populated with relatively progressive Mennonites, while neighbouring Shipyard Colony, with over 2,000 residents, was Old Colony. They were far more conservative and were not allowed to use motorized transport, and their houses did not have electricity. However, the colony was well-known for its carpenters, blacksmiths, and machining shops. Ed had a steel shaft that needed lathing, and several steel girders he wanted to sell, so we headed for Shipyard, where they would have the right tools to do the job and would know who needed steel girders.

"One time I had a broken hydraulic-drive pump for one of our earth-moving machines," Ed told me. "I had all the books, the manuals for it, and I read them again and again. I adjusted this valve, that one, I tried everything, but I couldn't get the thing to work properly. So I took it to a shop on Shipyard. I showed it to the owner of the shop, but he said he didn't have time to look at it himself. 'I'll have my boy look at it, he's pretty good,' he told me. This skinny fourteen-year-old kid in *schlaub'betjse* comes over. I was a bit annoyed. I figured, okay, fine, if this kid wants to tinker with it while I wait for a real mechanic, let him. He didn't even look at the manual I showed him. He starts fiddling with the pump. The pump is disconnected now, lying in the back of my truck. He can't even see how it fits in the machine. This kid, he had no clue what that pump was supposed to do on the machine. So I tried to tell him, this goes to this bit, this valve does whatever. And he was just quiet, sticking his fingers in here, there, feeling around. He played with it for a long time, and then he pulled out a screwdriver and made a few adjustments. 'There, it should work now,' he told me. I laughed, I thought, Ya, right. But his dad was still busy, so I took the pump home. And it worked! I have no idea how that kid figured it out. They don't go to school long, but they're not stupid."

We arrived at a shed that had started with wood, then grew with concrete and steel as the business flourished. Carriages littered the yard, the horses tied to posts in the shade of the trees. Next

to the horses were rows of modern machinery, gleaming beasts
of burden driven by the latest technology. But the red, yellow,
and green machinery stood on steel wheels from a century ago.
Some as tall as a man, others narrow and delicate, all made of steel
with treads welded from iron.

Old Colony Mennonites are not shy about embracing technology when it comes to farming, but anything driven by an engine
has to ride on steel. Anything pulled by a horse, or trailers pulled
by tractors, can ride on rubber tires. This forces a slower pace
of life, because even the relatively slow ride of a rubber-tired tractor might be too much temptation for young men eager to explore
the nearby towns. The shuddering ride of a steel-wheeled tractor
is not suitable for joyriding. The few tractors outside the shop that
were on rubber tires belonged to others—*weltmensch* or more moderate Mennonites—and had been brought here to this *schmiede*
for repairs.

Inside, the high-pitched whine of blades cutting into steel
was measured by the crash of metal being stacked and moved
from station to station, men shouting to be heard over the din.
The air was filled with the acrid smell of smoke, of hot metal
and grease.

Henry, the manager, had an ebullient red face held down
by a grubby white cowboy hat. A bright orange measuring tape
hung from the pocket of his dark trousers, and his legs shifted
and twitched with energy. He engulfed my hand in his thick calloused paw and pumped it heartily.

The shaft was unloaded from Ed's truck, precise instructions
and measurements were conveyed. But there was still the matter
of the steel girders. Ed had taken photos of the girders with a digital
camera, and now he, Henry, and a worker bent over the screen, discussing their potential uses. Henry knew a few people who might
want them.

He walked off through a side door of the *schmiede* and pulled
a mobile phone out of his pocket. He dialled a number and leaned
against the red flanks of a giant forklift with one hand, star-

ing alternately out to the fields beyond the tree line and down to his boot, which kicked at the dirt.

Henry made several calls, then turned back to the *schmiede*. He looked up and saw that I was watching him.

"I noticed you were using a mobile phone. That's allowed on an Old Colony?" I asked.

Henry laughed, his hand patting the phone in his pocket.

"It's not my phone. It's one of the workers', so it's okay," he said. "I use it sometimes, here at the shop. But I never take it home."

Old Colony farms and businesses often employed *weltmensch*, in part because they could bear the sin of carrying a mobile phone or driving the pickup truck to town. That distance from the activity—registering a phone or truck in someone else's name—was enough to negate the sin of using the technology.

"I've called a few guys who might want the girders," Henry said. "Someone will take them, I'm sure. They're perfect for building a nice strong trailer."

As we said goodbye and turned to leave Henry remembered something.

"Do I have your number?" he asked Ed. Henry fished his phone from his pocket and checked his contact list. "Ya, I have it. I'll be in touch."

I smirked at Henry. So it was his phone, not his employee's. Double lives, one for the church and one for themselves. It was a duplicity that I'd soon see the Old Colony Mennonites put to far more sinister use than mobile phones.

It was late afternoon when we returned to the farmyard. Ed excused himself to look after some paperwork in his office. Carolyn was not in the kitchen and the house was quiet. I walked out onto the veranda. The sound of machinery, the rev of a diesel engine, and the clang of metal drifted up from the meadow that held Chris's grave.

Ed's son Anthony had been working for days, mowing lawns and cleaning up the farmyard in preparation for his wedding. The wedding was to be held on the same open field where Chris was buried, and Anthony was removing the rusting hulks of old machinery, tangles of old fencing and vines. I walked down the hill and watched him behind the wheel of a tractor, lifting the remnants of steel machinery high in the air and then dropping them onto a trailer with a screeching crash.

Carolyn sat nearby, beside Chris's grave, her arms wrapped around her knees. I held back for a moment, and then went and sat down beside her. The grave was so fresh that grass had not yet overgrown it. A grey scar on the green meadow. Carolyn's eyes were red-rimmed, her nose running. We sat silently, letting Anthony and his machinery fill the void.

"He would have loved to be here for this wedding," she said. "The boys are all very excited, all playing a part, and we really feel Chris's absence now.

"It's a happy time, to see my son get married, to welcome a daughter into the family. But it's also hard, because the accident is still so recent. And it's a reminder, that there will never be a wedding for Chris."

Leroy was nearing his own wedding when he was killed. My parents had objected to the wedding—she wasn't a Mennonite, a born-again Christian. She was a *weltmensch*. But after his death they embraced her, and they mourned together until she was able to move on with her own life.

"What do you remember about our family and home from your visit after Leroy's death?" I asked.

"It's a long time ago," Carolyn said. "We weren't at your place for long, but I know it was important for Ed to come see your parents. I mostly remember the community, how they surrounded your family. Your parents were grieving, but you could feel the strength, the faith that was still there."

"That's the same thing I feel here, now, with you and Ed," I said.

"I can't imagine what it would be like without the community we have around us here," Carolyn said. "They, and our faith, have kept us going."

"My mom and dad, for years after Leroy died, they found a lot of comfort in supporting other families who lost children. Dad always said that you couldn't imagine what it was like to lose a child if you hadn't experienced it. We went to a lot of funerals and they took me along to some of them. A lot of young people that they barely knew, Mennonites and non-Mennonites. They visited people in their homes, wrote cards. I don't think they had much to say, no special advice or anything. They just wanted to tell these parents that others had felt this pain and lived through it."

The machinery was turned off and its noise was replaced by the creak of settling metal and the clatter of chains as Anthony secured the load. We alternated between watching Anthony at work and staring, blankly, at the overturned earth of Chris's grave.

Ed appeared, walking across the meadow from the house. During the day, as we'd driven across his land and he'd conducted his business, there were moments where his face would break into a careless smile, when the tasks at hand absorbed his full attention. He was a confident man, respected and well-liked in his community, and he carried himself with pride.

Now I watched as he approached. His body drooped as he neared the grave and saw Carolyn curled up in a defensive ball. He greeted me quietly, then sat down and put his arm around Carolyn's shoulders, and together we waited for darkness to fall.

CHAPTER 11

Central and South America

Fronteras

For the next few weeks I could forget about Mennonites. I knew there were few, if any Mennonite communities in the rest of Central America, so I focused on making miles south. I crossed from Belize into Guatemala and watched the countryside roll by. Shaggy fields of bananas and sugar cane were hewn out of the landscape by hand, and every bit of available space between the small homes and the mountains was turned to food production. Passing trucks groaned with loads of corn, melons, and palm fruit. I slowed to pass women walking on the sides of the road, colourful shawls wrapped around their shoulders and huge bundles of firewood and hay balanced on their heads. Children shouted and waved from schoolyards. Untethered horses grazed beside the road and bolted with a snort of alarm when I tooted my horn.

In the somewhat redundantly named city of Antigua Guatemala, in the country of Guatemala, I met two local riders who offered advice to passing riders via an Internet motorcycle forum. Richard and Suzanne were Americans who had moved to Guatemala to escape the rat race seventeen years earlier. They were just two in a sprawling fraternity of motorcyclists who welcomed me to their towns, directed me to hotels, helped me find repair shops, and allowed me to sleep on their couches. The simple fact that we all rode motorcycles meant we were never strangers.

Richard and Suzanne led me through Antigua's quaint Spanish Baroque streets and up a mountain road to the Earth Lodge, an eco-resort that overlooked the city.

"You have to try the sausage burger at this place. It's the best you'll ever taste," Richard said as we sat on the veranda with Volcán de Agua, Acatenango, and Volcán de Fuego all visible in the distance, puffs of white smoke against the clear sky.

I ordered the sausage sandwich and when it arrived I took one bite and grunted in surprise. The smoky, salty flavour and firm texture were unmistakable.

"This is *foarmaworscht*. Mennonite-farmer sausage."

Before setting off on this journey I had researched where I would find Mennonite colonies, marking them on maps taped to my apartment walls. There were no Mennonite communities marked on my map of Guatemala. We called the chef to our table, and he told us he had bought the sausage in a nearby village.

In the morning we drove to the village of Tecpán. We couldn't find the butcher the chef had told us about, but we were directed to a small bakery. The women behind the counter, including a few Guatemalan employees, wore long dresses and head coverings. Unmistakably Mennonite.

They told me there were a handful of Mennonite families living in Tecpán and nearby Chimaltenango, where American Mennonites had run a mission since the 1960s. The Guatemalan women wearing Mennonite garb were evidence of their success.

"*Tjenne jie* Plautdietsch *vestohne*?" I asked them.

They stared at me blankly. No, they could not understand

Plautdietsch. The mission had been set up by Swiss Mennonites from the US Midwest, descendants of Mennonites who had migrated to the Americas directly from Germany and Switzerland two hundred years before Johann had migrated. Their language was slightly different, and they didn't keep moving all over the Americas in search of cheap land and wilderness to hide in. The ethnic Mennonites in Guatemala were now outnumbered by the Kaqchikel and K'iche' Mayan people that had converted to the Mennonite faith.

I asked the women behind the counter if they knew about the large Mennonite communities in nearby Belize. They knew they existed, but little more. Swiss Mennonites have their own diaspora of missionaries, but not colonies like those created by Russian Mennonites.

The discovery that they were Swiss Mennonite rather than Russian instantly erased my sense of familiarity. Even though their lives would closely resemble those of conservative Russian Mennonites, their faith and religious practices nearly identical, their history was different. Their history did not include the vehement rejection of state control, the repeated international moves in search of seclusion, the cultural mix that created, which was cemented into our identity. At one time we decided we were different enough to split from them, and that was enough to destroy any sense of community I felt standing inside the warm bakery.

This was a very Mennonite thing to feel, this clannish view of people. The Swiss Mennonites really were still my people, but they were different, so I focused on the differences. Us and them. We built fences, and you were either on one side or the other.

In southern Manitoba the Mennonite community is divided by the Red River. Johann arrived on the east side of the river, but a large group of his shipmates soon moved to the other side of the river in search of better land, and Mennonite towns on both sides have prospered ever since. That created an us and them. They're *jant' sied*, the other side. In the western towns, they refer to the east as *jant' sied*. The term is not just geographical but is used to explain and describe the minutiae of differences that develop

among villages over time. Often it is used in jest—I've heard
my family accuse those on *jant' sied* of defiling hallowed Mennonite culture by adding syrup or using strawberries instead of plums
in traditional recipes. It's fair play to discredit someone for being
from *jant' sied*.

This was not one of the Mennonite traits I hoped to find
in myself on this journey, but there it was. Swiss Mennonites were
not *my* Mennonites. It dawned on me like an upset stomach that
this feeling was about as Mennonite as I could get. Dismay, familiarity, and a humbling acknowledgement of one's weaknesses.

I said goodbye and went outside, where Richard and Suzanne
were waiting on their motorcycles in the parking lot.

"Are these your people?" Richard asked me. "Do you know them?"

"Nah, they're from the States, not Canada," I said as I swung
my leg over my seat and put my helmet on. "Swiss Mennonites."

"But they're Mennonite, right?" Richard asked, shouting
now because I'd already started my bike.

I shouted back, muffled by the helmet: "Yeah, they're Mennonite, but a different kind."

In Mexico speed bumps were called *topes*. Sometimes the warning signs called them *reductor de velocidad*, and in Guatemala,
El Salvador, and Honduras the speed bump was darkly referred
to as a *túmulo*—a burial mound. Some were painted bright yellow,
giving me a chance to slow down or ride around the edge, but others
blended in with the road and announced themselves in a violent
collision that bottomed out the suspension on my overloaded bike
and left my spine tingling. More often, they lurked and hunted you.

The police and military manning the many roadblocks
weren't happy with simply slowing me down—they wanted more.
In Mexico a cop asked for my pocket knife. I said no. In other places
they boldly asked for payment. I declined. I had time; I could wait
them out. I had not paid a single bribe all the way across Mexico,
and so far, I'd dodged them in Central America. It was becoming
a mission.

I entered Nicaragua underneath the smoking peak of San Cristóbal, the country's highest volcano. The mountain roads were narrow, the oncoming truck traffic too heavy for me to make a legal pass, so I began passing on the shoulder. Dangerous, but very effective. It didn't take long for a policeman to stop me. He was sweating in a tight brown uniform, a squawking radio on his hip.

He said something about riding too fast, too dangerous. I played ignorant, which wasn't hard with my limited Spanish.

"*No comprende*," I said, shrugging my shoulders. "*No hablo español.*"

The policeman studied my papers, sucking on his teeth. He made a snaking motion with his hand, then wagged his finger in my face, scolding me in Spanish.

"*Ahh, comprehende!*" I said, pointing at the pavement, which was still wet with the morning rain. "*Mucho agua!*" I said, squatting down beside my bike and wiggling my bottom to mimic a fishtailing motorcycle. "*Mucho problemo!*"

"Managua. You come," the policeman said, tightly gripping my papers and beckoning me to follow him to the nearby capital, playing the old pay-now-or-come-with-me game.

"No, no," I said, shaking my head and pointing in the opposite direction. "Leon. That way."

"You pay here."

"You give me a receipt."

The look he gave me made it clear that a receipt would not be forthcoming. He went to his police truck, where I could see him shuffling through papers and speaking on the radio while I waited.

Ten minutes later the policeman returned, handing me my papers.

"*Vamoos!*" he said, and waved me off in disgust.

From Nicaragua I approached the Costa Rican border. Two kilometres from the *frontera* I felt my shoulders tighten, my jaw clench. I already knew what was coming. Every border was the same, teeming with fixers for hire to help you get your documents processed.

"Hey, amigo! Buddy! Hey brother!"

The young men tugged at my jacket and tank bag, grabbing the handlebars of my bike, which was still rolling forward, weaving between haphazardly parked trucks, women with crying children in tow, swarthy men wearing scowls and scuffed boots.

"Ten dollars, brother! Just ten dollars to do your paperwork!"

"No thanks, I'm okay," had no effect. "I'll do it myself," I repeated, more firmly. Still the hands picked at my jacket, worryingly close to my pockets, the crowd of agents, two deep around the bike, all shouting their offers so loud they couldn't hear my refusals.

The detritus, the dregs of society that each country produces, gather at the border crossings: beggars and cons, prostitutes and paper-pushers, bribe-hungry cops and lice-ridden dogs. Whether attracted there, pushed there, or abandoned there as the rest of society rushes across, they form a bathtub ring of life at every *frontera*. The ring differs in width and colour, in degree of grime and crime, but is unavoidable and ever-present.

The money-changers are there to feed off it, buying pesos and selling dollars on one side of the line, taking the opposite side of the deal on the other, their pockets bulging with rolls of cash.

"*Cambio dinero? Cambio?*" one enquired, coming close, engulfing me in a sour cloud of breath and sweat. He stood beside me flipping through a stack of currency held together with a thick rubber band. *Brrrrrrrrp*, it went as he brushed his hand against the edges, revealing a rainbow of notes and wealth. *Brrrrrrp. Greenredbrownpinkyellowgreenred* the bills flickered through his fingers.

"*Cambio dinero? Dollar? Peso? Quetzal?*"

He smacked the stack of money into his open palm with a *thunk*, the sound of a good day's business. His eyes never left my face: "*Cambio?*"

"Copy? Copy?" was the next thing I heard. I turned to see a teenager whose hands were suspiciously close to my tank bag zipper. Was I being paranoid? He moved his hands when I took a step towards him. "Give me your passport, I make copy."

Border crossings had fallen into a routine as I rode through the tiny states of Central America. A week in Guatemala, a hurried crossing of Honduras, El Salvador a blur of road signs. The process—immigration, copies, fees, stamps, copies, customs, copies, fees, currency exchange—was so dizzying and repetitive that at times I forgot which country I was entering and which one I was leaving. The faces of the guards, the officials, the money-changers and touts, the rows of dusty copy shops staffed by sleepy old women blurred into one another. Hey, didn't I buy quetzals from you at the Guatemalan border just a few days ago? Each *frontera* marked a different state, a different currency, and small shifts in the documents, fees, and stamps I needed, but they were also all the same.

Everyone at the border seemed to know each other. The fat-lipped money-changer walked through the border gate with only a nod to the guard, the copy boys criss-crossed the line with sheaves of paper, belonging nowhere. The children selling cold drinks shouted their prices in dollars on one side, and in córdobas on the other, the guards calling them over by name to run errands, fetch lunch and cigarettes, and to ask what the secretary in the Nicaraguan vehicle registration office was wearing that day.

Travellers ate their meals between states, standing up, or sitting on a bollard or on the steps to the office they were petitioning. They sat in cars and trucks, doors and windows open, throwing wrappers on the ground when meals were done. Peddlers pushed carts through the puddled nether regions, selling tacos and *caldo*, foods wrapped in grease-stained paper pockets and poured into Styrofoam pots. Wherever the carts stopped they attracted small crowds of people waving a variety of currencies.

"Want a taco? That will be a dollar, or twenty-five córdobas. Or eight quetzals, if that's all you have."

The heat made my thick riding trousers feel like a wet diaper. My T-shirt had last been washed some three countries ago. I could feel my socks sliding down inside my riding boots. A half-empty bottle of lukewarm water sloshed to and fro under my arm.

I headed for the immigration office with a plastic folder containing my passport and extra copies of it, bike registration and extra copies, insurance papers triplicated, and every other doc-

ument I carried, and some cash, all together in one packet, just
in case they asked. There was no queue at the office, only a horde,
with some of the horde closer to the wicket than others. The guard
at the door, leaning on the wall, smoking, fiddling with his phone,
only reacted when someone bumped into him. Then he responded
gruffly, ordering people to the back of the swarm, pointing
and barking at the bother of it all. I pushed, wedging myself
between an old man and a mother with two small children, to join
those at the front. The official ignored everyone except the person
directly in front of him, the one whose papers he was perusing.
And even then, that lucky person got only a heavy-lidded indolent
slice of his focus.

I presented my papers. The official perused them silently,
without looking at me. I had a small sum for some administra-
tive fee ready when his hand returned to the wicket, palm up.
He tucked the notes under his ledger and walked away from
the wicket. I looked behind me at the sea of faces and shrugged.
Should I just wait there? Wouldn't I get some kind of paper
or something to show to officials down the road? A moment later
he returned and handed back my documents—papers that gave
me the power to continue on my journey to the next *frontera*.

In Panama I reached the end of the continent, quite literally
the end of the road. Ahead lay a bigger challenge than any *frontera* I had crossed so far. The road was interrupted by the Darién
Gap, 160 kilometres of swamp and jungle separating Panama
and Colombia. It is the only bit of land connecting Central
and South America, and there are no roads through it.

The Darién Gap was the site of a failed Scottish colony, named
Caledonia, in the late 1690s. The fact that the hardy people
who broke the back of the Canadian wilderness failed at creating
a foothold here said something. The collapse of Caledonia sucked
up a third of Scotland's wealth and nearly brought the nation
to its knees, hastening its union with England. Even the Mennonites have never tried to settle this hostile strip of land.

Over the years a handful of crazy adventurers have ridden their off-road motorcycles through it, but that was a war I was not prepared to wage. Instead, I weighed my options—a cheap but sketchy coastal cargo ship, a fast but expensive ride on a cargo plane, or a more affordable and leisurely trip on a sailing yacht. I chose the latter, booking a berth, and a parking spot, on *Jacqueline*, a sailing catamaran skippered by an ornery Austrian. We tarped the bike and tied it to the yacht's railing and then set off across the Caribbean Sea.

For five days I and a handful of backpackers snorkelled, spearfished, and lolled in the sun as our sailing catamaran wound its way through the San Blas Islands towards Colombia. There were late-night rum-fuelled conversations, which of course led to stories of where we were from and where we were going. As I'd done in countless countries, cities, bars and buses over decades of travel, I repeated the familiar lines describing what a Mennonite was. I told the story that I had tailored to fit me. But this time I also described how I was starting to find the deep veins of Mennonite culture in myself. I started saying *we* instead of *they*, and *us* instead of *them*. I felt a tinge of pride when I told some parts of the story, a bit of embarrassment with others. I told these strangers-cum-confidants how I was beginning to get a clearer picture of which bits of me came from my Mennonite heritage, and how I embraced some of those realizations and loathed others. I told them I was starting see myself more clearly than ever before.

I told them how the Mennonites kept moving, again and again, all the way to South America. To a new land that they hoped would bring them the isolation and plentiful harvests they were forever seeking. And now I was following the Mennonites to this fresh, unexplored continent.

At each border I flattened and refolded the crumpled map of the country I'd just crossed. By the time I was done with a map it was puckered with rain spots and stained with greasy fingerprints. The bigger the country, the longer its roads, the more intimate the map and I became, and the grimier it became. I spread it out on

café tables and traced where I was going and sometimes used it to locate where I was. I opened it beside the road where the wind tried to yank it from my hands, tearing it a little bit more each time. At night in my tent I explored the next day's route by flashlight. The colours, contour lines, the names and typography all became familiar to me. I could glance down at the map in my tank bag and in a split second, while still negotiating curves and heavy traffic, check if this was the town, the turn, the highway I sought. The maps became the familiar face of strange new territory, an image of the places I'd seen and those I'd passed at highway speed. So it was a part of my border-crossing ritual to fold the old map, then dig through my panniers to find the next one and slip it into the clear map pocket of my tank bag. My ragged North and Central American maps had all been refolded and put away. When my bike rolled ashore in Cartagena, Colombia, I ripped open my plastic bag full of fresh South American maps.

The first few South American countries on my route were Mennonite-free. Some had small missionary communities, but there were no sprawling Russian Mennonite colonies. As I set off across Colombia, I wondered why the Mennonites had not settled there. Its valleys were filled with vegetable farms, with soil so deep and rich it seemed like anything would grow given just a few days of sunshine and rain. Neighbouring Venezuela also had no Mennonite colonies. I rode into Ecuador and across the equator the country was named for, where I found wide-open spaces and small subsistence farms. But no Mennonites.

Why, if Mennonites were willing to cross oceans to reach new land, would they not have settled in these countries? Mennonites have tended to move to remote, underdeveloped countries with fledgling or weak national governments. They have sought out governments that are willing to give them *Privilegia*, official or unofficial, but in any case, granting autonomy in exchange for badly needed agricultural production. Often these are places where the indigenous population has little voice and their land is easily expropriated. Mennonites abhor socialist, leftist governments, favouring business-friendly places with low taxes that allow them to become wealthy faster. Venezuela and Ecuador have both become more protective of their lands and indigenous people, limiting the kind of control Mennonites would be able to have over large tracts of land. Colombia, with its decades-long drug wars, was until recently too violent, and now that the violence has subsided it is too developed for the kind of colonialism Mennonites have in mind. These countries don't fit the profile of the types of places Mennonites settle in.

I grew lonely on the road. Ever since leaving Blue Creek I'd thought about Ed and Carolyn and how they had repeatedly spoken about the support of family and their community. The community was their lifeline. The words had struck a chord with me after having already spent a few months on the road, alone most of the time.

Community, where I'd grown up, was easy to define. It was those who attended our church and our school. Those who lived within a small radius of those institutions. And everyone within that community watched one another's backs, whether it was financial, emotional, or spiritual support. Every Mennonite community was like that. And membership in the community came with a responsibility to offer your own support to others when it was needed.

But in Hong Kong, where I lived on my own, anonymous in a foreign culture, in the heart of a jungle of a city, community was a much harder term to define. Responsibility was something you found in only the strongest, longest of friendships, often with people who lived on the other side of the globe. People came and went in and out of the city and my life. You accepted honest friendship when and where you found it, even when you knew it wasn't for long.

The longer I spent on the road alone, the longer my days became, with fewer stops. That left me too exhausted to socialize at the end of the day. The longer I was alone, the less comfortable I felt interacting with people I met along the way. I retreated into my helmet during the day and into my tent at night. Then I'd come to another Mennonite community, and jump back into that world. I went from hidden campsites in ravines and using a foreign language to order meals at roadside food stalls, to sleeping on clean sheets that smelled like those in my grandmother's guest room, sitting around tables sharing dishes I'd known since child-hood, and discussing our community in a language that I'd heard since birth. And then I'd return to the road, alone again. The con-trasts were dizzying, even as the feeling of loneliness became more familiar.

The dun land cleaved clean to blue sky in Peru. A hot black highway, the beige Andes to my left and the cold blue Pacific Ocean to my right. Roadside buildings of unpainted brick, concrete rubble creating little dunes of sand where the wind was forced to slow. Sometimes a plastic bag or bit of paper trash would break free, whirling and dancing across the open landscape like a drunken der-vish. My eyes ached for a glimpse of green. The mix of desert dust and sea salt created a haze that covered my bike and me in a grey scum, but the wind also carried the smell of the sea.

I turned inland a few hours south of Lima, where ancient geoglyphs known as the Nazca Lines traced vast animals and mystic designs on the desert floor. The road climbed from the sea and every metre of elevation brought a drop in tempera-ture and a feeling of dizzy breathlessness. I spent two days riding deeper into the Andes. The road dipped into pine-scented valleys that were warm with sunshine, where I'd peel off layers of clothing and eat my lunch stretched out on warm rocks.

Early one morning I climbed the steps to the ancient city of Machu Picchu. A thick fog enveloped the ruined city, hiding it completely. I joined a huddle of tourists and we all muttered similar expressions of dismay. "Such a shame." "Well, we can still explore the city, I guess." "I can't believe it, after we came all this way…wait! There it is!"

The sun climbed over the mountain tops, the fog disappeared, and Machu Picchu revealed itself. Built some six hundred years ago, it sits in a saddle on the eastern flank of the Peruvian Andes. No one is quite sure why Machu Picchu exists, whether for cer-emony, a summer retreat for rulers, or a planned last stronghold of the Inca. It was unknown to the outside world and covered in jungle foliage until 1911, when explorer Hiram Bingham was led to the site by a local herder.

I sat on a stone ledge overlooking the terraces, surrounded by dry stone walls that had remained straight and true through the years. As the sun filled the old courtyards and roofless houses I was struck by the sacrifice and work required to build this city high in the mountains. Was this the same thing Mennonites were talking about when they said they wanted to "build something" for themselves and their children? Most meant a farm or business, but they also meant a way of life, a continuation of the belief system their ancestors had carried from Russia to Canada to wherever they now lived. Working hard, leaving a legacy of values and a mark on the earth that showed they'd been there and played their part. Being Mennonite seemed deeply rooted in the struggle to secure the culture, cementing what was already past. If they wanted to preserve, unchanged, something as fleeting as a culture, they needed wealth to hold it in place. So building up wealth, farms, and land became synonymous with maintaining Mennonite culture.

Remaining separate from the society around them was a central tenet of every Mennonite community I'd been to. Yet Mennonites have also adopted local traits, from dressing for the environment, such as wearing sandals instead of boots, to adding chilies to their bland food and learning how to manipulate corrupt governments to get what they want. Our culture was constantly evolving whether we liked it or not, or even realized it. But Mennonites prefer looking back, clinging to old ideas, rather than looking ahead to see where that strong foundation of solid ideals and morals can take us.

In southern Mexico I'd passed through Mennonite communities where they were recolonizing land abandoned by the Maya a millennium ago. The Maya had created great wealth only to lose it all. Where had I heard that line before? It made me think of the Mennonites leaving their beautiful farms in Russia. The Maya had disappeared from the Yucatán Peninsula, as well as neighbouring areas, because of warring, drought, and overpopulation. Now it was the Mennonites' turn to own the land and use it to build their society. The Maya had expanded their knowledge of science and mathematics, trying to understand the world around them. The Mennonites chose ignorance and blindness, hoping it would help their culture survive. When I asked Mennonites about the remnants of Mayan civilization abandoned across their land, they shrugged their shoulders, unimpressed.

"There's just a pile of old stones left," they said.

Three weeks after arriving on the South American continent I descended from the arid mountains into lush green forest and the steamy tropics of southwestern Bolivia. Santa Cruz de la Sierra, with its traffic and throngs of people, was a shock after weeks of backcountry riding and camping. I had not spent time in a Mennonite community since Belize, two months and some 10,000 kilometres ago. Covering that distance, alone with my thoughts, had given me time to contemplate what I'd learned about my culture so far. I'd come to terms with the bits I saw in myself, both the pleasant bits and the jarring realizations. I was ready to see familiar Mennonite faces again— familiar not because we'd met before, but because we'd come from the same place.

Just inside the city limits I came to a major intersection, where I stopped to study my map. Left or right? I looked up to see a man standing on the curb near me. He was wearing dark *schlaub'betjse*, a plaid long-sleeved shirt, and a gleaming white cowboy hat.

"Hallo!" I shouted. "Which way to the center of the city?" I asked, in Plautdietsch.

He looked at me, surprised to hear a man on a dusty overloaded motorcycle speak to him in that tongue. Then he raised his arm, pointing the way. I had found my Mennonites again, this time in the heart of Bolivia, where I knew they harboured dark secrets.

CHAPTER 12

Bolivia
Secrets and Silence

There are more than 70,000 Mennonites in a cluster of colonies a few hours east of Santa Cruz, and they are among the most socially conservative in the Mennonite diaspora. Most of them are Old Colony Mennonites, who live nineteenth-century lifestyles and practise the strictest form of separation from broader society. They believe that their entire culture, from language to clothing, from education, village, and home design to their form of self-government, are all a part of the church and directly linked to their spiritual state. Being obsequious to the church is paramount, with disobedience seen as a rejection of faith itself.

A corrosive mix of isolation, poor education, and inept leadership had put Bolivian Mennonites in the spotlight and, as soon as I arrived in the region, I sought out David Janzen, a Canadian missionary to the Mennonites, to gain insight into what had turned into an international scandal. David had a fleshy face, an unkempt head of thinning grey hair, and the affable nature of someone who dealt with crises on a daily basis without getting much credit for it.

"It has been a struggle," he said as we drove along a grid of gravel roads with small, identical houses on both sides. He called out greetings to families sitting on their porches, sometimes raising an arm to wave to someone without pausing his words.

The streets of Villa Nuevo, a village in the heart of colonies, had a raw newness to them, just like its inhabitants. The planted trees were small and spindly, and the houses were clothed in a mix of tar-paper and siding. They were simple homes on small parcels of land. This was the most urban setting most of its residents had ever lived in and their gardens took up large portions of each lot.

All of the residents of Villa Nuevo had left, or been ejected from, strictly conservative Mennonite churches and colonies. Some of them were banned for disobeying their colony leaders. To be banned, or excommunicated, by the church means being rejected by the entire community, as nearly all activities are some-how related to the church. Family members are not allowed to speak or socialize with those who are banned, or they face the same censure. A banned person is lost, pushed out of the collective mind, cut from all relations. A person who dies while banned will go to hell. And everyone on the colony believes in hell, so Villa Nuevo represents a sort of renewed salvation for its residents.

To leave one's colony means to never return, like Walter turning his back on his brother Klass, in Belize. Sometimes people transfer to another colony, but transfers are rare, especially when families have been at the center of a scandal or had a reputation for challenging authority. Most families remain on a colony, even if it means being punished or ridiculed, rather than try to survive on their own "in the world."

"They don't understand the idea of a community outside of a colony, where people live together, pay taxes, and have a school, but also have some independence, like maybe going to different churches, or wearing different clothes. We tell them, don't worry about the neighbour, focus on your own new beginning."

Villa Nuevo had grown to nearly fifty families within five years, with a shelter for battered women and children, and a twen-ty-eight-bed alcohol and drug rehabilitation centre named Guia de Paz, or Path to Peace. The centre was still two months from opening and already it was overwhelmed with requests, primarily from Old Colony Mennonites. The organizers planned to add res-idential addictions counselling for women as well. The colony had built it because Bolivia's state facilities and services were scarce and poorly run, and anyway, Mennonite drug addicts didn't want to be associated with Bolivian drug addicts. Mennonites were different, but things were a long way from their ideal of a pure, simple life.

A big part of the problem was poor education. Catechism takes up much of the time in Old Colony schools, and children are lucky to be able to stumble through a short Bible reading and do basic arithmetic by the age of twelve or fourteen when they leave school. Science and humanities are ignored entirely. The schools also do a poor job of teaching German, the language they've gone to such lengths to protect. While Sunday church services are conducted in High German—Plautdietsch is the vernacular form—few people are proficient in the language.

The Mennonites had moved from country to country to defend their right to a low level of education in the fear that better education would only encourage challenges to authority, pique interest in the outside world, and unravel a community that had remained tightly knitted together for centuries.

"The more you read the Bible, the more you know, and once you know more, God expects more from you. So it's better to not learn," David said. "That's the way they think."

David slowed his truck as we drove past the Bridge, Villa Nuevo's school with space for 130 students. It offered a nationally approved curriculum all the way through grade twelve, including Spanish and the sciences.

"This school here, this is our hope," David said. "This is what we hope will make the difference over the long term. It won't happen overnight though."

When Mennonites first came to Bolivia, they agreed to teach their children basic Spanish while the government agreed to leave colony schools under community control, operating largely in German. However, over the years the colonies ignored the clause to include basic Spanish instruction. In fact, community leaders so effectively ignored Spanish that most people came to believe that their original agreement with the government exempted them from teaching their children Spanish.

Now the government was putting pressure on the colonies to raise their educational standards and teach their children Spanish. Colony leaders grumbled that this was all the fault of Bolivia's increased "socialism," which in their minds was the same as communism. And everyone knew that communism, whatever that was, was bad, because it came from Russia.

The Bolivian government had some leverage with the Mennonites because many of them were still Canadian and Mexican citizens through their parents, and they remained in Bolivia on expired temporary visas, although by now about three-quarters of the Mennonites had been born in Bolivia. The government threatened to throw them out of the country if they didn't comply with educational reforms, and the situation escalated to the point where the Mexican and Canadian consulates intervened to broker a deal.

Canada was present in their lives other ways as well. Manitoba Colony, one of the best-known Bolivian colonies, was named after a colony in Mexico, which was named after my home province. And David and his wife, Lisa, were two of many moderate Canadian Mennonites who came to Bolivia in an attempt to open the closed colonies and offer help to those who wanted to escape. They were supported by Mennonite churches in Canada, missionaries to their own people.

David managed a Christian radio station, Radio Trans Mundial, which broadcast sermons, religious music, and news in a mix of German, Plautdietsch, and Spanish.

"Radios are officially banned on the colonies, but a lot of people have them hidden in the barn or in a backroom and they listen to them secretly, *up plietch*."

Up plietch. Secretly, hidden, behind closed doors. I'd hear that term a lot in Bolivia.

Old Colony churches do not preach salvation through a religious conversion such as being "born again" but rather through obedience to the old ways, by living a quiet, family-centred life. More-moderate Mennonites in Canada and the US therefore see it as their duty to convert Old Colony Mennonites to a more expressive and evangelical form of Christianity. The Old Colony leaders were having none of it.

"*Betjeare* [conversion, 'born again' in their Christian faith] is almost a curse word on some of these colonies," one missionary told me.

Old Colony leaders said their communities had no greater social problems than any other society. They didn't need saving. There was no darkness in need of light. They just wanted to be left alone to live a peaceful and productive life.

But there was plenty of evidence to the contrary. I'd read newspaper reports about Manitoba Colony and its new-found infamy months before I set off on my journey. The reports said that starting sometime in 2005 a group of Mennonite men had used a spray-based animal tranquilizer to incapacitate families in their homes at night, and then raped the women and children. They were accused of carrying out rapes in many homes, on various colonies, until they were caught in 2009, tried, and given prison sentences of between twelve and twenty-five years. The case had been labeled the "Ghost Rapes" of Bolivia due to the use of the amnesic spray.

I rejected the story as wild hearsay when I first read it. It was too outlandish, too dramatic, to have taken place on a Mennonite colony. Then, as I learned the details, and as David and Lisa described the situation on the colonies, my disbelief turned to horror. I felt a tightening at the back of my throat, a strong desire to scream, a disgust and loathing, as I listened. And once I'd heard, I struggled to look at any Old Colony man the same way.

In addition to being a case of gross male chauvinism, it had become a Mennonite version of the Salem witch trials, where a theocracy built on isolationism and religious extremism had led to false accusations and tragic lapses in due process. There were also reasons to doubt the stories.

"Most observers doubt a lot of the factors in this case," David said. "There are a lot of political forces at play that make it hard to believe some of the claims."

The most glaring of the doubtful factors was that colony vigilantes, often the heads of the very households the men were accused of targeting, had tortured the accused to produce confessions. The claims that they had used a "magic spray" were dubious, and women still complained about incest and sexual assault, even with the accused in prison. These factors made David doubt the official narrative, and he, and others, suspected the arrests were a guise to cover up a long-running problem with incest on the colonies.

The story was a devastating one, no matter which version you heard, regardless of which details were included, created, or forgotten. It had torn through the community, which had quickly closed ranks; a wound healed at the surface but still festering deep inside. But most important, to me, it revealed the bigger truths, and the grander lies, that all the stories about Mennonites as great colonizers didn't include.

Would I want to abandon my search for identity after digging into this festering sore? Would it make me abandon the identity that I was feeling increasingly confident in with every mile and community I saw? We Mennonites or those Mennonites? I wasn't sure yet.

....

Every Saturday, Old Colony families flooded into Santa Cruz on buses and in the backs of grain trucks driven by *weltmensch*, or in the colony's own wagons, pulled by tractors. The wagons were one form of motorized transport approved by the colony leaders, as their people weren't going to go anywhere far, or fast, on a flatbed trailer towed by a chugging Massey Ferguson. Once in central Santa Cruz, the Old Colony men stood around in packs, hands on hips or slouched against shopfronts, in their dark *schlaub'betjse* and white cowboy hats, and watched the world go by. Some of them bartered with Bolivian shopkeepers over the tools of nineteenth-century farming, such as harnesses, milk pails, and wagons. The women bustled from shop to shop, buying pots and pans, bolts of fabric, brooms, and soap. Children—boys dressed as miniature versions of their fathers while girls wore straw hats with bright ribbons—gawked wide-eyed at the *weltmensch* all around them. They took long, sensuous licks of their ice cream cones and soaked up the big-city life.

Lisa ran a small women's counselling office down a back alley near the city's central market, and Saturday was her busiest day.

"I have a phone that they can use, and sometimes they use my office for other things, so they have an excuse to come see me," she said. "It takes time for them to feel safe enough to talk to me."

Her discreet space was filled with heavy Mennonite women wearing serious faces, their round bodies swathed in dark, suffocating dresses. The reek of sweat permeated the warm air.

Lisa was a spring flower among them. She was petite and sported a broad smile and girlish charm. She was eager to hear new stories, meet people, and try new things. I took an instant liking to her. The Old Colony women must have overlooked her sparkle—overtly sparkly for a Mennonite woman—for they did confide in her. They told her stories of dark deeds done *up plietch*, terrible secrets borne by women who saw no escape.

"It's very hard to just listen sometimes. I feel terrible, so helpless sometimes," Lisa said. "The things they tell me, they're not just sins, but the men that do these things should get locked up in jail. But it doesn't help us or them if we go to the police each time. The women won't come to me anymore, because they don't want it public, they don't want me to take things that far. We have to try to make changes from the inside. And if we interfere too much the leaders will just pack up and move somewhere else. That's a real risk."

But the women hinted at the truth. Mothers who were afraid to leave young daughters at home alone with their fathers and brothers. Girls who refused to use the outhouse at night, because their father or brother might attack them in the darkness. The young girls were confused, as all they knew about sex was gleaned from watching the horses behind the barn. Now they were becoming infected with sexually transmitted diseases even though they considered themselves virgins—they had, after all, never given themselves to a man.

"Some of the men visit the Bolivian prostitutes," Lisa said. "And, of course, most of them know nothing about condoms, so then they come home and use their daughters, and the diseases are spread without anyone understanding what is happening."

Silence was the key. Secrets kept from leaders, from other women, from outsiders, from all. Mothers and their daughters would wake up with bleeding vaginas, with their nightgowns torn and soiled. One woman said she awoke with ropes on her wrists. They couldn't remember what had happened, but they felt funny in the morning, with headaches and foggy minds. Mothers and daughters were both waking up to the same horror, but they kept it a secret from each other out of shame.

"On the colony everything is done *up plietch*," David said. "Everyone uses cell phones *up plietch*. They listen to the radio *up plietch*. If you get an offer to do some work with your tractor off the colony, for a *weltmensch*, you put the rubber tires on and go do the work *up plietch*, and then when the work is done you put the steel wheels back on. As long as people don't find out, it's considered okay."

If bad behaviour did come to light, a mumbled apology to the men in the church—only the men had the power to dole out God's forgiveness—would bring them back into the good graces of community leaders. I was taken aback by the pervasiveness of it, and by the sinister raping of women so naive and sheltered that they were taught by their mothers to accept this as part of being a woman.

"It keeps happening because there is no punishment for it," Lisa said. "If the punishment were the same as it is off the colony, as it is out in the world, where they'd go to jail, it wouldn't happen so much. But here they don't even always get banned by the church, and that's the worst that could happen. They pay something, or they talk to the preacher, and everything is okay. And then there is the silence. The women, even though they know what has happened and that it is wrong, they're terrified to talk about it, because these things are not talked about. Even the words themselves, for sexual organs or acts, they can't even say them to me."

The men said the women were filling their heads with silly thoughts, expressing their own devious sexual fantasies. Or maybe the men were telling stories to cover up their nighttime dalliances. And anyway, sex was not a topic to be discussed publicly, outside the family home. So be quiet. Ignore it, and it will go away.

But it didn't go away.

....

Manitoba Colony's flat fields and pastures were divided into a regular grid of dirt roads. The ditches on either side had been torn up by the steel wheels of tractors, which drove in the ditches to save the roads for the horse-drawn carts.

Every kilometre or so a driveway led to a small farm with a modest house and a few outbuildings. Gardens held straight rows of green vegetables that varied in shade like paint samples. Women were bent over the rows, hoeing, picking, planting. Instead of recorded music or the cacophony of mechanization they lived amid the lowing of animals, the clank of dishes inside a house, the creak of a passing horse-drawn carriage. The land here was so rich that farmers could raise crops without the use of artificial fertilizers. Manitoba Colony was thriving, with 2,000 babies born every year.

There was a steady trickle of traffic on the roads. Women driving single-horse buggies averted their eyes as I passed them on my motorcycle. The children stared at me, open-mouthed. I waved and shouted hello at everyone I met, but only the men responded. They drove rougher, unpainted work wagons pulled by two horses. Some of them drove tractors, making their jolting way through the ditches on steel wheels that had spade-like paddles for traction. The men grinned at me, and if they were with friends they'd burst into laughter, sharing a joke about this stranger who drove through their quiet land.

I put myself in their place, on the narrow buggy bench, forward view blocked by a giant horse's ass, or on a tractor shuddering along on soul-saving steel wheels. In a long dark dress or forced to wear the hot, constrictive *schlaub'betjse*. Before them was a man, wet and muddy up to his knees from bucking his motorcycle through the squelchy roads. Black motorcycle with a huge black bag slung across the back of the seat, black riding clothes, black boots, black helmet with dark glasses covering his eyes. And strangest of all, the man spoke to them in Plautdietsch. *Weltmensch*, those from the outside, they didn't speak Plautdietsch.

My great-grandfather Johann probably knew their great-grandfathers. They shared the escape from Russia to the New World, but then their paths took different directions in the Canadian Prairies. These Mennonites went south, trying life in Mexico, Paraguay, and other lands in between before planting their wheat here. I knew all this about them even though they remained silent, just as they were taught.

I found Abram Wall, one of the colony leaders who had helped push the rape case through the courts, on his farm. He was a successful Old Colony farmer and business owner with nine children. He lived in a comfortable, airy home, his barns and sheds were large and well-built, and the modern machinery parked inside was fuelled and ready for planting season.

He invited me into his home, and we sat in rattan rocking chairs on the veranda, a wall of greenery and flowers around us. He rocked to and fro, his arms set stiffly on the armrests. He was tall and wiry, with stick-out ears and a nose with a flattened end.

Abram's eyes lit up when I told him I lived in Hong Kong. He and several other Mennonite men had recently gone to China to buy agricultural chemicals, solar panels, and a deep freezer for his wife. They had spent three weeks holed up in their Shanghai hotel, venturing forth to visit factories and then retreating to their rooms. He had previously travelled throughout the Americas, and that had always been pleasurable, but not China. They had seen little or done little other than strike the necessary business deals.

"We ate at McDonald's a lot," Abram said. "The food there, it's always small bits, never a good big piece of meat. And there were too many people. I don't understand how a Mennonite could live in a place like that, but I guess a person can become accustomed to anything if they are forced to."

But I hadn't come calling to ask Abram about his travels. I told him David had suggested I speak to him about the case that had put his colony in newspapers around the globe. He cleared his throat, paused for a moment, and then spoke.

"We heard complaints of things that were happening. Then a boy was arrested and interrogated about what was happening, and he said exactly what they had been doing, and with whom. So they drove to those boys' homes to ask them, and they said the same thing as the first boy, which places they'd visited, what they had all done, and with whom."

Boys. The accused were grown men, most with families of their own. Abram also avoided using any words that might suggest he was talking about a sexual act, the most common euphemism being that the women were "used." Not raped. No one said rape, and so neither did I. The boys had "done things" to the women and children, there had been "trouble" in a home. I only learned the Plautdietsch word for rape, *vejewaultje*, with force, later, when I looked it up in the dictionary. So I adopted the euphemisms I heard everyone else use. Lies are sneaky like that.

"All of us Mennonites are very sorry it happened," Abram said. "But if this has indeed happened, to keep it quiet would be very bad as well. The saddest part is that it happened. That's the way it is."

Abram looked down at his lap, pain showing in the slump of his shoulders. His large hands were wrapped over the ends of the armrests, hanging on for strength.

"When we questioned them, they described the houses, the people that were in them. The boys said exactly which farms they went to, which houses, and then inside the house, they could tell us how the beds were placed in the room, and which bed the fat girl was in, the skinny girl, which rooms the children were in, everything."

Abram said the stories had started changing once the vigilantes had taken the accused to the police. Then they began denying everything they'd told the colony leaders and the story became muddled, like it was now.

"Of course the story changed, because you got their confessions out of them by torturing them," I said. I suspected Abram was trying to elicit my sympathy. It wasn't working.

"I wasn't there when they were questioned, but they said that no one has tortured them, no one laid a hand on them, no hitting," he said. His voice rose an octave and he gripped the armrests of the rocker even tighter. "They were interrogated, but no one tortured them. They made all of that up."

Later, I'd learn that there was a dead body to prove Abram was lying. But I didn't know that as I watched his face pucker with emotion.

Abram regretted the bad reputation this was giving Bolivia's Mennonite colonies, but he denied there was a larger problem of incest in the community. No one he knew did that. It was all just talk.

"We brought a lot of women to the doctors in the city. But then there were a lot of children we were wondering about, underage girls, so we brought the doctors from the city here, to the colony. The doctors could say exactly which ones had been used, and which ones not. It was over one hundred, in total."

Abram rocked back and forth and looked me straight in the eye. I waited for him to continue, but he said nothing. He gave his head a little tilt, shrugged as if to say, "What's done is done."

Over one hundred young women were raped, but there were no pregnancies. Abram said the rapists had used condoms. I found that hard to believe because sexual education was non-existent and birth control was frowned on as an interference with God's will. Abram shrugged his shoulders.

"No, thankfully there were no pregnancies that I'm aware of."

I asked him if he could introduce me to some of the women. Abram shook his head.

"They are tired of talking about it, too ashamed. We had all kinds of reporters here when the court case was on, it was very bad for the colony. I can tell you everything you need to know," he said.

"So how could they do this? Why did no one wake up? How did it take so long for everyone to find out about this?"

"They had a spray," Abram said, raising his hand and wiggling his index finger, as if operating a spray bottle.

While Abram didn't believe anything else the accused had said, he did believe the story of a magic spray, told during interrogation. No one had actually found any samples of the spray.

"I haven't seen the spray. They just said themselves that they used such a spray. People also said they had sensed something. Some said that after those nights they woke up with a big headache and they could feel it in their heads that they hadn't had a good night or had had a different kind of sleep than usual."

"It all sounds so unbelievable. Like something someone made up," I said.

"If we wanted to make up a story there are a lot of stories that are easier and better to make up than this one," Abram shot back.

"The main proof was that children woke up and were bleeding in the morning. And that the boys were seen. The women are almost positive they saw them, although they can't be totally clear because they were sleeping. But they were certain enough. One little girl even woke up and saw someone there, beside the bed, and then he hid under the bed. She went and looked under the bed and"—Abram made a snakelike motion with his hand—"he slipped out the door."

Abram's yard was ripe and green in the warm sun that blazed beyond the shade of the veranda. I could hear someone working inside the house, the occasional enquiring voices of children. A cock crowed somewhere beyond the bushes. It was cool and peaceful in the shade.

"It's hard to believe that here, in this place, among Mennonites, that this kind of stuff can happen," I said.

"It will never be quiet and tranquil again," Abram said. "A lot has happened, and no one will come back 100 percent to where they were before."

"There are many people who wonder who is telling the truth," I said. "I'm guessing that when I go see the men in prison, they'll say you're lying. But who is telling the truth?"

"People that do those kinds of things don't care about the truth. The truth has no worth to them, and they are willing to lie. It has nothing to do with money, with the poor or the rich. It's only related to what they did. If rich people had done what they did they'd be sitting where these boys are sitting now. They deserve to be in jail."

CHAPTER 13

Bolivia

Palmasola Prison

My taxi came to a halt in the middle of a large mud puddle. Above me towered a red-brick wall with a green gate. And over the gate, a sign in bold white lettering:

CENTRO DE REHABILITACION
SANTA CRUZ—PALMASOLA

About thirty people were crowded in front of the gate, and they all turned to look at me as I got out of my taxi. Women on the left, men on the right. Tired women with whimpering children clinging to their skirts. There were also women dressed in miniskirts and jeans so tight that I sucked in my own belly in empathy. One wore a scarlet top that showed off a smooth brown midriff and dizzying cleavage. She caught me looking at her and winked at me. The gate opened a crack and a guard poked his head outside. The women surged forward, shouting, petitioning. The guard stared at them for a moment, glanced at me, expressionless, and then pulled his head back and closed the steel gate with a decisive clang.

The waiting men looked much less exotic, less purposeful, than the women. They leaned against the wall, hands deep in their pockets, hats pulled low over their eyes. Many had bundles, tied up in ragged plastic bags, at their feet. The bags contained fruit, soft drinks, and loaves of bread. My own hands were empty, and I regretted not bringing something to offer to those inside.

I gave a small nod of greeting to the men who took notice of me and was about to join the back of the queue when a young man with spiky gelled hair waved me over to his spot near the front.

"You American?"

"No, I'm Canadian."

"Is this your first time here?"

I nodded. He laughed.

"Ya, I could see that. My name is Eric. Stay with me, I'll show you what to do," he said. I was relieved and happy to comply.

Eric was there to visit a man whom he alternately described as a cousin and his sister's boyfriend. I asked him what his cousin had done to land him in prison.

"You know...children," Eric said, wincing and shrugging his shoulders to emphasize the delicacy of the matter. "Doing bad things to children."

What? Another pedophile? Was rape really that common here? I looked at Eric, unsure how to react. Should I show sympathy that his sister's boyfriend was despicable? Disgust? And then I realized I hadn't considered how I'd react to the Mennonites accused of rape. Should I express my disapproval? Eric interrupted my anxious thoughts.

"And you? Who are you here to see?"

"The Mennonites," I said.

"Menna—who?" Eric asked, looking confused.

"You know, Mennonitas. The gringos. There are eight of them."

"Ahh yeah," he said. "Are they your relatives or...?"

"No," I said, cutting him off. I shook my head vigorously to make sure he understood. This was not one of those times when I wanted to be recognized as a Mennonite. "I'm just here to meet them. To interview them."

After half an hour of watching a slow trickle of visitors enter the prison gates it was our turn. Immediately after stepping through the gates we were confronted by a guard who made us stand spread-eagled and patted us down. We were pushed through a narrow door into a small shed. Inside, in the stifling heat, sat another guard with dark circles under the arms of his tan uniform. Eric instructed me to slip ten bolivianos into my passport and hand both to the guard. The guard deftly separated them, slipping the crumpled money under his ledger before he recorded my details in clumsy handwriting. Then he scribbled *X 51 34* on the inside of my forearm in blue ink, mixed up with what looked like a smudged postage frank. I felt like a steer being led to slaughter.

We walked across the large outer yard of the prison. It was a no man's land of mosquito-breeding puddles and heaps of fetid rubbish. A herd of unbridled horses grazed at the patchy grass. Their coats shone in the sunshine, manes thick and untrimmed. They looked like they had stepped out of a poster on a teenage girl's bedroom wall. *Live free, like the wind.*

At the inner wall yet another guard took my passport. He scribbled more letters on the inside of my forearm, which was now covered in multicoloured stamps and squiggles that formed some kind of code of visitor registration. I was patted down once more and then pushed towards the gate, which was crowded with men shouting greetings to the incoming visitors.

This wasn't my first time in a prison. The first time—the only other time—was more than thirty years ago. All that remains of the memory is the clanging of steel doors, a fluorescent-lit room of shining linoleum, and the desire to stay close to my father's side. We were in Stony Mountain, a federal penitentiary not far from our home, there to visit prisoners as part of a church-organized outreach program.

Dad had been assigned to Andre Gilderbloom, a man I remember as lean, with dark stubble and slicked-back hair. Andre served a long sentence for armed robbery, and when he was paroled and in a halfway house Dad invited him to join us for Christmas. A whole weekend with a violent convict in our house! A real *weltmensch*! How exotic, we thought. Andre arrived—smelling of tobacco and aftershave and wearing a tan leather jacket—with a handcrafted gift: a miniature fireplace, complete with stone masonry, a wooden mantel, and a small light bulb instead of a fire.

We sat down at the dinner table and began passing the dishes around, but soon there was an awkward silence. Andre was pocketing every serving spoon and fork before passing the dishes on to my brothers and sisters. When he saw that we saw—we were curious and surprised but too polite to say anything—he laughed.

"Oh, sorry! I'm so used to being in prison, where you grab anything you can get your hands on because you never know when you'll need it."

He stuck the spoon back into the mashed potatoes and retrieved a fork from inside his jacket and returned it to the sliced ham. It was probably a ruse he put on for our entertainment, but he'd just secured his legend with the Dueck children.

Years later my father would reminisce about his visits to Stony Mountain and pull his old visitor identity card out of his wallet to show to people. "Ya, I've got proof that I've done my time," he'd joke, holding his thumb over the word *Visitor*. Everyone would laugh. Good joke. Of course he hadn't been to prison, he was a good Mennonite.

Palmasola was not Stony Mountain. Here there were no bars or cells and very few guards. The prisoners were dressed in normal street clothes. It looked like a poor and overcrowded urban ghetto of about 4,000 people. Palmasola had a well-structured real estate market where prisoners paid for their own cells, or "apartments," as they called them. Apartments became available when a prisoner was released, the guards skimmed a transaction fee, and everyone made a bit of money except for the poor. If prisoners couldn't pay for a bed they ended up sleeping in an alleyway on the fringes of the prison. It reminded me of the Hong Kong property market.

Eric guided me through the streets to look for the Mennonites. Pedestrian streets wriggled between ramshackle buildings painted in a riot of blue, pink, and green. Laundry and tangled electric cables reached across the alleys under a hot clear sky. Small shops sold drinks and cigarettes. The smell of fried food filled the air. Men hung out of second-storey windows, smoking and calling

to friends below. Women and children milled about in a dizzying, colourful rush, all of it drenched in noonday sun. Swarthy
men slapped each other on the back and shared choreographed
handshakes and fist bumps. I felt conspicuously white and square.
I wished I hadn't shaved that morning. Or worn my clean jeans.

We rounded a corner to find a group of Old Colony Mennonites gathered in the shade of a tree. They were even more glaringly
out of place in this ghetto than I imagined I appeared. The women
wore long dark dresses and black kerchiefs despite the heat while
the men were in their clean going-to-town *schlaub'betjse* and white
cowboy hats. They stood in a tight circle, backs to the chaos
around them. I recognized one of the men from the newspaper
photos and introduced myself. But how do you greet a man like
this? Hello, I saw your face in a newspaper clipping that described
how you raped a bunch of your neighbours, how do you do? No,
that didn't work.

"I see you have some visitors. Your family?" I asked him in
Plautdietsch.

He nodded. His guests remained quiet, watching me. I tried
to make small talk but met only stares and murmured replies.

"Where are the rest of the Mennonites, the ones that live here?"
I asked him.

He pointed down the street at a restaurant. A handful of Mennonite men were sitting around a table on the veranda. One of them
raised his arm and waved at me.

Tall, trim, and about fifty years of age, Peter Wiebe appeared
both older and more confident than the rest of the men. I had seen
newspaper pictures of him, and I could see he had lost weight during
the three and a half years he had already served in prison. With
wire-frame glasses and a neat yellow shirt, he looked like a casual
businessman. He was their leader in prison, just as he was accused
of being their leader on the colony. Peter was a self-trained veterinarian, and he was accused of manufacturing the magic spray that
was so powerful that an angry bull would fall asleep like a baby with
one squirt to the face. The spray that had earned him a twelve-and-
a-half-year prison sentence.

Peter shook my hand and welcomed me to prison. The other men offered muted hellos and then fell silent, staring into their empty coffee mugs as Peter took control.

"Have you had lunch?" Peter asked.

I hadn't, and realized I was hungry. There were only dirty plates on the table. Peter stood up and shouted an order through a doorway, and within seconds a short, pudgy Mennonite with a blank face that glistened with sweat came and set a plate of rice and meat gravy before me. I thanked him in Plautdietsch and he replied with a confused look and a low grunt.

"Who's that?"

"Jacob Wall. He's the one that's not quite there," Peter said, tapping the side of his head with a forefinger. "He didn't do well in school and then got into some trouble on the colony. He's the one they grabbed first, the one that gave them all our names when they threatened him."

In June 2009, Jacob was caught on a property at night and he could not give an explanation for why he was there. After some rough interrogation and threats of lynching he agreed to everything that was put before him. Yes, he had raped women in their sleep. When presented with names of possible co-conspirators he agreed: yes to him, him, and him.

A band of vigilantes formed, led by some of the wealthiest, most powerful men on the colony, and began rounding up the named suspects. Within a few days ten men from Manitoba Colony and neighbouring colonies were arrested and locked up in sheds, wellhouses, and pig crates.

"Weren't you mad at him for getting you into this mess?"

"It's not his fault. Everyone knows that he isn't smart enough to have thought this whole thing up. They used him because they knew they could get him to say anything they wanted."

Conversation drifted to prison life, about those who had visited, those who would come soon, and the quality of the food. All I could think of were the rapes. I wasn't sure how I expected the men to act, but now that I was sitting next to them, I was taken aback by how relaxed they were. Their initial shyness towards me was no different than if I'd arrived, a stranger, on their colony. We were having a regular old Mennonite *spezeare*, catching up on the latest gossip. I knew the case against them was in doubt, but still, I expected them to look more remorseful. While they might be in jail on trumped-up charges and forced confessions, David said several of them had been accused of incest previously, making it harder to believe their claims of innocence.

They certainly acted as if they felt no need to prove their innocence. If they were innocent, I wanted to know what unlucky series of events had landed them there. If they were guilty, I wanted to know how men who chose to live nineteenth-century lifestyles in the name of spirituality could stoop to such wretched lows. I wanted them to say it out loud.

"So, this whole story that brought you here. I'd like to hear more about it," I said nervously.

To my surprise they were eager to tell me their version, leaning into the center of the table as Peter took the lead.

"Everyone knows that most of these men were just easy targets, the easy ones to blame," Peter said, pointing at the men around the table, who nodded in agreement. Most of them were underdogs on the colony. They were all short on money and influence. Peter, with his important work and his twelve children and eleven grandchildren, had more respectability to his name than the rest combined.

Abram Peters was in his early twenties and the youngest in the group. He had sandy blond hair and his eyes flickered towards the floor whenever I looked in his direction.

"Why did they come after you if you didn't do anything?" I asked. I was surprised at the hard, accusing edge to my words. I resented Abram's sullen, pimply face, even though I'd just met him.

"I mean, if you're innocent, they must have had something else against you," I added.

"I was targeted because I was making trouble," Abram said. "I was unpopular and poor. I was falling behind in school, and I even ran away once. They accused me of leading a bad, sinful life."

A bad, sinful life. That could mean everything or nothing.

Maybe he was caught drinking beer or kissing a girl. Maybe he was caught with a mobile phone or a bicycle. Maybe he'd played sports, *up plietch*. That could have been me, a bored young man. I'd snuck cases of beer into the house when my parents weren't home, tried to lure neighbourhood girls into the night for some grabby-grabby, grown my hair too long, strutted with an attitude I couldn't back up. But I wasn't a rapist. Was he? Regardless of his guilt, he said the vigilantes had locked him in a hot, airless shipping container, choked him until he passed out, then hooked a 220-volt electric fencer to the chains binding his body and given him a shock that made him confess to everything they accused him of.

Jacob Wiebe, Peter's veterinarian assistant, was dark haired with sideburns and a blue striped T-shirt that was one size too small. He was accused of having peddled the spray to the other men, but he'd long been a thorn in the side of powerful landowners.

"The rich farmers on the colony would buy two pieces of land, one big and one small. They'd pay the tax on the small piece and then pay bribes, so they didn't have to pay tax on the big piece," Jacob said. His spoke in a high-pitched, plaintive tone that made me feel sorry for him and distrust him at the same time. "I said something about it, and they didn't like that. Now I have to be quiet. I'm in jail, so who will believe me?"

The spray had become an easy explanation for all the inexplicable aspects of the case. They had used the spray to sedate entire households in the dead of the night before they crept through windows and raped the women and young girls. Why didn't the farmyard dogs bark when the rapists approached the house? Because they were sprayed with the magic spray. How could a girl sleep through a rape and wake up confused about whether she was raped or not? The magic spray had wiped her memory clean. Why did the men of the house or the teenage boys sleeping in the next room not hear anything? Because the spray was so powerful that with one squirt through a window screen the entire household was knocked out cold.

"They say that if you sprayed it in the air dogs would fall asleep within fifty metres," Jacob said to guffaws from around the table. "At first, when we came into the prison, the other inmates teased us and said they wanted magic spray too, it would make it easier for them to rob people."

At one point in the investigation a group of Mennonite vigilantes had come to Peter's farm to search for the spray. They seized several bottles from the house. Peter said one was perfume, and another was Maxman, a spray-on remedy for premature ejaculation bought in Santa Cruz on one of his Saturday shopping trips. I didn't ask him if that spray had worked as advertised.

"They held the bottles up and said, 'Aha, we found the spray!' Of course, it wasn't true, and my daughter grabbed one of them out of their hands and before they could stop her she sprayed herself right in the face with it. And, of course, nothing happened."

Magic spray, suspicious shadows, and a handful of misfits and whistleblowers. One girl claimed to have seen a man outside her window at night. She said the man's eyes glittered in the darkness, and her testimony became evidence that he had had evil intentions.

The accused were handed over to Bolivian police, battered and bruised, along with the confessions collected by their neighbours-turned-vigilantes. At first, they were kept in the nearby Cotoca county jail, where security was light. One man, who confessed he had raped his own daughters but denied attacking women in other homes, escaped to Paraguay. In 2011 the case went to court and, after a two-month trial—a single trial for all the men—Peter was sentenced to twelve years in prison while the others got twenty-five years each.

The men fell silent, looked at their hands, picked at their nails, or fidgeted with the cups on the table. There was a cocky, defiant quality to them that I found both irksome and reassuring. As outlandish as the accusations sounded, as weak as the facts against them were, I also struggled to believe their version. Would Mennonites really create such a story, fabricate such lies and accusations, and ruin so many lives, to cover their own dirty deeds? And could they have convinced the courts, even ones as corrupt as Bolivia's, to play along? Clearly the men weren't beaten, not by a long shot.

They didn't look guilty. They didn't sound ashamed. Or were they that callous?

"Do you want to see the prison?" Jacob asked. "I can give you a tour."

He led me to a back corner of the prison wall where half a dozen filthy inmates rooted through heaps of smouldering rubbish. The stench crawled up my nostrils and made me breathe in shallow gasps. Gibbering, wobbling lunatics in blackened rags stared at us as we passed. One man had his hand down the front of his trousers, unabashedly tugging at his penis as we watched. He gave me a rotten-toothed smile when our eyes met. A few small children, nearly naked and streaked with grime, played games among the detritus, their shouts competing with the deafening cacophony of the prison. This was the bottom of the prison ladder, the last station for those rejected even by their fellow criminals, those too poor and shunned to claim even a spot on the floor.

"We shouldn't spend much time here," Jacob said. He led me around a puddle of black water and quickened his pace. "It's very sad, these guys. They're all on drugs, so you don't know what they'll do. I don't like to come here."

Jacob and the others were doomed to life behind bars for the next quarter century, but their Mennonite sense of otherness remained undiminished. They did not join the other inmates in the woodworking shop, even though Mennonites are renowned for their wooden furniture. They conducted their own church services under the guidance of a sympathetic missionary. Some of their isolation was fear of the unknown, with several of them expressing a desire to stay clear of prison politics, but the us-and-them mentality of the colony was also at play.

"Are you scared of the other prisoners?" I asked. The Mennonites, even though no longer wearing their identifying *schlaub'betjse*, stood out in the prison. Too white and clean-cut, like me. I wouldn't want to be here and have everyone know it was for raping children.

"We haven't had many disagreements with people," Jacob said. "We just mind our own business. It's very peaceful in here, maybe even more so than in Santa Cruz. In the city you hear of killings and problems every day, but here it's calm. It's not so bad."

It was calm except when you crossed invisible turf lines or caused offence. Jacob told me about an inmate who was suspected of taking pictures of another inmate's child with his mobile phone.

"They thought he was doing it for bad reasons, so they killed him. We saw it all. They beat him to death with an iron bar," he said. "Now there are no pictures allowed, and you have to be sure that no one thinks you are taking pictures with your phone."

We passed a dusty soccer pitch filled with bare-chested men in the throes of a match, their families packed along the sidelines, cheering raucously. The spectators licked ice cream cones and sucked at straws stuck into soda cans. Some of the children beside the football pitch lived in the prison and passed through the gates to and from school every day, while others were here for the day to visit inmates. Wives and girlfriends moved into the prison to join their partners and left for their jobs every morning but came back at night in order to keep the family together.

Jacob's tour ended in his room, a small but tidy space that felt more like a college dormitory room than prison cell. A small barred window looked out over the prison roofs and brought a flood of fresh air and sunshine. Underwear and socks were hung out the window to dry. A few small stools doubled as bedside tables. Jacob wove colourful hammocks to pass the time and earn pocket money, and a bundle of them hung in a corner. A Plautdietsche Bible and a few hymn books were stacked atop one of the tables alongside a modest collection of toiletries and combs. On one wall hung a small picture of Jesus, uncommon in a Mennonite home because displaying crosses or pictures of Jesus was considered a Catholic practice. An old television, a forbidden pleasure on the colonies, sat atop a wooden cupboard. There was no need to do things *up plietch* here, without the church leaders looking over his shoulder with their oppressive rules.

Jacob had recently bought his apartment for US $1,400. Two beds were taken up by other Mennonites and one was used by a Bolivian who was in prison for raping his daughter.

"His wife accused him," Jacob said. "He's a good guy, I could see that right away. He's got a good spirit, and he's poor, so he didn't have a place. I said he could stay here for free."

Jacob's wife, Otta, came to visit him for a week at a time, and he had rigged a thin curtain around his bunk for privacy during her visits. She still lived on the colony with their youngest son and two daughters while the older three sons had moved away.

"One of my older boys worked in the colony cheese factory and he heard the workers talking about how we should have been killed rather than turned over to the police. It hurt him very much to hear that, so he quit his job and moved to another village," Jacob said, his face pinched with concern.

It sounded harsh, but I knew that there were numerous threats against the men's lives if they dared to reenter the colony. Mennonite pacifism only went so far.

"It's not bad staying here, but it's very hard to stay patient," he said as we sat down on his bunk. "I don't feel alone here. We know many people support us and pray for us. I thank God that I am here because here we've learned a lot about the Bible and about life, and we wouldn't have learned these things if we were on the colony."

Jacob grew quiet. He looked more vulnerable in the privacy of his room than he had outside.

"So, did you do it?" I asked, hoping I'd get a better glimpse inside his head now that we were away from the rest of the men. "They say you confessed, and then changed your story. So which story is true?"

Jacob looked at me sharply. He shook his head, still staring at me with defiance in his eyes. "I would not take on a sin I have not done. There's no way I'd admit to something I have not done. If I had done that, the things they say I did, I'd end my life. I would not welcome visitors here and look them in the eye," he said.

Jacob was looking me in the eye, watching the impact his words had on me.

"I'd often come home from work late, because I'd work on cattle, help with calving, these sorts of things," Jacob explained. "Someone saw me come home late one night and they said I was out making this trouble."

"How about the others, do you believe them?" I asked. The men appeared remarkably unified given that some of them were arrested based on the accusations made by the others. I wondered if that united front was just for my benefit.

"I believe them that they did not do these things," Jacob said. "They did not use their daughters, or others. If you're in prison with someone for three years you talk a lot, about all kinds of things, and about the case, and the stories are always the same, never changing. If they were lying the stories would change a bit. Just a detail or two would be different. But not with these guys, it's always the same. But the story on the colony, the story told by those that have accused us, their story always changes. It's different every time."

Jacob's shoulders were slumped forward as he sat on the bed. He looked like a victim. I tried to picture him creeping through the colony in the dark, magic spray in hand, raping women and children. It was a picture that refused to draw itself in my mind. Still…I found myself trying to weigh the facts, the versions, and my head ached with doubt.

The other men were gathered in Peter's apartment and Jacob suggested we join them. Peter, who had more money than the others, had a room three times as large as Jacob's, with its own toilet. The men were lounging on beds and chairs when we entered, and the conversation soon slipped into the comfortable rut of complaint.

"We're here because the ones with money and power got scared, because they were afraid people would find out what they were doing. They were the ones who used the women. So this way they can say they've fixed the problem," said Cornelius Thiessen, a ponderous man with dark, lank hair slicked back off a shiny red forehead. He was sweating in a pair of ill-fitting black trousers and a dark, long-sleeved shirt.

"All those things that they said we confessed to, well, we had to because they tortured us," Cornelius said. "I was hung by my arms for hours, and my shoulders still give me pain, they've never healed. I'm not even sure what I said to them, I just thought I was going to die there."

He was lucky not to have died. The men told me how Frank Klassen, a thirty-seven-year-old father of nine children on nearby Belize Colony, was not so lucky. When vigilantes came to his farm to arrest Frank he refused to confess. They strung him up from a tree by his arms and left him to hang for nine hours. Nine hours in the Bolivian sun. By the time they took him down, he was bleeding internally. They brought him to the hospital, where he died five days later. Lynched by his own people.

"They did the same thing to me, but I survived," said Cornelius, rubbing his shoulders for effect. He looked uncertain about whether or not he'd gotten the better deal. He had not hung long, the pain was too much, so he had confessed and agreed to everything the vigilantes accused him of. And that was the confession that was used in court and put him in prison.

"Do you ever wish you hadn't confessed? If you hadn't confessed, you might not be here."

"Of course," Cornelius said. "But...there was no other way. I thought I would die. I thought they were going to kill me, they were that angry. I wish I could have stood the pain more, but..."

I listened, dumbfounded. In my mind, the balance of truth had just tipped in favour of the men. Surely, the fact they were tortured undermined the value of their confessions. But would the colony, and the leaders of the church, really go this far to cover their own tracks?

Bitter accusations against community leaders served as a temporary salve for the men. Crude allegations embellished through boredom and desperation. Sins that were committed and covered up, sins that the jailed men said they were paying for, instead of the guilty.

"John Neufeld, he fucked a cow," Cornelius said, earning a round of snickers from the others. "And he was messing around with other women, Spanish women. Because of that he had a wife to spare so he shared her with others. He was banned from the church for a week, but he confessed and now he is back in the church."

Others chimed in with their own vitriol, stories that had festered and grown over the years, accentuating the injustices the men felt. Confirmations that came from someone who had spoken to someone who had heard something someone had once said to someone. The same rumour mill that had ballooned the rape story beyond credibility was easing their own consciences.

"One of the leaders accused us of these things until it came out that his son had made his daughter pregnant. The baby died, and after that he wasn't involved as much."

"Another one, a rich one, he owns a big *schmiede*. He said to someone that all of this was wrong, locking us up, but he was scared to step in because he was scared it would hurt his business if he did."

Each accusation was met with a round of nodding heads. It was so, for they had all heard it. Just as their own cases and stories became harder and harder to refute each time the accusations were repeated. No matter how mendacious the propaganda, if repeated often enough it became the accepted truth. They were angry but they also gloated over their victory. They had escaped colony life. The world outside the colony, albeit one behind prison walls, was a lot less intimidating than the preachers had said it would be, and now they knew something the others didn't. They knew that *weltmensch* weren't half the devils that they were made out to be, and that Christian faith was not the exclusive domain of the Old Colony Mennonites.

But even behind bars, the men were not free of the colony's clutches.

"They say someone is watching us, from inside, but I don't know who. Maybe it's not true," Jacob said, fear in his voice.

"But on the colony, we were taught that the *weltmensch* are like cattle, that's it. Just animals. And the preacher would say wearing these clothes makes me lost, that I will go to hell," Jacob said as he tugged at his short-sleeved shirt. None of the men wore *schlaub'betjse* any longer. "Now I know that it makes no difference at all, as long as you dress properly, decently, it doesn't matter what you wear."

"There was always the threat that if we disobeyed, or were caught doing something, or in possession of a phone or a radio, then we'd get locked out of the church. And that meant we'd get locked out of heaven as well. Now we know better, but my family still wears the old-fashioned clothes on the colony to keep peace, for now."

"There are so many rules on the colony, about rubber tires, the clothes you wear, listening to the radio, using a phone. You're so busy following the rules you can't even think about anything else in life," Jacob said. "Here, no one bothers us. We just have to make sure we follow the rules and don't get caught with a phone. You can't use the phone outside, you have to be in your room when you use it, hiding."

"I guess that maybe it's a little bit like the colony in that way, always *up plietch*," he said, joining the others in laughter.

These men were descendants of Russian Mennonite immigrants to Canada, like me. Their great-grandparents had left Canada and moved south. Some in giant leaps, others in fits and starts of church splits and crop failures. But Canada was still considered a distant motherland for many of them. This had piqued my interest in the case.

"Are any of you Canadian citizens?" I'd asked. There was a round of head shaking, until I got to Jacob.

"Ya, I have a Canadian passport because my grandparents came from there, but I've never been there. I always knew it was important, that it was worth something but…does that still count?"

"Have you told the consulate, the Canadian government, that you're here?"

Jacob shook his head. "I was scared to tell the Canadian government about all of this. I thought if they knew maybe they would take the passport away."

"I don't think so. I think they'd be interested to know that a Canadian citizen has already been in a Bolivian jail for years. This case, and all of you, were in the papers in the US and Canada. So you should contact them."

Jacob looked uncertain. "Well…I wouldn't know where to start with all of that."

Instead, he gave me directions to his farm. "I'll call my wife and tell her you're coming. She knows where the papers are, she can show them to you."

The sun had sunk low in the sky, casting long shadows across the prison walls.

"*Na yo*," Jacob said as he stood up to walk me to the gate. The soccer game was still underway, but many visitors had already left, and the prison was much quieter than it was during the day. When we reached the gate, Jacob gave a small nod of recognition to the guard.

"I have to stay here, I can't go any farther," he told me with an apologetic smile.

My mind whirled with the quandary. Each man was utterly convincing in his testimony, passionate in his claim that his was the true version of a story where the truth was long ago buried under hearsay, superstition, and gossip. They'd gained my pity, even if I didn't fully believe them. I struggled to believe that Abram Wall and the rest of the colony would have orchestrated all this to protect its most powerful members. Maybe the truth lay somewhere in the middle?

"Thank you for showing me around, for telling me everything," I said, shaking Jacob's hand. His eyes met mine. "Thank you for telling me your version."

"It has become more complicated with time, this story," Jacob said. "You can't believe everything you hear. Everyone has their side of the story."

I walked out into the street, a free man. But my mind was caged by the conflicting stories, by the confusion over what was true and what was false. Which bits were true because they'd happened, and which ones became truth because they were repeated and believed by so many? Was I becoming the latest captive in this suffocating web of doubt and suspicion?

CHAPTER 14

Bolivia

Shunned by the Colony

Otta was expecting me. Her screen door shrieked as she opened it for me. It had no handle, only a hole in the screen by which to pull it open, made grubby by countless fingers.

As soon as I entered the house Otta disappeared into the bedroom and reappeared cradling a torn and creased envelope in her hands. She laid the envelope on a scratched Formica table-top, so old its blue was worn white at the edges.

I opened the envelope and shook its contents onto the table. A Canadian passport, a Bolivian identity card, and a few photo-copied documents. Jacob Wiebe. Green eyes, born 1968, May 12. The same Jacob I had met in Palmasola. In the photos Jacob stared wide-eyed at the camera, the flash glaring off a forehead kept white by his ever-present cap.

"The passport runs out in February. Does that mean it won't work anymore?" Otta asked. "We didn't know what to do with it. I thought, once, that maybe Canada could help, but then I thought, he's never even been there…"

I photographed the documents while Otta stood and watched. When I was done, I put them back in the envelope. Neither of us said anything as I did these things, and the silence was uncomfortable. I felt like I was invading, but I only wanted to help. She carried the documents to the bedroom and, as she returned, she stood in the doorway and held the curtain aside to show me. The bed was neatly made up with a yellow patchwork quilt.

"This is where we slept when he was here. Now we all sleep upstairs. I felt so alone here so I decided to go sleep with the children."

Otta had a severe, drawn face. Her eyes were set in dark hollows. Her hair was pulled back tightly, a black kerchief tucked behind her ears. A dark dress with purple flowers hung loosely on her thin body. Her voice had a hard, persistent edge to it.

"When the preacher married us, he said that no one should separate us until death. Now they've done that very thing," she said.

Otta stood before me, defiant but also resigned to the realities she could not change. "So, what do you think the Canadian government will do?"

"I don't know. There's probably not much they can do, but still, it would be good to tell them."

I didn't want to get her hopes up. Her eyes were hungry for answers.

Otta insisted I eat and waved aside my protests as she pushed me towards a seat. They had already eaten, she said as she set the table. Her twelve-year-old son stood to one side and watched silently. He had completed his schooling and learned what he needed to know to continue in the old Mennonite ways. Whippet-thin with wide beseeching eyes that peered out from underneath a blond fringe, the little lad was now the man of the house.

"Hello." I reached out for a handshake. "What's your name?"

He stared at me for a moment, then gave me a shy smile and stuck out a narrow hand.

"Tell him your name," Otta chided.

"Gerhardt," he said in a hoarse whisper.

The house felt empty, and too quiet. As if it were waiting, holding its breath. The main room held a small gas-powered refrigerator and a few sideboards with chipped dishes. There were wooden benches on two sides of the worn table. Thin curtains were tied back to allow more light in. A boldly branded wall calendar from the Manitoba Colony was the only decoration on the walls. Two small frilly dresses printed with bright flowers, and unlike anything I'd ever seen a colony girl wear, hung on the kitchen wall. I stared at them for a long time, confused as to why Otta would have such dresses, and why she would hang them in the kitchen. Then I realized the dresses weren't meant for wearing, instead their many pockets bulged with ladles, spatulas, and sauce bottles.

Otta's three older sons were unable to get work on Manitoba Colony—perhaps due to the stigma caused by their father, Otta wasn't sure. They had left the colony and lived in the nearby Mennonite community of Chihuahua—named after the Mennonite capital in Mexico. Her sons gave her some money to pay the bills, and she had sold some of their land to support Jacob in prison.

I apologized for eating from her scarce resources.

"Nah!" she scoffed. "We're poor but there's still leftovers. This is nothing special I have for you."

She set the table with reheated beans, cold egg noodles, slices of canned meat, pickled vegetables, home-baked bread, and a cup of powdered drink mix. She continued to talk as she set the table.

"Ya, well. It was a Sunday, June 21. This was back in 2009, of course. They came on the yard, a big group of men, at four in the morning, and asked my man if he wanted to come along and see the boys that had been arrested. They were being held in the cheese factory. That's all they said.

"At first I got up when they came on the yard, and then my man got up, still in his nightclothes, and he told them, 'Let me get dressed first.' When he came into the house to get dressed he told me, 'Maybe you should go to church with the children on your own, I'm not sure if I'll be back in time.' This was the first we'd heard of this whole story, when they came to our house. So I went off to church, happily, with no worries. I came home, made lunch, and he was still not home, so I lay down for my *meddach'schlop*. I left some lunch on the table for him, expecting him to return soon. I woke up at two in the afternoon, and saw he still wasn't home and had not had his lunch, and then I became worried. It wasn't until that evening that someone came and told me that they'd locked him up as well. And he hasn't come home since."

Jacob had come under suspicion because he had been an apprentice to Peter, working with the colony's livestock. He was accused of distributing the magic spray supposedly made by his mentor.

"They came to the house once to search for the spray. I went outside, I told them I knew everything that my man did and that he had not done these things. I said I knew everything that was in my house, and that there was no magic spray, and that they need not came back. I turned around and went inside and they left."

Otta's eyes narrowed and her chin thrust forward. She had sat down at the table with me as I ate. Now she stood up and walked to the kitchen, where she pushed a few pots around on the counter. Gerhardt's big blue eyes were full of apprehension as they followed his mother's nervous movement. He was at an age between being able to protect his mother and needing her protection himself, and their connection was palpable. Whenever Otta looked at him the lines in her face eased a tiny bit and the tightness of her eyes would relax. Then she'd begin to speak and the anger came back.

She was as much a victim as the women who were raped, just in a different way. I had the overwhelming sense that without her breadwinner at home penury was just around the corner.

"The leaders of the community, of the church, do they not look after you? I mean, you're basically a widow. Isn't that one of their responsibilities?"

"They don't help at all. Nothing. It's very hard sometimes." Otta's voice took on a querulous tone. "Ya, I've told the children, if there were expensive habits we could quit, it would help, but it's hard to stop the habit of eating. But I've noticed that if we pray, there is help. Many times it's felt like there's no way forward, but then we pray again, and God listens and he helps."

"What do you mean he helps? How?"

"Well, we still have food to eat," she said as she gestured at my plate. "And he comforts me. I'd be very lonely otherwise."

Just like the rape victims themselves, Otta was badly served by the silence and refusal to properly clean out the wounds before bandaging them up. The real truth didn't matter to the leaders, what was important to them was that the fragile balance of power was maintained. Digging deeper and showing some sympathy could only upset that balance by encouraging people to speak the truth.

Single mothers with young children are a rarity in Mennonite culture, particularly on a colony. Divorce was unheard of when I was a child, much as it still is in Old Colony communities. I remembered Klaas and Greta on Spanish Lookout. Greta's mother and Klaas's father both passed away, leaving behind large families, and the two families soon became one as a matter of survival in a society where gender roles were clearly defined. Even if Otta had sided with the church, condemned her husband, and divorced him, the church would not have allowed her to remarry, and she would still have been branded with shame for life. But that wasn't an option anyway, because capitulation wasn't Otta's style.

"The colony shares meat when big animals are butchered. First one farmer, then it's someone else's turn. The poor, and those families without a man in the house, they always get meat, even if they don't have a cow when it's their turn to butcher. Well, the church came to me, and said they could see I no longer had a cow to give. They said that if I would alter my life, if I would do things the way they did them, then they would still give me meat." Otta laughed, a dry cackle. "I said, for ten kilos of meat I won't stoop to being part of those people who did those things, who made up these stories to put my man in jail."

A mobile phone sat on the windowsill. That was a forbidden technology on the colony, especially inside a home. Calls were sometimes made *up plietch*, outside in the yard, or from the barn, but not in broad daylight, and certainly not in the house.

I pointed at the phone. "Does stuff like that, having a phone inside, does that make them go against you?"

"I put it there because it doesn't get a signal in the house, because of the tin roof," Otta said. She shrugged. "What the colony says, the rules it has, they don't mean so much to me anymore. I have to be able to speak to my man."

"I go to the prison as often as I can, every few weeks. But the trip takes money and the journey makes me so uncomfortable.

Driving to the city with all those people looking at me."

At first, I thought she meant the people in the city and in the prison itself were staring at her. Jacob had shown me his room in Palmasola and its lack of privacy, and she had stayed in that room with him overnight. All those people in the prison looking at her. But no, she meant those people looking at her were other Mennonites, because of Jacob.

"There's a big bus that comes through the colony in the morning, and everyone who wants to go to Santa Cruz goes on that bus, and then in the evening it comes back. It's all full of people from the colony. And they don't speak to me. But oh, how they stare at me, because they know where I'm going."

Now that I knew the curiosity the community had for Otta and her troubles I thought of my own entrance into her corner of Manitoba Colony, how I'd stopped and asked where she lived, by name. The defiant wife of a rapist was entertaining a strange man who had arrived on a motorcycle. That would get them talking.

"It's been hard to speak to any women on the colony. You're a lot braver than most," I said.

Otta waved her hand, it was nothing. "Before this, I wouldn't have let you come in like this, without my man here. Now, it doesn't matter."

I couldn't imagine my mother going it alone like Otta was doing. It was rare for my mother to drive to town by herself, let alone to the city of Winnipeg—of similar size and distance away as Santa Cruz was for Otta. Matters of money and interaction with non-Mennonites were entirely left to my Dad. If a stranger came on the yard, the first thing she did was send me to fetch Dad.

"I'm not scared. Not of anyone," Otta said, forcing out another dry laugh. "What should I be scared of, they've taken it all. They've already done their thing. Ya, I live here, my house is on the colony, but I'm not part of the colony. I go to a church off the colony and I have very little to do with people here. They leave us alone."

She looked at Gerhardt for confirmation, but he said nothing. He leaned on the table, thin shoulders hunched up to his stick-out ears, and gave his mother a wan smile.

Otta had two young girls who still attended the colony school.

"I'm very surprised that they still allow the girls to come to school. There's another family, when they bought a car and started to go to another church, the leaders said the children could no longer come to the school. But my girls still go to school."

Otta paused. "I think it's very good that they let them come," she added. "They don't do the things they could do to help, but at least they allow us that."

She laughed, heartily this time. She took a breath and laughed some more. At the luck of it, or at the unpredictability of censures handed out by church leaders, I wasn't sure. Her eyes never left my face as she laughed. When she took a breath and pitched into a third cackle I felt uncomfortable, but joined her with a stiff smile. I tried to imagine life at school for the girls. Some of the rape victims were classmates. Everyone at school knew their father was in prison, and why.

"They learn almost nothing at school. It's a shame. They learn to memorize stuff, but they don't learn how to think. Only memorization. I sometimes ask them things when they come home, to see that they're learning to think problems through, and they haven't learned a thing. But what choice do I have? Where else will I send them? I have no car, no money.

"I think that if people here would learn things, like how to think, this situation would not have become such big story. The men stuck in jail and the girls, they were told what to say, again and again. The men were told what they should say to confess, the girls were told what to say when they got in front of the judge. I know very well that many of the girls and women did not know what they were saying. They don't know Spanish that well, they just allowed themselves to be taught what to say. It's the same as in the schools here. They are told things, the children don't understand what it means, but they memorize it."

Despite the poverty and the critical stares of her neighbours, Otta saw the whole case as having a positive outcome. The whole sordid case, the accusations and bribing of officials and convoluted stories had drawn back the curtains on colony life, and her family had been set free. Just as Jacob had also said.

"Ya, things are so much better now. My children have become *betjeared*. The attitude, the spirit, of the whole family has changed."

The issue of becoming *betjeared*, or converted, scored to the heart of colony ethos. To become a "born again" Christian was to snub the Old Colony church. The stagnant church taught yielding to God, the onerous guilt of sin and following the "old way" as dictated by its overbearing male leadership. Being *betjeared* or "saved" was considered selfish and prideful. To claim such a conversion showed a sense of daring, of reclaiming one's spirituality. It was a personal expression that raised the leaders' hackles.

"The children say everything just feels so different now. We are not just focused on the sins we're committing. We're free from that now. We don't just measure everything by our short-comings, like it is here without understanding the scriptures. Now we can have joy too."

I looked at Gerhardt for confirmation, but he gave me no signal that he agreed with his mother. His eyes flitted up to meet mine and then returned to the tabletop, where he pushed a crumb in circles with his small finger. He didn't look very free to me.

"I'm glad to hear that you feel freer. Jacob, and the others in prison, said the same thing. But still, now you're alone, without the community you had before."

What I didn't say, but thought to myself, was that she had nowhere to go. Her education was no better than her children's, she was barely literate, unable to communicate in the national language. There was little chance of her getting a job off the colony to support herself and her children.

"It's hard, very hard. To have the patience, waiting for him to come out, not knowing when it will be. Someone said maybe in time for Christmas, which would be a very nice present, but I don't have my hopes up. But even though I'm alone now, our lives are better, freer."

It was time for me to leave. We went outside, where Gerhardt played with a pet turtle that lived in his sandbox. The turtle pulled its head into its shell when he picked it up, and Gerhardt tapped at the shell and tried to coax his friend out.

"When I'm alone he doesn't hide like that," he said, disappointed at the turtle's timidity. It was the only thing he'd said in my presence, other than his name. His voice was soft and high-pitched.

"Maybe he's doing something bad *up plietch*," I said. Otta snorted at the joke; Gerhardt didn't get it.

Being twelve meant Gerhardt was expected to work and help the family put food on the table. Most boys his age would work on the family farm for a few years before they were qualified to work for neighbouring farms, the cheese factory, or a local *schmiede*.

"He's done school, so he could be out working, but with his pa gone he has no one to teach him," Otta said. "And he's too small to go work for others. Anyway, I told him I need him at home to keep me in good cheer. And he charges the batteries, operates the water pump, things like that."

Otta patted the man of the house on the head. He smiled shyly.

Theirs was a small yard by colony standards. A black horse-drawn buggy was parked outside the shed. Laundry flapped on a clothesline, white sheets hung next to dark dresses. A large tree beside the shed had a rope swing hanging from a low branch. A modern multi-speed mountain bike was leaned against the outside of the house; another forbidden convenience. Bicycles were viewed in the same light as cars and trucks, they tempted youth to travel outside the colony to explore sinful temptations. Old Colony Mennonites removed the pedals, sprocket, and chain, then cut and welded the frames to convert bicycles into giant scooters. That made them inefficient enough that they would not tempt young people to stray. But Otta's bike was complete, with gears and brakes. Now Otta and her family were free to ride a bicycle.

CHAPTER 15

Bolivia

Unanswered Questions

The stories haunted me at night. I was staying in a small cottage near David's radio station, in the countryside on the edge of the colonies. At night I sat on the porch, nursing a bottle of cheap whisky, staring into the darkness of the Bolivian savannah and wondering who lurked and preyed there. My house had electricity—bugs crashed into the porch light until they made tortured circles in the dust—but all around me the land was pitch-black and quiet. There was little traffic, no commotion or nightlife—at least none that I could hear. Who knew what was going on in the darkness. The stillness left room for imagination.

I had built walls in my mind. Walls that separated the rose-tinted memories I had of growing up in a happy, healthy, moderate Mennonite family, my version of Mennonite, with what others saw as being Mennonite. Other rooms contained different Mennonites, varied in tone and dress. Some rooms contained those varieties I found in the South, who took Mennonite faith and culture and tailored it to fit them the way they wanted to wear it. I'd always known those other rooms existed, but I'd never opened the doors to see inside, and I'd certainly never considered that we were all in the same house. I had trouble associating myself with what I found in some of the rooms.

The dangers of mixing heretical zeal and isolation were well-documented in our Mennonite history. At times the wild, heretical streak in Anabaptist culture led to an austere and pious life, but repression also gave way to orgies of sex and killing. Not long before setting off on this journey I'd read the story of Jeronimus Cornelisz, whose family was of early Frisian Mennonite stock. He ran away from his debts and became a Dutch East India Company merchant at sea. In June 1629, his ship, the *Batavia*, was wrecked on the remote Morning Reef off the west coast of Australia.

Cornelisz and his gang lorded over the islands and the two hundred *Batavia* survivors. As food and water became scarce the killing began, with the mutineers murdering about one hundred and twenty people over a two-month period. The men enslaved and raped the women. Eventually Cornelisz and fifteen of his men were discovered and hung by the trading company.

Now the story of Cornelisz felt a lot closer to home than I liked. When I was in Santa Cruz, I'd noticed the look people gave me when I said I was Mennonite and that I was staying on the colonies. I felt embarrassed, and always hastened to add that I was a "different kind of Mennonite," though I wasn't sure myself what I meant by that. There had been times on this journey where I was very proud to identify as a Mennonite, however tenuous other Mennonites might judge that connection to be. I thought of Klaas and his family in Belize, and their willingness to break conventions in order to bring change to their colony. The hard, honest working success of the Mexican Mennonites, a trait I reminded myself of when things got tough. In every community I'd visited I'd seen a willingness to help others and give generously. But now all those good things were pushed aside by the ugly results of repression, isolation, and ignorance.

....

I called the Canadian consulate the day after meeting Otta. They knew about the rape case, but were unaware one of the accused was Canadian. I gave them Jacob's name and passport number, and they said they would contact him. But there was little they could do besides visit him in prison, and offer him medical care and moral support as a corrupt justice system and reclusive community had their corrosive effect.

The rapes were bad enough—spawning pity for each Old Colony woman I saw. Who had done what to them, how, when, and where—the facts would forever be cast in doubt. Real justice could never be served. But what had happened after the rapes were discovered also gnawed at me. Speculation, torture, coercion, and lies. It was this that evinced how ignorance fed vengeance in a vicious cycle. This part of the story hadn't been told in full by the international media that had come here to hear about the "Ghost Rapes."

I'd never encountered anything near the darkness of this case in my own community, but the obstinate closed-mindedness felt familiar. That blind dedication to tradition and culture, no matter the cost, made the outside world seem scarier, but also more seductive. Us and them. I explored the latter first through books, then through travel—and both made me realize that the world and its *weltmensch* weren't as evil as I was taught they were. For me the isolation of mind and society were an inconvenience and perhaps a catalyst. But here in Bolivia, I'd found these played out to the darkest, most sinister effects. The darkness disgusted but intrigued me. It coloured everything I saw and heard. Each time someone declined to make eye contact, every person who gave an evasive answer, each uncomfortable silence and awkward exchange made me wonder: Victim? Rapist? Or just wounded by the witch hunt?

There were still many questions left in my mind, and those questions, the confusion between superstition and hearsay and truth and fact—all that doubt was what made everyone on the colony a victim of these crimes.

I spent hours riding my bike through the colony and on the roads surrounding it. Sometimes I was searching for a certain farm, a person I'd heard was willing to tell their story. Other times it was aimless riding, taking comfort from the steady buck and weave of

my bike on rough roads. The bike felt light and free without her usual load of luggage. The full-throated roar of the engine ripped apart the silence of the colonies, and I imagined a raw open wound that lies could not hide.

My cottage was just outside the town of Pailón, a grimy little outpost fifty kilometres east of Santa Cruz. Pailón was the nearest commercial centre to the colonies, and on most days it was filled with Mennonites on business. It also contained a string of greasy barbecue joints that were hugely popular with the Mennonites. The restaurants belched out clouds of blue smoke, their glaring fluorescent lights making the diners appear sallow and ill. I tried each one before I realized they were all equally bad. Over-cooked meats, limp french fries, sweet sodas. I recognized faces I'd seen on the colonies and waved hello to them. Most gave me only a shy nod before moving on, herding fat wives, bashful daughters, and gangly sons to their table.

One Sunday afternoon I was invited to join a *zangfast*, a community song and worship event held in an open-air hall. It was a rare mix of Mennonites from across the spectrum of conservatism, possible because it was held on neutral ground—not on any one church or colony's territory. The hall was packed, standing room only. Old Colony Mennonites of good reputation in the church wouldn't be caught dead there—with musical instruments and wayward Mennonites who might pollute their minds—but there were many who still wore the Old Colony garb while they searched for a life beyond the colony, like those who lived in nearby Villa Nuevo. Others came from more liberated Mennonite churches and communities.

The day was blistering hot and muggy, but only the missionaries wore shorts. Women sweated in long dresses, men plucked at their thick trousers and shirts buttoned up to the collar. The seats were filled mostly with young families and teens—this was a safe and acceptable place for young people to meet and socialize, so they came in droves. The Canadian volunteers who had come to work on the new school in Villa Nuevo were the stars of the show as they led the singing with their guitars and harmonicas. Songs about simple faith, honest living, hope, and humility. Each song was followed by polite applause. The applause marked this as an entertainment event—no one would clap for music played in a church. People sipped at soft drinks and cups of cold yerba maté and coffee poured from Thermos bottles they stashed under their seats. There was an earnest wholesomeness to it that made me feel homesick.

"This next song speaks to my heart," one of the missionaries said in Plautdietsch, strumming his guitar for effect. "There are days when I'm lonely or scared, or I just don't feel joy. And then the words of this song give me comfort."

He began to sing, his strong tenor voice carrying the flat Plautdietsche tones over the crowd, through the open-sided hall out into the grassy parking lot and beyond.

> *Länen, länen*
> *Guanz vesecha kaun ekj met ahm gohn'*
> *Länen, länen*
> *Länen gaunz aun Jesus siene Oarms*
> Leaning, leaning
> I am secure walking with him
> Leaning, leaning
> Leaning fully on Jesus's arms

The next morning, I lingered over my breakfast, picking every crumb from my plate, drinking every last drop of coffee, not wanting to leave my comfortable little cottage. Over the past weeks I had unpacked my bags, cleaned and reorganized everything, made it my temporary refuge. I changed my mind half a dozen times during breakfast. Go, don't go, go, stay. The house was cool, and a gentle breeze whispered through the open windows.

The *zangfast* had put me in a good state of mind. It had distracted me from the dark stories, suspicions, and angry accusations. I had met people who refused to succumb to that darkness. Now, with the last crumbs of my toast gone, I was forced to once again return to the darkness.

I had become less bothered by questions of innocence and guilt as I'd heard more about the case. Instead, I was thinking about how sexual naïveté and suppression of knowledge had made the communities more vulnerable to abuse, and to the mad witch hunt that had followed. Obsessed with sexual control and told to remain quiet and ignorant, this community was fertile soil for such a tragedy to grow in. I agreed with David's theory.

"Did some of those in jail abuse their daughters? Many, or maybe all, did. But did they rape the women they're accused of raping, in the way they're accused of doing it? Not many people around here believe that those stories are entirely true," David said.

I believed that there had been incest and rape, and maybe even by some of the men in prison. A lot of women had been sexually assaulted, but some of the stories had grown over time. But who had the authority to tell a woman who fully believed she had been raped that the facts as presented by the powerful masterminds were not the facts as they'd happened?

The men had been tortured, there was a dead body to prove it, so their confessions were worthless. That meant there was a high probability that some of the men in prison were innocent. That meant that some of the perpetrators were probably still on the loose, and, when I stood back for a wider view, there were good reasons to think that some of the men who had led the witch hunt might be the guilty ones. That meant that if the rapes had poked a hole in the fabric of the community, the way the case had been handled had torn these people in two.

David believed the charges had been trumped up to draw attention away from the more powerful leaders in the community who were suspected of incest. The rapes had not stopped. Girls were still being molested by fathers and brothers, even as community leaders proclaimed that the guilty had been caught and punished. The women who came to confide in Lisa were still scared of the men in their own homes. The whispers had not stopped.

"The fact that it's still happening, that we still hear about cases, says that it wasn't quite as simple as the leaders want to make it look," David said.

I'd lost track of who the victims were. They were all scape-goats of the colony, of the old way. Everyone was pushed farther back, deeper into the darkness. Disgust and unease had grown to the point that I wanted to walk away, but there was one more person, someone who I was told was impartial, even if only by the convoluted standards of this case.

"They owe me US $12,000 for the chemicals they bought from me, so I am holding their tractor," Peter Fehr said as he pointed to a chunky green machine parked in the middle of his yard. One of the tires—rubber tires, I noted—was flat and the tractor slouched to its left. "I've had it here for a long time and still they don't pay. Now they need the tractor for seeding, so they come begging for it, but they still haven't paid."

He shook his head and laughed, as if recounting the silly disobedience of a child. Peter sold agricultural chemicals and fer-tilizers, and his business had grown beyond his colony and made him rich and powerful. The debtors were his Brazilian neighbours, who, like himself, had come to Bolivia for its plentiful and rich land. Now they'd come to ask for grace on their debts.

He excused himself to talk business with the petitioners while I tried to eavesdrop. Peter was tall and lean with an angular face. He had a boisterous confidence and chattiness about him that was rare among Old Colony men, many of whom tended towards the stern and dour. Now he was using that charm on the farmers, sprinkling the negotiations with smiles and the occasional chuckle. After fifteen minutes of to-and-fro Peter walked away to call their boss. He went into a small office in the corner of his shed and hid himself from view as he pulled a mobile phone from his pocket. *Up plietch.*

I was standing outside in the sunshine when I had the sensation I was being watched. I looked towards the house and saw the cur-tains twitch as a pale face pulled back from the light. A few moments later I glanced back at the house and again the watcher retreated into the shadows.

Ten minutes later Peter returned and shook the Brazilians' hands—he had struck a deal with their boss.

"If they don't have the tractor they can't plant their crops, and then I'll never get paid," he explained as he led me to some lawn chairs beside his house.

"So, you came here to talk about those boys that are locked up, right?" Peter said as he turned to me. Boys, not men. He clapped his hand on his knee as if calling a meeting to order. Peter had known who I was when I arrived on his yard—people had been talking about the Canadian Mennonite writer on a motorcycle.

"As soon as I heard about it, I felt so sorry for the boys that I hoped it wasn't true," Peter said. "I imagined what it was doing to the parents. I'm a parent too. What if one of my boys had done that? Then I was hired to translate, because they saw me as impartial, but that was very hard to do."

One of the accused had once been Peter's daughter's teenage sweetheart, while another had worked on his farm, but in a tight-knit community of intermarriage and blurred lines of authority, he was considered impartial.

"When it started, I was sitting there in the court and I thought I knew which side was true. I thought, this can't be. It's just not possible. And if you listen to different people talk about it, as I know you have, listen to those who were involved in it, you'd also believe that it's not true. Right?" Peter paused just long enough for me to take a breath in preparation of my answer, and then he barrelled on. "Then you go and listen to the other side, and again you are 100 percent convinced that it's happened exactly how they say."

Exactly. Every time I left an interview, I felt I had hit upon the crux of the story, that I could see it all clearly now. But then, half an hour later, riding my motorcycle through the colony back to my refuge, thinking about what had been said, I always began to doubt. I replayed their comments in my mind, compared them to what others had said, and saw the gaps, the contradictions. The outlandish claims that had seemed reasonable when matched with the earnestness in their eyes began to look flimsy upon second examination.

"I have heard both sides now," Peter said, his voice growing quieter. "I believe it happened, yes. It's hard to believe, but yes, it did happen."

Manitoba Colony was not the only crime scene; attacks had taken place on other colonies as well. More than a hundred families were targeted, Peter said. The number of rape victims varied, depending on whom I asked. Some said a hundred, the court documents said a hundred and thirty.

"I'd say the number that were used is around a hundred and sixty," Peter said. "There were more that came forward after the court case."

Victims ranged in age from eight to sixty while court-ordered medical exams found that a three-year-old girl had a broken hymen, which suggested sexual assault. One victim was mentally handicapped, another was pregnant at the time and went into premature labour after she was raped by her brother.

The Mennonite Central Committee (MCC), an international aid group, had offered to provide counselling, particularly for the women, but they were rebuffed. One bishop had said the women did not need help because they were unconscious when the attacks had happened and therefore remembered nothing, so no emotional scars remained.

"Were they used by men after the court case, or did the women just begin to talk about it afterwards?" I asked.

I could see that Peter understood the real question in what I was asking, and he paused before answering.

"That I wouldn't know. It's hard to say."

I'd heard that some boys were raped as well.

"Ya, we have heard those things," Peter said. "But it wasn't discussed much. I don't think the victims want to talk about it."

Between one hundred and one hundred and sixty young women were raped, but there were no reported pregnancies resulting from the rapes. The accusers said the rapists had used condoms, but this was a society with zero education on issues of sexual health and pregnancy prevention.

And always, the magic spray. A can of spray was produced as court evidence, but its origins were unclear. Bolivian farmers had testified at the trial that Peter Wiebe, the cow doctor, had used the spray to sedate bulls on their farms, and Peter Fehr, the translator, said a sample had been sent to the Instituto de Investigaciones Forenses, Bolivia's national crime lab. The lab found it contained formaldehyde and scopolamine, an odourless, tasteless drug discovered over a century ago and used to treat motion sickness and postoperative nausea and vomiting. Until fifty years ago scopolamine was mixed with opioids such as morphine to put mothers into a semiconscious state during childbirth.

"If no one has seen this spray and no one I've spoken to knows of an actual sample, what was sent to the lab? What did they do the tests on?" I asked Peter. He shrugged his shoulders. He didn't know.

Scopolamine was once a common over-the-counter sleeping pill ingredient, but the US Food and Drug Administration pulled it from shelves in 1990 because it was not proven effective. In higher-than-therapeutic doses it can cause amnesia and fatigue, and can cause people to lose their free will while still remaining conscious. There are many reports of it being used criminally, much like Rohypnol, the date rape drug.

A US government report said there could be as many as 50,000 cases of scopolamine used for robbery in Colombia per year, and that the drug could be administered through food or drink or even, in powder form, blown into a target's face.

"It's the same drug that the FARC [Fuerzas Armadas Revolucionarias de Colombia] use when they rob banks," Peter said. "They put the drug in powder form on a banknote. They know a man has come out of the bank after making a big withdrawal. The FARC are looking proper, even wearing a tie, and they go up to the man," Peter said as he stood up, back straight, adjusting an imaginary necktie.

"*Señor*, is this note a fake, do you think?" Peter asked his imaginary prey.

"The man takes the note, like this, to look at it." Peter held an imaginary banknote in front of his face. "And as he does that, *puffff*, the powder goes up his nose. And although his eyes are open he does not know what he's doing."

Peter stood still, holding the imaginary banknote, eyes wide open, zombielike.

"And the man that used the powder on him, the thief, says, 'Please give me your money.' And the man hands it over. He'll do anything that is asked of him. And he's left standing on the street, or maybe the thief told him, 'Walk that way.' And then later, he'll come to and not have any idea of what happened. None. Well, maybe a glimmer, he'll know something funny happened, but nothing more."

In large doses, scopolamine can cause respiratory failure and death. While some women on the colony complained of headaches and confusion in the morning, there were no deaths or respiratory problems attributed to the magic spray.

"The amount that put an adult to sleep, to make them unaware like this, would be enough to kill a child," Peter said. "No one asked— and it wasn't my job there to ask questions, I was just translating— but I thought, why then are there no dead kids? Because the rooms that it was sprayed into, those rooms had people of different ages in them, from adults to small children, and yet they are said to have sprayed enough of this stuff through the window to knock the grown men out cold. But the children were fine. I have often wondered about that."

Peter stared at me, his eyebrows arched, eyes wide. He shrugged and shook his head.

"But even despite that, you still believe that it all happened?" I asked.

"I can't explain that, but yes, I think in general, this story... well, something happened. Maybe we'll never know exactly what, but those boys did bad things."

"Peter, what happened to those boys, I mean the men, in the backyard sheds where they were held? In those few days

before they were taken to the police? When they were questioned…
what went on there?"

Boys instead of *men*. *Sin* instead of *crime*. *Used* instead of *raped*.
Lies instead of truth.

"Those boys were not tortured. No one tortured them, I know
that for sure. Abram Peters told me that he was not shocked.
They'd threatened to shock him, yes. The man holding him said,
'Well, go get that livestock shocker, then he'll talk.' They said that
to scare him, to make him talk. But he was never shocked. And his
father has admitted to me that he lied about that as well. I had to
go into the jail cell at one point to interview them, for the court.
I asked Abram, 'Did they use a shocker on you?' He said no, they
had not.

"They did scare them. They held them," Peter said, pretending to hold a person against the wall. "They scared them, and that
has often bothered me. And they may have said things they should
not have said to scare them more."

But how about Frank Klassen, the man who had died after
he was hung from a tree to make him confess? Everyone agreed
Frank was a drunken abusive father and husband. He was known
to viciously beat his family. It wasn't long before his name
was added to the list of men who were accused of creeping around
the community at night, raping innocent women and children.

"That was terrible," Peter said. "He's my brother-in-law, his wife is
my wife's sister. I was there, I saw him. I took him to the hospital
and came back from the hospital when he was dead. They say no, he
didn't die from that, but we know better. That was terrible, what
they did to him. He did die from that."

"So if they tortured him, why should we believe they didn't
torture the others?"

Peter again arched his shoulders, made a frown. He had
no answer.

"I do know that those who hung Frank from the tree were
arrested and held in jail for a short time until the colony paid US
$25,000 to have them set free," he said.

Peter had access to the colony's financial records, and he said the colony had spent US $330,000 on the case against the eight accused rapists. The money had come from colony taxes, not from donations to the church, as some people had speculated.

"But I'm not sure where all the money went, to whom exactly. Some of it was paid to the judges, and maybe some to some of the women, the witnesses," Peter said.

"And the laboratory that wrote a report about the spray? Were they paid?"

"That I wouldn't know," Peter said.

"But Peter," I said, more loudly than I'd intended. I was frustrated. Peter struck me as more intelligent, more open-minded than many of those I had interviewed, and I suspected he was reverting to cluelessness at his convenience. "The men were frightened, and probably tortured, into confessing. And you know that the money was paid to get the case through court, to put these men in jail. You don't know who all was bribed. No one seems to have seen the spray. How can you be sure which parts of this story are true?"

"Well, there are some things that still are not clear, but you don't understand. We don't want to have to give people money for this thing to be settled, but that's just the way it works here in Bolivia. If you don't pay the police and judges, they won't do anything."

The Mennonites had moved to Bolivia because they wanted to escape from the pressures of social progress in Mexico. They thought that seeking out even greater isolation would protect them—but it hadn't. In each place Mennonites moved to, whether it was Russia, Canada, Mexico, or Bolivia, the cultural influences found their way into the community. Here it wasn't better education or a foreign language, but the insidious criminality of this country's crooked legal system. Their isolation had worked against them, allowing social rot to fester for years, hidden by imposed silence.

"I heard that one of the judges did not officially sign off on the sentencing, and that the colony has to keep paying him so that he will keep the men in jail."

"Hmmm…well, there were some problems there at one point, yes," Peter said.

Peter was chosen as a court translator because he was a prominent member of the community and, without any of his family in the list of victims, he was considered impartial. But of course the truth—whatever that might be—was more complicated.

"It was Wall, the fat one," Peter said. He jumped up from his seat and beckoned me to follow him as he walked behind the house. He pointed up at the rain gutter, which had a few small dents in it. Directly above the dents was a window that led to a second-floor bedroom where he said his daughters slept.

"Those dents are from a ladder. And look at the window screen, there are still holes in it. He tried to burn the screen with lighter, he thought it was a plastic screen, but it was steel. And then he tried to poke holes in it so he could reach in and open the window. The girls woke up and shouted. We ran out, and the ladder was standing here. And I don't remember putting the ladder there. Later Wall admitted it was him. The spray didn't work that time."

Peter grabbed my elbow and pulled me closer to him.

"I don't want them to hear, it's very difficult," he said in a low voice as he nodded towards the house. From inside, I could hear muffled female voices, young and old.

"The court case was already under way when my wife told me that the boys had been in our house, after all. I didn't know, she was too afraid to tell me. Two boys climbed a tree to get on the roof."

Peter led me to a tree that grew beside the house. "They crept across the roof and through the window into the girls' bedroom and climbed down onto the bed. You could see the footprints the whole way. And a big footprint, right there on the bedding."

"He came and used my daughter and my maid. And the next day the maid had a horrible fever, and was very sore here," Peter said, patting his hips and buttocks. "That's how hard he was on her, like a rabbit."

His maid told him she had awoken with her underpants pulled down and her nightdress over her head.

"My wife said you could see the fingerprints on her clothes," Peter said. "Their hands and feet were dirty from climbing on the roof."

"Fingerprints on clothes? Footprints on the blanket?" It sounded far-fetched as evidence. Peter stared at me, wide-eyed, as if to emphasis the severity of his story.

"May I speak to her? Is she inside?" I asked, nodding towards the kitchen door, from which came the clink of porcelain and the splash of dishwater. I had asked several different leaders if I could interview some of the victims. Each time I was turned down.

Peter shook his head and pursed his lips in refusal. "No. It's better not, they want to forget it."

Peter was concerned that his own nineteen-year-old daughter had been raped, so he took her to Santa Cruz to see a doctor, who told Peter her hymen had been broken, an unscientific and inconclusive but widely accepted sign she was no longer a virgin. The doctor had not shared his findings with Peter's daughter directly.

"On the way home, I said, 'Well, that's a relief, the doctor says that nothing has happened to you.' And she sighed a breath of relief. I didn't want her to worry about it and feel bad."

"But your daughter is nineteen. Is she that naive?" I asked. "Don't you think she knew what had happened, if she was 'used'?"

Peter shrugged his shoulders. "I don't know."

"So you believe your own daughter was used. How does that feel?"

"And maybe even my wife, we don't know. She once said to me she was suspicious that something had happened," Peter said in a hoarse whisper. He lifted his hands and held them in front of him as if pushing against a wall. "I said no. That's enough. Stop it. I don't want to hear any more."

And neither did I.

CHAPTER 16

Paraguay

The Green Hell

I began the next day in a foul mood. My bike was acting up. Bolivia's crappy fuel had clogged my carburetor and I hadn't found time to clean it, so the bike was sluggish and unresponsive. But truthfully, my bad mood had festered and brewed the entire time I was in Bolivia. My mind had been occupied with other people's rape and ignorance for too long, and it had left a sour memory. The entire Bolivian experience had confused me, sidetracked me from my mission to learn more about the Mennonite in me.

It was mid-November. I'd been on the road for five months and was becoming exhausted. Dirt ingrained every part of my body, bike, and luggage. On some days I revelled in the physical challenge of the ride, but not on this day. My bike seemed to agree.

By now I knew the bike's weaknesses, when I'd find the power I needed and when I wouldn't, when the tires would grip and when they'd skid. I'd learned to ignore the noises, vibrations, and small flaws that had become part of her, and to notice new, temporary ailments like a rattling chain or spongy brakes. I could feel her weariness, her sullen resentment at where this journey was taking us as we set off that morning.

Still, I felt a tinge of pride at what I was about to do, the honour of the struggle.

"Riding solo across the Chaco. This'll show them," I thought, not bothering to complete the thought to include who would care, why, or what I'd show them.

The Gran Chaco plain is unbearably hot, hotter than almost anywhere else on the continent. In the west this flat lowland is dry, filled with bottle trees, thorns, and cacti. This used to be a seabed, and the water that comes from the ground is salty and undrinkable. To the east the Chaco becomes wetter, even swampy in places, and quebracho trees grow large enough to be used for timber. In the whole, the Chaco is a wretched, bug-infested hell that breeds disease and malcontent.

This alkaline wasteland, sometimes called the Green Hell, sprawls across borders into Brazil, Bolivia, Argentina, and Paraguay. Similar to France in size, it is walled in by the Andes Mountains on the west while the Paraguay River bounds the misery of the Chaco in the east. Yet-to-be-discovered tribes of hunter-gatherers hide from modernity in its depths, choosing to share their lives with jaguars, howler monkeys, and giant peccaries. There are other shadowy figures seen in the bushes at dusk, revealing themselves so rarely that scientists have yet to identify and name them.

This was the place Mennonites left Canada for. They gave up a comfortable, safe, and democratic home to search for the big dream in one of the most hostile environments on the planet. Paraguay granted them a generous *Privilegium*, but even so, the first years were brutally hard. There were no roads, schools, doctors, or easy food supplies. The soil, climate, plants, and animals were all foreign to the Mennonites, who had to build everything from the ground up, in a place never before successfully colonized. They nearly starved to death in the early years.

They were so hungry they learned to eat carob pods—which the Mennonites call by the local name *algarrobo*. Sweet with a dry, mealy texture, they're often used as livestock feed, and are also a popular health food as a syrup or substitute for chocolate in baked goods. But to the Mennonites carob pods were foreign and eating seeds off wild trees instead of wheat and meat was a sign of just how desperate they were.

But moving all the way to Paraguay gave them a badge of honour for perseverance. No one could think of a more horrible place to start a new life, and there was pride in that. Righteous suffering. Here they'd be left alone to run their schools and colony as they saw fit. The Chaco became a real test of faith, a purifying struggle of unrelenting misery that showed the world just how determined the Mennonites were to live the life God intended for them.

And obviously, being led by God to a new Promised Land should not be easy. The Chaco validated just how promised it would be for that first wave of colonialists. If God had prepared a utopia for them, there had to be some kind of wall around it to keep the sinners out. Just as Moses and the Israelites had become lost in the desert in their escape from slavery, the Mennonites would fight the natural elements of the Chaco to reach their new nirvana.

The farther away from Canada, the more conservative and reclusive it seemed the Mennonites became. I thought of the people I'd met in Mexico. Despite the radical motives for their move there, they were so close to Canada, so connected by family and business to their northern cousins that a strong sense of familiarity remained. In Belize, the Mennonites were a bit farther away, their lives more adjusted to the tropical, Caribbean lifestyle, but there was still a sense of connection. In Bolivia, I'd felt like I was far away from home, and the Mennonites there, while maintaining their Canadian roots, were mostly of a radical, ultra-conservative variety that I had trouble associating myself with. But those in the Paraguayan Chaco went beyond that. From what we'd heard in Canada, it sounded like they'd moved to another planet entirely.

Now I was riding my motorcycle into the heart of this horror. A case of misunderstood directions found me on a secondary road through the wilderness, compounding my difficulties. There were few villages and the way stations that did cling to the roadside were simple muddy lots ringed with small shacks and hand printed signs. *Gasolina. Taller.* A *Restaurante* serving fly-specked grilled chicken and bottled sodas that had never seen the inside of an icebox. They were all as impermanent as the wind.

The Bolivian *frontera* was guarded by a small yellow-brick building half hidden in the trees. The painted crest on the front was peeling off the wall and there was no other signage to hint that this was an international border. The thump of my boots echoed in the empty office.

"*Hola!*" I shouted. No answer, just the bugs and birds and hum of the Chaco.

"*Frontera? Imigración?*" I walked back outside and saw a guard leisurely sauntering across the yard, picking at his belly button.

"*Aduana?*" I asked, pointing at the building.

"*Si, si,*" he answered, as if it were obvious.

He wore no uniform, and he looked like he'd been left at this station alone for far too long. His unshaven face was greasy with sweat, his dirty shirt unbuttoned halfway down a round, hairy belly. He took my papers and walked behind the counter, where, with the *kathunk kathunk* of a stamp, he cleared me out of Bolivia.

The tarmac road was destroyed in many places in preparation for rebuilding works that had not yet occurred. And then it had rained heavily for several days. The parts of the road that were supposedly intact were a patchwork of hard-rimmed potholes that were hidden under soupy mud. I was riding on a bald rear tire, which was causing my bike to spin and fishtail through the mud. Every few kilometres, machines had torn the roadbed away, leaving large hummocks and a wide, soggy ditch to cross. I was still relatively fresh from the morning, having started out in dry clothes, when I reached the first of these ditches. I stopped and pondered the physics of 250 kilograms of luggage, fuel, and Kawasaki engineering on an insecure surface, and then gunned the engine. I was halfway through the mess, legs splayed to each side to catch myself, weaving and lurching drunkenly, when the rear end went right and the front wheel went left. Sitting on my ass in slick Chaco mud was still not the pleasure one might have imagined.

The humiliation only intensified my bad mood. I gritted my teeth and growled with effort and rage as I lifted the motorcycle from the mud. There was no one to around to shock with my curses, which robbed me of even that satisfaction. There was nothing to do but remount and ride on, suspecting that this would happen again before the day was over. It did.

The solitude of the Chaco was disquieting. But I was not entirely alone. A rustle in the underbrush turned out to be an armadillo, which scurried away when I approached for a closer look. Rheas popped out of the foliage and stretched out their grey scaly legs to beat a tempo as they galloped down the road. Lizards a metre long whirled around and scuttled for cover as I passed. A dead snake as thick as my leg lay rotting in the heat, its black skin torn apart by vultures. Above me, the vultures spread their giant wings and surfed the updrafts while flocks of smaller birds swept across the landscape like thunderclouds. Doves, plump and round, sat on the road by the hundreds. They thrashed their stubby wings, frantic to gain the altitude to escape as I approached. I ducked my head in fear again and again until one dove wasn't quite fast enough. It smacked into my helmet with a loud thud and a scattering of feathers. I didn't bother to stop.

The Chaco's vast aquifers of salt water fed a bitter, withering vegetation. Ropelike liana crawled out of the ground and intertwined like a nest of snakes to create impenetrable walls fortified by stunted palms with bluish-green leaves. Thorns and vicious sharp leaves sprouted from every plant. I examined my tires for punctures at every stop.

The cattle grazing beside the road, some behind fences while others wandered free, matched the sullen colour of the land: mottled brown and grey and miserable. They took complete ownership of the road and stood in the centre with curved horns lowered. I slowed and edged around them, weighing the risk of slipping off the road against the chance of a horn through my fuel tank.

I rode with my visor open to enjoy the rush of air. I had long ago learned to swallow mosquitoes and flies whole and had earned countless welts from those that bounced off my face. Then, out of the corner of my eye, I caught a split-second flash of black, and then the sharp smack of impact. I felt the bug burrow itself between my cheekbone and the helmet padding, squirming against my skin. I was clawing at my face with one hand while trying to keep my bike upright in the muddy tracks when I felt a numbing sting of pain.

By now I was tossing my head like a startled horse, trying to dislodge the creature. I veered to the side of the road, tore my helmet off and dislodged a bee as big as my thumb. It fell to the ground and buzzed in drunken circles for a second before I squashed it with my boot.

My cheek was hot and swollen. I felt a stab of fear. Months earlier, riding through Alabama, I was bitten by a mystery bug. The bite had caused my nostrils and ears to swell shut. My eyes had been reduced to tiny slits as I gasped for air and fought off a wave of terror. A passerby spotted my dilemma, gave me his own emergency antihistamines, and saved my life. I'd had chills and a fever for two days after the bite. It was the first time I'd had an allergic reaction to anything.

Since then I had carried a packet of antihistamines tucked into my breast pocket. I swallowed two of them now, washed down with a gulp of warm water from my canteen. I took a few deep breaths, worried that I might soon struggle for air, as if I could stock up on it for later. Without the throb of my motorcycle engine and the comforting safety of motion I felt very alone. I had not seen another vehicle or human for several hours. I opened and closed my mouth like a landed fish, then blew air through my nose until the snot flew. It all worked just fine. So far. Waiting on the road for my airways to close wouldn't help. I restarted my bike and rode on, reminding myself that the Mennonite pioneers had suffered far worse.

The perseverance of the Mennonites who moved to the Gran Chaco was remarkable, even by Mennonite standards. Getting to the Chaco had nearly killed them, and although passing years made escape easier, the vast plain was still a barrier holding back the outside world.

When Paraguayan Mennonite families returned to Canada on visits, we viewed them with a mix of curiosity, awe, and derision. Curiosity, because they were obviously our relations despite their different accents and exotic origins. Distant relations to be sure, but my grandmother could have explained the blood-lines. Awe because we'd all heard stories of just how tough life could be in Paraguay, and these were the people who had experienced it. They loved Jesus so much they'd moved to the Chaco, where they nearly starved and the wind blew dust over everything. Derision because they were so different. Their clothes were outdated, their teeth were bad, and they were dreadfully uncool, even by our own culturally stunted standards. Now I was following them down that hole.

I'd had my fill of the dark underbelly of Mennonite culture in Bolivia, but now I was fighting my way through one of the earth's most inhospitable patches, knocking a hole through the basement floor in order to find the very darkest corner of Mennonite retreat. My mind's eye—made all the more creative by the hours spent alone on the road—was filled with Mennonite hillbilly families, mouths full of rotten teeth, spilling by the dozen from clapped-out Econoline vans, too many children to feed or educate properly.

Paraguay has long been a wild frontier where men with cash and big dreams come to make a fortune or create their utopia, far away from prying eyes. It attracts oddballs and dreamers much in the same way that Alaska does, but with a more sinister edge. All that empty space—well, except for the aboriginals, but they're easily moved—screams potential to people gullible enough to think they can make it here, just as it does to the few that actually do find success.

People have come from Europe, Australia, Asia, and across the Americas to build their own ideals of peace, socialism, and pure living in Paraguay. Most settlers have failed. In the 1880s Elisabeth Nietzsche—Friedrich's sister and a rabid anti-Semite—together with her husband, Bernhard Förster, founded Nueva Germania, a colony in the jungles of eastern Paraguay. The country swatted away their Aryan greatness, and the place drove Förster broke and mad. Within two and a half years he had poisoned himself, Elisabeth returned home, and their little kingdom fell into ruin. Then Germany's Nazis came to hide there in the jungle after World War II, creating fertile ground for tales of espionage and manhunts.

In 2000, Reverend Sun Myung Moon, the self-proclaimed messiah who led the Unification cult known as the Moonies, bought large tracts of land in the Chaco to build a paradisiacal community and eco-resort. The plan failed and the land was soon back on the market for the next wide-eyed optimist.

I could understand why they'd failed. By late afternoon my bike had tipped me into the mud a half-dozen times. I'd stopped cleaning myself after each fall. The seat was covered in a slick of muck, daubed on coat by coat each time I remounted. But my anger was spent. Not even my most creative curses would make this any better. The Chaco had beaten the ugly mood out of me, and in its place there was a growing curiosity over those who called this Green Hell home.

By the time I arrived in Loma Plata, the town at the centre of Menno Colony, the sun was setting, and I was ten hours and 450 kilometres from where I had started the day. I was bewildered when the road went from mucky chaos to smooth tarmac. The business centre appeared, an oasis, a small slice of Europe. Shade trees in straight rows escorted me towards the downtown. Sturdy red-brick buildings were adorned with flowering vines, wide roads were filled with orderly traffic. Concrete monuments graced the roundabouts.

A shiny SUV pulled up beside me at a stop sign, and through the tinted windows I could see a blond woman wearing dark sunglasses. She saw me staring at her and waved, flashing a pearly smile. Two teenage boys, dressed in shorts and T-shirts, came out of a shop and walked down the street bouncing a basketball between them. I passed a museum, a hospital, and a handsome school. I looked at my map, a nagging feeling in my stomach that perhaps I'd made a wrong turn.

I found my way to Pension Loma Plata, the cheapest of the town's lodgings. It was surrounded by a red-brick wall, with the hotelier's family living in an adjacent house. My boots dropped clumps of muck in the shiny foyer as I entered.

"Ohhh, you must have come from a long way," the receptionist said in hesitant English.

"From Bolivia. I came through the Chaco," I said.

"Oh ya, that road is terrible when it rains. Welcome to Loma Plata."

"I wasn't expecting the colony to look like this."

She laughed, like she'd heard other visitors say that. "It's changed a lot from the early days."

I was exhausted and was about to retreat to my room when she called after me.

"The Wi-Fi is the name of the hotel. No password."

I shucked my riding clothes off in the shower to clean them, and then looked into the bathroom mirror. My face was black with dirt, and the right side had a cartoonish bulge to it, as if I'd been in a brawl. But I was smiling.

CHAPTER 17

Paraguay

The Cost of Success

The rain was another pleasant surprise. Instead of an arid and dusty Menno Colony I found Mennonites luxuriating in an unusual, inconvenient, but very much welcomed rainy season. The water collected in puddles on the road and the ditches were filled with it; even the mosquitoes flourished. The farmers smiled—this was more than they'd hoped for. This weather was different from what it was at the start.

Menno Colony felt more like a town striving to match the rest of the world than one hiding from progress and integration. In its shops you could buy televisions, computers, designer furniture, and motorbikes. Or you could walk into the hospital, where doctors, Mennonite and non-Mennonite, offered professional treatment. The schools rivalled the best in the country, where teachers—again, Mennonite and non-Mennonite both—taught secular courses in Spanish and German. And if you had trouble finding some of the powerful business leaders who had helped build all this, it might be because they were in Asunción, the nation's capital, where they sat in the boardrooms of national banks and corporations and jostled for political positions in the halls of power.

The harsh landscape hadn't changed. Farmers had learned to put two rubber tires on each wheel, one over the other, double-clad for protection against razor-sharp thorns. They carried small electric shockers in their pickup trucks, as they'd found the shockers to be the most effective way to treat victims of poisonous snakebites, even though the treatment defied medical explanation. The treatment consists of four or five high-voltage, low-current but very painful electric shocks, applied as close as possible to the bite. The positive results were documented in *The Lancet*, the British medical journal, but they couldn't explain it.

But despite the persistent thorns and snakes, the Mennonites had become rich enough that they no longer needed to eat *algarrobo* pods. The Menno Colony cooperative, which ran most of the biggest businesses in town, produced revenues of US $750 million a year. On the outskirts of town stood their new eight-hundred-head-per-day cattle abattoir, which exported beef around the world. Mennonites made up only about 1 percent of Paraguay's population, but they produced a huge share of its agricultural goods—they were, on average, more than ten times as wealthy as other Paraguayans. The proceeds enabled the colony to build thousands of kilometres of roads and electricity lines.

The Mennonites I met were proud of their accomplishments, offering to take me on tours of their expanding farms, new businesses, schools, and hospitals. They pointed out that their students were going off to university and leading Mennonite institutions to new heights. Strangely, no one mentioned the relief of having escaped Canada's education standards, or the spiritual balm the Chaco had provided. No one mentioned the need to remain separate from the *weltmensch*. But they hadn't forgotten about the heroic struggle they'd gone through to get there eighty-five years earlier.

Nowhere in Mennonite history was there a story of suffering and perseverance more worthy and hallowed than in Paraguay. Nowhere was the story of the beginning, the struggle that was endured for God's glory, more tied to Mennonite identity. After a week of bewilderment at the about-face of Menno Colony I was offered a chance to revisit that story in person. Peter, a middle-aged Loma Plata businessman, invited me on a day trip. He brought along his taller, balder brother David, as well as Rudy, their brother-in-law.

It was raining as we set off. The windshield wipers swished back and forth. A scum of grey water swept over the truck in a whoosh as we plunged through a puddle big enough to bathe an ox in.

Peter was hunched over the wheel of his brand-new Nissan extended-cab 4x4, muttering encouragement to the truck as he peered from underneath a baseball cap. He was soft-spoken and his salt-and-pepper goatee twitched when he smiled, warning that a wry wisecrack, delivered in a low, monotone voice, was on its way.

The road to Puerto Casado cut a muddy and rutted two-hundred-kilometre-long blaze through the Chaco, running east in a straight line from the Mennonite colonies. Had there been traffic, we would have seen it from far away. But there was no traffic. Deep green forest on either side of the road disappeared into a narrow apex on the horizon, both front and back. An apex we chased for hours on end.

Everyone was in a jocular mood, relieved to have escaped family and work obligations for the day. David filled any silence with his constant stream of quips and observations, while Rudy added colourful commentary in a nasal, impassioned voice.

"We should have taken my Toyota," David said, grinning at Rudy, who sat in the back seat with him. "A Nissan will never make it there in this mud!"

"Well, we should have at least brought your Toyota along to drag this thing out if we get stuck. Peter can still drive his new Nissan, just for show," Rudy added.

"In Canada the roads are never this bad, are they?" Peter asked.

I laughed. "Sure they are. But we don't drive Nissans, so it's not a big problem."

Peter snorted, and the brothers in the back slapped their knees and guffawed. Ford versus GMC, John Deere versus Massey Ferguson. They were the rivalries I'd grown up with, a substitute for the pro sports we never watched. I felt as if I was on an outing with my uncles in Canada. These men had the same puckish sense of humour that played with the Plautdietsche language, stories that relied on self-deprecation but were backed by deep pride.

The men from Loma Plata were proud of what they'd achieved, especially when compared to the wilderness around them. Each kilometre looked the same as the previous one we'd passed. Parts of the bush had been fenced in by enterprising farmers. Small tumbledown huts, where the caretakers of the lots lived, stood naked and alone in muddy yards.

David was busy in the back seat making *tereré*, the Guaraní version of the herbal drink yerba maté. First, he scooped finely mulched leaves out of a plastic bag and into a tall cup made from a bull horn, decorated with a steel base and rim. He put the cup between his knees and filled it with ice water from a large thermos. Next, he fished around in his bag and pulled out the *bombilla*, a silver pipe with a wide screen scoop at the end, like a tea infuser attached to a straw. He tamped down the leaves with the *bombilla*, mashed and stirred, added some more water, and then sucked on the straw. He repeated this a few more times, adding water and crushing the leaves until the cup was full of sodden mash.

"We Mennonites are sometimes too stubborn to learn from others, but we have learned to drink maté," Rudy said as he took the cup from David.

He drew deeply on the *bombilla*, then held the cup as David refilled it again, working the *bombilla* like a mortar at the same time. It was passed on, and whenever the *bombilla* made a gurgling sound David added more water. The drink had a refreshing bitter taste, like green tea, and the caffeine perked me up. Too much of it could give you diarrhea, but that didn't hamper their intake. They passed it round and round, unhurriedly. At times it would rest in someone's hands as they became lost in the telling of the story before resuming its rounds.

Ironically, as the Mennonites are ardent pacifists, war was a big part of their story. Once again Mennonites were pawns in a conflict, but this time it had played out in their favour. In the late nineteenth century, Paraguay lost a ruinous war with Brazil, Argentina, and Uruguay that forced it to give up half of its territory. After the war the government resorted to selling some of its remaining land to raise cash.

Carlos Casado del Alisal, a swashbuckling businessman from Argentina, bought the land we were driving through, about 5.6 million hectares in total, for tannin and timber production. The tannin, used to tan animal hides, came from the quebracho tree, an extremely hard, blood-red wood that grows only in the Chaco.

"Casado was a terribly rich man," Peter said. He said Casado's name like he knew him, but I couldn't tell if he was accusing or admiring. "By the mid-1920s his son was running the company and was selling some of their land."

It was perfect timing, because some of Canada's hard-working pioneer Mennonites had become disillusioned. Many had already moved to Mexico, but the bravest souls chose Paraguay and the *Privilegium* that offered them the isolation they so craved. Nearly 2,000 Mennonites—most of them from the Old Colony sect—sailed from Canada down the east coast of the Americas and travelled to Asunción. There they boarded boats that churned up the Paraguay River and deposited them at a bend near the Brazilian border. They stepped ashore in the Chaco on New Year's Eve, 1926.

The town—officially named La Victoria, but commonly referred to using the district name Puerto Casado—was a booming company town at the time, bustling with traders and tannin workers. It was now a swampy, remote village built around the abandoned factory and a disused port. There was little industry, and most of the 6,500 inhabitants wore a sullen, bored expression.

The Paraguay River was the town's main feature. Like the Red River, where Johann's journey had ended and mine had begun, the Paraguay also flowed smooth and brown through flat, flood-prone land. Both had muddy, overgrown banks that bred mosquitoes and both places had received Mennonites at the end of epic journeys. It was wide with eddies and currents that rippled the coffee-coloured surface like taut muscles. Tree branches and clumps of tangled water hyacinth, unmoored by recent rains, floated by. Wooden skiffs were pulled up on the banks to unload cargo.

We stood on a rotting old dock and looked out over the water, relieved to be out of the truck. The air was heavy and damp. Suffocating.

"So, this is where our parents and grandparents stepped ashore to make a new life," David said. He pointed up and down the river, reminding me of the corporate public relations people I'd had to deal with as a financial journalist. So completely and utterly committed to sticking to their script that they never questioned the narrative or wondered who had written the words they were repeating. I found his dedication to the storyline tiresome because after a week on the colonies I couldn't see what that struggle had achieved beyond more land, more cattle, more wealth.

"The people who came through this port would barely recognize you as Mennonite now. Apart from the Mennonite food and Plautdietsch, your lives aren't that different from other farmers, here or in Canada. What do you think they'd say if they could see what the colony has become?" I asked. I didn't bother to hide the challenge in my voice.

I'd seen little evidence of the advertised motives of this move that had taken place eight and a half decades earlier. They might have set out to prove their piety and follow "God's will," but along the way they'd changed tack and proven that integration and breaking down walls didn't kill off Mennonite culture and success, but instead enhanced it. Maybe my moving away and exploring the world had made me more of a true Mennonite than I would have been if I had remained.

"I think our parents would say it was worth it," David said. "We appreciate it, that they dared to do this, to come to the Chaco. We like it here now. We want to stay here. I'm very thankful to my parents that they did it."

Rudy had never visited Puerto Casado before, and he shook his head in wonder. He, like me, ignored David's enthusiastic exclamations.

"Man, oh man. So this is it, eh?" he said under his breath as he shielded his eyes to look across the river. "This is where they landed.

"I have lived there, in Canada, for two years, and I can't understand what our fathers' complaint was or why they moved away," Rudy said. "I can see it a bit better now, the goals that came from that kind of life, but those objectives exist here as well. It is the same here now.

"I always say, God can take the crooked line and write it straight, and here he has shown that. It depends which side you see it from, but I think it would have been better for us to stay there."

Rudy laughed as he saw the surprise on his brothers' faces. These exoduses, from Russia to Canada, from Canada to Paraguay, were rarely looked back on as mistakes. God was leading them, after all, and God wouldn't make such mistakes. In the end, as the struggles paid off and life became more comfortable, the stories of suffering were shaped and retold until they added a touch of glory to it all. That was the Mennonite way.

"We have been able to create work for a lot of people here," David said, now speaking to Rudy as much as to me. "For a long time, we thought that, as Mennonites, we should live on our own, separate and quietly. Today I see that differently, because I've seen how we can help people by giving them jobs and teaching them skills and how to work."

"Yes, we took this land and made it productive, and made ourselves some of the richest people in the country," Rudy said. "That was not the goal, but that is the result. By making our home here and developing it we have made progress. But the original intention is gone."

Bolivia had also been mired in wars, losing its Pacific Ocean coast to Chile, and, like Paraguay, it became protective over the territory that remained. Both countries claimed the northern part of the Gran Chaco, at the time considered a barren, unprofitable scrubland. When Paraguay offered Mennonites a *Privilegium* to colonize the Chaco it became a potential source of agricultural production, which raised the stakes. The Mennonite settlements also helped validate Paraguay's claim to the Chaco, which Bolivia protested at the League of Nations to no avail. The resulting Chaco War of 1932–35 became South America's most bloody conflict with more than 100,000 dead.

The Mennonites were already settled on their new land by the time the Chaco War kicked off, and the front lines went right past their farms. The Mennonites began to trade their food and water to the Paraguayan troops, while Bolivia struggled to get supplies to their front lines. The Mennonites helped Paraguay win the war and take ownership of two-thirds of the disputed territories. Today, the Mennonites point at that early trade as a key factor in why their colony had opened up to the world. But since then the changes had come from within. When the Mennonites saw that their schools weren't equipped to produce the kinds of citizens they needed to colonize the Chaco, they improved their schools, and taught Spanish so that they'd be better at negotiating on a national level. The change was intentional, so much so that those who disagreed packed their plows and bonnets and moved to Bolivia, refusing to accept the changes. The opening up of Menno Colony wasn't an accident, and it had worked. Menno Colony turned out better than anyone could have hoped for. Their growing influence and interaction with the Paraguayan community was a positive change, but it undermined the isolationist intentions of their immigration story.

"I don't know how important it is to keep the culture, but it is important," Rudy said. He fell silent for a long time, and then sighed. "A lot of the culture is disappearing, and that is the way of the world. But in the end, I think it's important that bits of it remain. But most important is that we remain Christian, because without that…"

Rudy made a half-hearted gesture towards the town behind us, as if the same fate would befall the Mennonites if they dropped their guard. Puerto Casado reeked of mould and rot. The cornerstone buildings of the town's glory days—a cathedral and several large homes—still stood straighter and taller than those that had come later, but their yellow paint was streaked with grey and the buildings were home to pigeons and cobwebs. We snooped around the stone cathedral and admired the heavy wooden beams in the roof.

"Still perfectly straight after all these years," Rudy said as his eyes roved the shadows high above him. "It could still be repaired. If this building was on a Mennonite colony we would do something with it, make use of it somehow, you can be sure of that."

There was a touch of selfish satisfaction in seeing Puerto Casado wither away, as it was a place of bitter memories in Mennonite history.

"The plan was that the land they'd bought would be surveyed when they arrived, and they'd move directly into the Chaco," David said as he again took on the role of official narrator. "But the railway was not done, and the survey was not done. They moved into tents pitched next to the tannin factory, and some of them had to stay there a year and a half. In Canada in December it was cold, but here it was very hot, and they became sick. They lived about a kilometre from the graveyard, and they had nothing to drive, so they put the bodies on a wheelbarrow or whatever, and as soon as they'd returned from burying one there was another death. It was a very sad situation, but they did not give up."

They waited and negotiated with Casado's company men and made exploratory trips into the Chaco to see their recently purchased land. And they waited for the transaction to be completed. Typhoid, malaria, diarrhea, and a host of other tropical afflictions took their toll. They were instructed to bury their dead in the Catholic cemetery near the river. It was a huge affront to the Mennonites to lie next to the Catholics in death, but they had no choice.

Now the cemetery was as waterlogged and fetid as the rest of the town. A sickly-sweet smell emanated from the mauve blossoms of the lapacho trees, mixing with the dankness of sodden earth. But the air screeched with life. Birds, high above in trees with trunks blackened by humidity, called out like church bells. Mosquitoes buzzed in our noses and ears. Cicadas thrummed in the trees.

The Catholics were buried in large tombs covered in ceramic tiles and crosses and praying figures. The tombs were decrepit now, decorated with faded plastic flowers, but they still had a stately quality. The Mennonite graves were overgrown mounds and broken rings of concrete, with cheap concrete-cast headstones that were sinking into the swamp.

"Imagine people rising up," Rudy said, raising his arms as if lifting angels to heaven. "The concrete, it will all just crack up, and it won't matter how big and strong and fancy the graves are."

A donkey wandered by. It stopped to watch us for a moment, then nibbled at the grass between the graves and continued on its unhurried way. The men stooped low to read each gravestone and look for familiar names. Both Mennonite and Catholic graves had a startling number of young women and children. The Mennonite dates of death were regular, a few each month, enough to keep sorrow near and raw. By the time they left Puerto Casado they'd buried 168 bodies, a tenth of their original force.

The dates and names were hard to read on the weathered headstones. We lifted them out of the mud to expose their faces, grunting as we fought against the will of nature. Some of the lettering looked like it had simply been scratched into the wet concrete with a nail.

"This woman was born in 1902 and died in 1925? No, that must be 1927. A young woman. Maria Wiebe. No, not Maria... Agatha, must be...A...gath—ya, Agatha," Rudy mumbled to himself as he crouched down to examine a headstone, tracing the letters with his fingers.

"Ah, this is our dad's sister that lies here," said David as he brushed moss off a stone a few metres away. "*Hier ruht in Frieden Sara Fehr.* It's a child, one year old. That was my aunt."

The stone was leaned against another grave, so we couldn't be sure which grave it belonged to.

"Why has no one come here and fixed these graves up?" I asked. "It doesn't look good, you know, that the Mennonites left these graves like this when you live just a few hours away. Where is your pride?"

David hmm'd in noncommittal agreement. "We don't come here much, so I guess no one thinks about the graves."

It wasn't a very glorious part of the story, this graveyard. Same as those pioneers who gave up and returned to Canada. Their story was also rarely mentioned.

Eventually, the surviving Mennonites travelled inland on the narrow-gauge railway built by the Casados to haul wood to the tannin factory. The railway extended 145 kilometres into the bush. We piled back into the pickup truck to follow their route and stopped at the railhead, named Kilometer 145. Bits of twisted rail and rotted sleepers poked through the undergrowth. The old wood-fired train itself was nowhere to be seen.

"I always imagine how it was when our poor people arrived and Casado was a rich man. Look at this house here," David said as he slapped his hand against a solid wood post of the train station, which had been refurbished as a museum piece. The buildings were whitewashed, the yard orderly and neat. An ox cart with giant wheels, designed for the rough Chaco trails, stood beside the old railway, as if waiting for more Mennonites to arrive.

"Casado said he would build the rail the whole way, but he never did, so the last ninety kilometres they had to go by ox cart," David said. The Mennonites still grumbled about the bad deal their ancestors had received.

Women and children, tools, household goods, and sacks of seed were taken off the trains and reloaded onto ox carts and dragged deeper into the Chaco. Some of the furniture and quilts had travelled all the way from Russia to Canada, then were bundled and packed up for yet another fresh start. The deeper into the Chaco they travelled, the more difficult it became. Many became dismayed when they realized that this was what they had waited for: a dry and thorny place where scrubby bush made travel hard, where snakes and wildcats and endless tropical afflictions waited to pull you down into the dusty ground.

A series of way stations were built along the ox path, where the drivers rested their livestock, sheltered from the heat, and recovered from the brutal travel. A Mennonite historical society had restored the main shed and a few small adobe outbuildings at Hoffnungsfeld (Field of Hope), little more than a rough clearing with packed earth that faded into the surrounding bush. The buildings had hand-hewn wooden doors and were dark and dank inside. The brothers gravitated to the shed, filled with antique farm machinery, harnesses, and wagon wheels.

David stood in the middle of the shed, arms outstretched.

"In here, with family and children. In the heat, with the flies. Just terrible," he said, and then clucked his tongue. "This was the only route into the Grand Chaco back then. Everything had to come this way, and if you became sick, you had to take this route to Asunción, which took ten days round trip. Now you just take your phone, and you can be connected in seconds."

We'd spent all day reminiscing, debating, and poring over a history whose glorious portrayal could not cover up the suffering and loss at its core. Our mood, so jovial at the start of the day, had become sombre. Had it been worth it? Were the Mennonites in Paraguay any closer to heaven than those they'd left behind in Canada? Or did they endure all that suffering only to end up back where they started?

We trudged through the prickly trees to return to the truck. In the morning I'd seen the brothers put fishing rods in the truck. When I'd enquired where we'd go fishing, they'd answered with a sly wink.

"*Na yo*, let's go fishing," David said now as he clapped his hands in an attempt to stir us from our melancholy. "We can always still go fishing."

We returned to the long, narrow road that slashed across the Chaco. The sun had broken through the clouds and dried some of the puddles, leaving hard ruts in their place. The truck swung and lunged through the ruts, kicking up stones that clattered against the fenders.

Beside the road were large pits, dug to provide soil to build the road, and then turned into fishing ponds. With the recent rains they were filled to overflowing, which had multiplied the fish, or at very least the fishing stories.

"I spoke to someone who said he'd fished in one of these ponds last week. He said he caught so many fish that he couldn't even relax. Every time he sat down, he had another one on the line," Rudy said as he tried to revive our mood.

"Well, that sounds like work," David said. "I don't know if I feel like working today."

"Ah, a bit of work for some nice fish. That's not a bad deal," Rudy said.

Peter slowed the truck at several ponds to peer through the

trees that ringed them. Most were impossible to reach, blocked off by ditches full of rainwater. Peter was given rough directions to one that was both accessible and reportedly home to fish. He watched his odometer as he measured the distance from Puerto Casado accordingly.

"Eighty. It must be a bit farther," he said.

Then a few minutes later we came to another pond and Peter tapped a forefinger on the odometer. "Well, this is the one, according to the numbers anyway."

He steered us down a rough track that led to the edge of a pond that was larger than the others. We dug out fishing rods and tackle boxes.

"We need to make room in the truck box for all the fish I'm gonna catch," Rudy said as he tied a hook to his line.

"Ha! We should have brought a trailer to haul them all home, because I plan to fill the truck box myself," David answered.

"I feel bad, coming all the way from Canada to catch all your fish. I can just watch, if you'd prefer," I said.

"After ten fish you can stop and leave the rest to us," David said.

Peter said nothing. He was already walking through the knee-high grass to the water's edge. Soon everyone had found a spot along the shore and fell silent, casting their lines into the glassy pond. Water spiders, their legs cartoonishly long for their tiny bodies, skittered across the surface. The shallow pond was filled with purple water hyacinth and our hooks snagged their roots if we didn't reel in our line fast enough.

"Psst," Rudy whispered, as he pointed across the water. "Look."

Two herons, stark white against the lush green vegetation, pranced along the edge of the pond. Their long necks undulated with each step. Then they took to the air, skimming over the water before they soared higher, trailing long dainty legs.

First Rudy caught a fish, then David, and within an hour each of us had at least one. Sometimes the fish escaped before they were pulled ashore and the men muttered as they cast their lines in pursuit. The air had begun to cool. The insects that had put up a deafening clamour at high noon were falling silent. The light

turned a deeper orange with each degree the sun fell towards the horizon. The trees filtered it into a dappled glow that made us squint to see where our lines had hit the water. For the first time the Chaco seemed bearable to me, even pleasant. It must have been the unseasonable rains that did it.

Rudy broke the peacefulness. He yanked on his rod, tip pointed at the water as he bowed it with effort. He paced up and down the water's edge, jerking at the line.

"Argh! This one isn't coming loose," he said as he tried to pull the hook out of the weeds.

"Maybe it's just a big fish. The one you said you were gonna catch would be about that size I think," David called from down the shore, grinning.

Rudy already had his jeans down to his ankles, revealing skinny white farmer legs. He hopped on one foot, then the next, as he pulled off socks and shoes. David and Peter hooted with laughter, but Rudy ignored them. He waded into the water, fishing rod in one hand, his other outstretched for balance. The water reached his crotch and he yelped.

"I should have known to bring clean underwear on a trip like this," he shouted. David and Peter snickered and carried on a whispered derisive commentary as they watched from the shore.

"Dip in and out a few times and those ones will be clean enough. Not dry, but clean," Peter shouted across the water.

Rudy waded deeper until he reached the spot where the line was snagged on the bottom. He yanked it free and waded back to clamber up the bank, wet grass stuck to his bare legs. His underpants hung heavy and wet like a full diaper and he looked down at them in dismay.

"How are we gonna explain your wet pants to your wife?" David asked.

"She knows better than to ask questions," Rudy said as he pulled his jeans back on and resumed fishing.

David set his rod down and returned to the truck to unload lawn chairs, a cooler, and a few armfuls of firewood. I started a fire while David rummaged around in the cooler. Once the fire was crackling, he positioned a steel stand over it, and atop that a cast-iron pot. Then he added noodles, tomato paste, chilies, and ground beef.

"I thought you had better taste real Paraguayan *giso* while you're here," David said. "It's a stew the ranchers around here make when they're out herding cattle."

The smells from the pot wafted to the water's edge, where Peter and Rudy cleaned our catch.

"Well, we didn't even need to bring the *giso*," Peter said as he held up a bag of fish fillets. It wasn't quite enough to fill the truck box.

"Ya, it's good we caught some. But I wasn't confident that we would get anything, and I didn't want our guest to go hungry," David said as he filled bowls and passed them to us with a few *galletas*, the hard water crackers that had evolved from ship's biscuit.

Here, not far from the Paraguay River, the Chaco was wetter and more lush than in the east, and the moisture allowed larger trees to grow. A light breeze whispered through tall palm, eucalyptus, and white quebracho trees. The red quebracho was long ago chopped down to make tannin, but the white ones remained, even though they were highly sought after to make fence posts and for timber. The sun had slipped behind the forest and the heat of the day had faded.

"Ahh, this is Paraguay. It was terrible at first, but now look. What a place," David said. He reclined in his lawn chair and wiped *giso* from his chin.

"I wonder if our parents could have imagined that someday we'd have time to go fishing like this," Peter said. "Not because we're hungry, but just for fun."

I grunted to show I was listening, my nose deep in my bowl of *giso*.

CHAPTER 18

Argentina

The Farthest Wheat Field

I was ready to accept that there was no clear Mennonite identity that I could frame and hang on my wall as a certificate of me. Some Mennonites made me feel like I belonged and others made me want to shed my cultural identity. Just like how I embraced the company of the biker fraternity, but didn't call myself a biker. *Mennonite* was a label I liked to give myself, and I was gaining confidence that I had the right to do so. There were others who used the same label, and their use gave it new meanings, and that was okay.

Just like the second- and third-culture friends I had around the world. Born to Chinese and English parents, raised in another country, with different passports. Their grandmothers didn't share a common language. "Which one do you identify with more?" I'd ask. They always looked back confused at having been asked for an answer that didn't exist. My travels had taught me that identity can be complex, but I'd somehow thought my identity would be much simpler. I was a white English-speaking male from Canada; my only unique label was *Mennonite*. How complicated could it be?

In the end we all pick and choose whether we want to keep the buggy or buy a car, choose an English name or use our Chinese one. Language, faith, family traditions. As soon as we expose ourselves to any foreign culture—and we Mennonites expose ourselves every time we move—we have to start choosing. It's an inexact science, what we keep and what we pass over, so everyone ends up with a different quilt.

Sometimes we find others with matching quilts, but often they're hard to find. My trip had helped me see how many different patches there were to choose from when we made our own quilts. And my quilt was far from colour coordinated, some of the patches clashed with the others. There were a lot of quilts out there that didn't look anything like mine, and that made me feel a bit *Oot bunt*. *Oot bunt*, mismatched, like Greta described herself on Spanish Lookout. But I'd seen enough quilts. I had all the context I needed to know who I was.

I was ready to go home, but there was one more colony to visit. When I'd plotted my journey on the maps taped to the walls of my Hong Kong apartment, I'd had to get on my hands and knees to study this last spot, way at the bottom of the map, where Mennonites had gone to be themselves. The most southerly colony. I'd drawn a black circle around its name: Remecó, on the northern edge of Patagonia.

I knew no one on Remecó, so I drove up and down its dirt roads, asking for the *vorsteher*—the reeve or administrator of the colony. It was the week before Christmas, but there were no decorative lights or Christmas trees on the colony, no angels on front lawns. Just neatly trimmed yards, flower gardens, and trees, everything a bright midsummer green.

I was directed down the road to Hans Loewen, and when I found him he invited me into his house, where he introduced me to his *mumtje*—his quiet, smiling missus.

"What's your name?" I asked her.

"Na, I'm *mumtje* Loewen," she answered, looking at me quizzically.

"No, I mean your own name."

She gave a short laugh and looked at Hans, confused.

"My name is *mumtje* Hans Loewen."

"No, your first name. The name your parents gave you."

"Oh. Na, it's L—Lena," she said with a stammer. "My name is Lena."

Hans and Lena had come here as newlyweds with about eight hundred other Mennonites from Mexico more than twenty-five years ago, for all the usual reasons. Now there were twelve hundred Mennonites on the colony. No electricity or cars, just sticking to the Old Colony ways. They had five children, ranging from their eldest daughter, who was married with two children of her own and lived in a small house on the edge of the farm, down to four-year-old Peter, the apple of everyone's eye.

"It was hard at first," said Lena, who I soon discovered could be quite chatty once the ice was broken. "The stores here didn't have any of the things we knew back in Mexico. In fact, we still import cloth from Mexico to make our clothes, because here they don't have the patterns and material that Mennonites use."

But what they did have was privacy to live the way they wanted to. The landscape was so expansive it made me gasp. The blue sky was impossibly large and present, a constant factor. Ripe grain crops shone golden in the sunshine. Fat doves squatted on the dirt roads by the hundreds, taking flight as I rode by. It was warm by day, with dew falling in the cool of the night. And there, with fertile soil all around, they hand-milked their cows, butchered their own pigs, grew grain and vegetables, and drove tractors with steel wheels.

"You are welcome to stay for a few days," Hans said.

I was happy to eat at their table, but I preferred to sleep in my own tent, beside the shed. As soon as I began to erect it the family crowded around, having never seen a modern camping tent before.

"Look, Sush! You can crawl right in!" Helena, one of the daughters, said as she held back the flap and bent over to peer inside the tent, gathering her skirt around her knees.

A white, fringed scarf covered her hair and neck, and over that she wore a wide-brimmed white hat with a purple sash that kept her pretty face in shadows. Her dark dress ended at her pale ankles. Heavy black leather shoes, grimy with dust, completed her outfit.

Nine-year-old Sush, bespectacled and shy, worshipped her seventeen-year-old sister, her eyes never leaving Helena. Sush knelt in the entrance of the tent and twisted her neck to look up at the mesh ceiling.

I showed them my foam sleeping mat and the children took turns squeezing it and feeling its odd waffle-like surface.

"It's not very thick," Helena said with a giggle.

Next, I unpacked my sleeping bag and fluffed it up. I showed them how to crawl in and zip it up.

"A blanket with a zipper!" crowed Sush.

"When I'm on the road I set my tent up wherever I find a good spot, and that's my home for the night," I said.

They looked at each other and laughed. I showed them my set of nesting camp pots and the collapsible stove and gas bottle. I set it all up on top of a bike pannier. With the click of a lighter I had the stove hissing and a blue flame licking at the bottom of a saucepan.

"Just that, that's all you have to cook on?" Helena asked. "Just one burner?"

"People who live in cities sometimes pack all this stuff up, put it in a big sack on their back, and leave the city to walk in circles in the hills for days on end," I said, standing hunched over as if I was carrying a house on my back.

That had Hans's attention too. Until then he'd stood back, laughing as he watched his daughters discover my odd equipment.

"But they have cars, right?" Hans asked. Perhaps he wondered if there were non-Mennonites who shunned convenience just for the piousness of it.

"They have cars, but they choose to walk for exercise and fun," I said. "They walk for ten, maybe twenty kilometres a day through the mountains and then they set up their camp, just like mine here. And then the next day they pack it all up and walk some more."

"But why? If they have cars, why do they do that?" Hans wanted to know.

We were only 700 kilometres from Buenos Aires, but Argentina's capital could just as well have been on another continent. When the Loewens referred to the "city," their voices filled with awe, they meant Guatraché, half an hour's drive by car—one of which they did not own—and boasting a population of about 5,000 people.

The fun came to an abrupt end when Hans realized it was late afternoon. They had spent their afternoon ogling my camping gear when there was work to be done.

"It's milking time," Hans declared. Helena straightened up, grabbed her sister by the hand, and marched off towards the barn.

"Can I come help?" I asked.

Helena stopped, looked at her father, and then walked away without replying. I zipped up the tent and followed her.

The cows, with swollen, pendulous udders, bumped their noses against the back gate of the barn. Helena and her brother Heinrich opened the gate and ushered the cows to their stalls. Heinrich, Hans's oldest son, was lean and wiry, and his face looked much older than his twenty-one years.

Sitting on low wooden stools, shoulders pressed against warm flanks, they began to milk. The small barn was filled with the thump of hoofs when the cows shifted, the rattle of a chain, the swish of a tail, and the steady *tzzzzt tzzzzt tzzzzt* as milk hit the bottom of the empty tin pails. The sound deepened in pitch as the pails filled with frothy milk.

"Do you know how to do this?" Helena asked me, blushing just because she was speaking to me directly.

"No. Can you show me?"

She showed me how to begin each squeeze at the top of the teat and work downward in one deft stroke. I fumbled and pinched and pulled. The cow stamped her feet as she sensed that something was wrong. With practice I caught the rhythm, and each squirt became smoother than the last.

"It's just like dancing," I joked. "Don't focus on the steps, just feel the rhythm."

Helena didn't laugh. Dancing was more foreign to her than milking a cow was to me. I soon relinquished the stool and still-swollen udders to her.

"Your arms will be sore in the morning because you are not used to the work," she said, laughing. She sat down and began to expertly massage the teats again: *tzzzzt tzzzzt tzzzzt.*

Helena was a pretty girl, and she was nearing marriageable age. "Do you have a *schatz*?" I asked. A sweetheart.

Helena only blushed more deeply and shook her head as she leaned closer to the cow, hiding behind its flank. All I could see were her pale forearms, which were ropy with muscles.

"Maybe you don't have a *schatz*, but I bet a few boys wish you were their *schatz*," I teased.

I couldn't see Helena's face, so it was hard to tell just how horrified she was that a strange man would talk to her about such a delicate matter.

Outside, the half-dozen steel milk containers that stood on a handcart were filled one by one, their tops screwed shut when they were full. Heinrich lifted Peter onto the wagon beside the milk. The blond boy was the pet of the family and he spent much of his day riding around the farmyard on a homemade tricycle built to look like a Massey Ferguson tractor, complete with red paint, decals, a tractor seat, steel wheels, and a spittle-spraying engine sound made by the operator. He was dressed the same as the men, in *schlaub'betjse*, a plaid shirt, and a brown unmarked baseball cap.

Heinrich pulled the wagon, loaded with milk and little brother, across the farmyard. They were late with the milking, and the colony milkman was already waiting at the end of the lane. Instead of delivering milk, this milkman drove his horse and trailer around the colony and collected milk twice a day, taking it to the colony cheese factory. Once the milk was loaded the day's chores were done.

The family was slipping into Sunday mode. I'd felt the subtle shift earlier in the afternoon. The already quiet life of farm and colony was slowing down even more, matching the stillness of the wide-open land. But everything had to be clean and tidy for the Sabbath.

Hans and Lena washed the family buggy in front of the shed,

preparing it for the weekly trip to church. It had a single backless bench seat in the middle of a shallow rectangular box frame with a small arched roof. The buggy had narrow rubber tires—allowed on horse-drawn wagons but not on anything with an engine.

Buckets of water, rags, and floor mats were spread across the lawn as Hans and Lena scrubbed the buggy, which glistened in the early-evening light.

"The buggies all look the same to me," I said as I admired it. "What would happen if you painted your buggy red, so you don't get it mixed up with others?"

Lena snorted with laughter. She straightened up from her task of scrubbing floor mats, hand at the small of her back, and shielded her eyes against the low sun to look at me. She laughed again.

"Would that be wrong? Is a red buggy sinful?" I asked, goading her into another burst of laughter.

"It wouldn't be wrong, but we'd be embarrassed. No one uses a red buggy," she said before bending down to scrub the mats again. Better to just fit in with the rest.

The low sun bathed the farm in a gauzy golden glow, and the air cooled in perfect rhythm with the falling light. I sat down under a tree near my tent and opened my laptop on my knees to write. I could hear the buggy creak and rattle as Hans and Lena pushed it into the shed. A few minutes later Hans appeared at my tent, a kettle of hot water in one hand and his maté cup in the other. We handed the maté cup back and forth, and Hans refilled it each time the straw began to gurgle.

Beside us grew a field of ripe wheat that glowed white in the dusk. "Looks like this is about ready to harvest," I said. I took a head of wheat and rubbed it in the palm of my hand to separate the seeds.

"Ya, maybe next week," Hans said.

"What kind of wheat is it?" I asked.

"Hmm." Hans screwed up his face in thought. "It's the hard wheat we always plant. I'm not sure what the name is."

"Hard red wheat? The wheat that's good for baking bread?"

"Ya, that kind."

"It's probably a descendant of Turkey red, the wheat that came from Russia with our forefathers," I said.

Hans shook his head. "This seed didn't come from Europe. It's just seed we kept from last year's crop."

"And where did last year's seed come from?"

"We always keep some of the grain for seed. That's how we do it."

"The original seeds, years and years ago, probably came on the first shiploads of Mennonites that came from Russia," I said. "That wheat was the parent of the different hard red wheats grown across the US now. My family was on those same ships, and so was yours. So we're all from the same place, we've all travelled to different places, and now we're all here together."

Hans wasn't impressed with my allegories. The quietness of the land, his family's strong bond, and their simple life made me proud to associate myself with Mennonite culture again. The bitter taste of what I'd seen and heard in Bolivia was not entirely gone, and the useless piousness of moving into the Chaco was still at the back of my mind. But hey, who likes everything about their culture? Embrace what you have. And anyway, it was never my choice to begin with, so I might as well just be proud to be Mennonite. I'd slipped into a reverie of camaraderie and belonging when Hans asked:

"So what do you think of Mennonites? What do you think of the way we live? Do you think we're crazy?" His question reminded me that he still saw me as an outsider. The *bombilla* in the maté cup made a sucking sound, extra loud in the stillness of dusk. Hans added more hot water, mashed the leaves, and handed the cup to me, waiting for me to answer.

"I don't think you're crazy," I said before taking a sip of the hot, bitter liquid. "I'm not sure if I would want to live this life, but you have a peaceful, healthy life, surrounded by family. You have a good house, you eat well. You have a good life."

Hans dismissed my compliments with a nod. This too was uncommon talk for him, and it appeared to make him uncomfortable.

"How old are you?" I asked.

"I'm forty-four, and with two grandchildren already!" He

laughed and shook his head in disbelief. "I don't feel old enough to be a grandfather, but that's what I am."

"Have you achieved what you hoped you would achieve at this point in your life?" I asked. It was a common thought and question in the busy, goal-oriented urban society I lived in, but as soon as I asked, it struck me how odd a question it was in the context of Old Colony life.

Hans laughed, and then hummed and hawed. "It's hard to know. I'm not sure what I dreamed of when I was young.

"My dream now would be to start a new farm on the new colony we've started to the northwest, and to have the money to do it properly. Not do it poor like my first farm here. I'd do it for fun, instead of for survival like we did it the first time.

"And you, you're not married? Why not?" he asked.

Now it was my turn to struggle for an answer. I made noncommittal noises, as single men of my age are wont to do when asked this question.

"Don't you want a family?"

"Well, it's hard when you travel a lot," I said, offering up the only flimsy excuse I could think of that wouldn't need hours of context. The way Hans looked at me suggested he thought I must have made some mistake, have some tragic flaw, one that had prevented me from having my own family. He might have been right, but I tried to explain that journeys like this one made me happy. Travel, that hallowed goal of the middle class everywhere, didn't seem such a worthy goal to him.

"So, you'll just stay an old *jung*, then," he said, using the term for a boy, an unmarried male. But *jung* meant a lot more, with sexual, social, and maturity connotations. How could I explain to Hans that while in his world a male only became a man when he had a wife, his own family to feed and defend, in my world being single had no bearing on your maturity? I shrugged and said nothing.

"Isn't it lonely, all alone in a big city, with no family?"

"I have friends," I said, hearing the note of defensiveness in my voice.

My months of visiting tight-knit Mennonite families

and communities had made me question my solo existence in a metropolis. I envied the strong community support Mennonites enjoyed. But I doubted I could ever go back to that kind of life and give up my personal preferences and freedoms, my choice to change my lifestyle as life itself changed. I couldn't go back and live the way Johann had lived in Russia, just like Hans knew he wouldn't be able to return to his Old Colony life if he adopted the ways of the world. It was a one-way street.

"I'd like to live like this, a simple life on the colony, and I know a lot of other people who live in big cities who dream about this as well," I said. I'd barely completed my thought when Hans broke out in a cackle of disbelief.

"That's what you think now, but this would never work for you," he said, passing the maté cup to me.

"Well, only if I'm allowed to keep my computer," I said, grinning at him. "Don't you think it would be possible to live like this, quietly, in a Mennonite community, but still also have better education, maybe a car, lights you can turn on at night?"

The farmyard was nearly dark now. There was no yard light, no light on in front of the barns. Each of the day's chores was completed before the last of the light was gone, and once it was dark activity was over for the day.

"Once you have cars, people are always on the road, going somewhere, and they're never home to eat as a family. And going to the city becomes too easy. Once you have electricity you have more lights at night, so people come out of their homes at a time when the family should be at home, together. And with electricity you can have television and all that stuff. It would make our life much more complicated. Once you start allowing those things, it never ends.

"It's easier for us to live the old way out here, where no one bothers us," Hans said. "Staying away from that life, living simple, it makes it easier to live a Christian life."

Hans scraped the sodden green pulp out of the maté cup, threw it into the bushes and turned for the house.

"*Na yo*, it's time for supper," he said.

Inside, the floors were mopped and waxed, and the house smelled of soap. A battery-powered light cast garish shadows on the kitchen walls as Lena and Helena prepared dinner. The dining room was lit by a hissing gas lamp. The family sat down in their regular places while I sat at the foot of the table. We bowed our heads as Hans prayed.

> *Segne, Vater*
> *diese Speise,*
> *uns zur Kraft*
> *und dir zum Preise.*
> *Amen.*

Lena had made *reahre ei*, a hybrid of scrambled eggs and pancakes, an easy meal to make on an evening when work was kept to a minimum. She apologized for the simplicity of the meal; I thanked her for making a dish I had not eaten since I was a young boy, back on the farm in Canada. Lena served it with tomatoes and onion, a slice of cold sausage on the side.

"This is good, but my mother always served *reahre ei* with Rogers Golden Syrup. That makes us different—a big enough difference for me to start a new colony, I think."

Hans and Lena both laughed, but the children only grinned, too shy to laugh at the joke.

We ate the last of the meal in silence, and when we were finished, I thanked Lena and began to rise from the table. Hans looked at me and cleared his throat. Helena broke into giggles, which she tried to stifle when her mother shot her a stern look. All the children sat with their hands folded in their laps. I dropped back into my chair, embarrassed. I'd forgotten the tradition in many conservative homes, where they prayed both before and after the meal. I bowed my head and Hans said a quick prayer. When he was finished, I raised my head and looked around, unsure if there was more to come.

"We're done," Hans said, chuckling.

Helena's face was red with suppressed laughter as I thanked them for dinner and turned for the door.

A nearly full moon had risen, so bright it cast shadows. The tipa trees shone with the lustrous patina of old silverware. In the middle of the yard, where hoofs and steel wheels held the grass at bay, the packed earth glowed like hallowed ground. The dog, lying beside the house, lifted his head as I passed, and then dropped it on his paws with a gentle clink of his collar. Christmas crickets, called that because they sang the loudest at this time of the year, buzzed and hummed their wavering tune.

I walked down the driveway, stepping carefully to keep the silence. Across the road a dim yellow light flickered from a window, but the rest of the village was dark. I stood in the lane for a long while, breathing in the smell of dust, hay, and livestock. I could hear the muffled sounds of sleeping farms all around me. The shuffle of horses in the barn, the slow creak of a turning windmill, the hollow thud of a closing door. Sounds and smells just like those Johann knew in Russia more than a century ago. The farm, the layout of the colony, the language and foods, the nineteenth-century conveniences, all very like they were when Johann migrated, and it was the only life that Hans and his family would probably ever know.

I craned my neck and stared, open-mouthed, at the wide sky. Constellations so bright they pushed aside the darkness, other segments of the sky where the stars were nearly drowning in black, but still blinking, twinkling. This patch of Patagonian soil, the sounds and smells and people, felt as close as my heart and as far away as the stars. It was me who was caught in the middle. I'd come looking for myself in other people's lives, in other people's interpretations. Yes, I'd found my people, made new friends, and discovered things about us, and about me, that I'd never known before. But the answers, what there were of them, weren't as neat and tidy as I'd somehow imagined they might be. Those expectations seemed naive to me now. But I felt satisfied. Content. I didn't feel the need to ride on, to search any further.

I opened the zipper on my tent, frozen for a moment by the loud screech it made, and then I fell onto my sleeping bag. My ears reached out beyond the thin dome of nylon to search out the night sounds, seeking out those that I knew as I drifted off to sleep.

On Sunday morning I awoke to the clank of milk cans. Beside my tent was a small water tank. Hans and Heinrich set the tall steel cans of milk into the water to keep them cool over the Sabbath until the cheese factory reopened on Monday.

When the chores were done the whole family disappeared into the house to get ready for church, and I retreated to my tent to get dressed. The best I had in my wardrobe was oil-stained jeans, a black shirt, and my black leather riding boots. I looked like a biker. I crawled out of my tent just in time to see Hans stride across the yard. He looked like a true gentleman, in a dark suit with a tall white cowboy hat. He climbed aboard his buggy carrying a small wooden box of hymn books, which he gently tucked under the seat.

Lena was decked head to toe in a heavy dark dress with a black head covering. She and Hans were dressed almost exactly as they would have been 150 years ago in southern Russia.

The buggy seat wasn't designed for three adults, so I had to put my arm around Hans and all but sit on his lap to keep from falling off. The road filled with other horses and buggies, all carrying soberly dressed couples riding to church. It was a quiet, dusty scene, broken only by the soft plop of horse's hoofs and the creak of wheels.

We rolled into the churchyard and parked at a hitching rail. Hans opened the wooden box and took out their hymn books. There were quiet greetings exchanged with neighbours, but there was none of the socializing that I'd grown up with at church. The church had several doors, and Hans pointed out which one I should use, determined by a confusing mix of age, sex, marital status, and position within the church. Hans was a song leader, and he used a special entrance reserved for church leaders.

I had attended many church services on my journey and each one varied in its degree of austerity in the name of tradition. This one, I knew, would be at the extreme end of the spectrum.

I felt a hundred pairs of eyes on me as I entered and trod on other people's toes on my way to an open spot on the backless benches. Men sat on one side, women on the other. The most aged worshippers sat on benches set against the dais, facing the rest of the congregation, so they could lean against the low wall separating the dais from the rest of the church. Each man gave a slight, silent nod to his neighbours as they entered, and then, before sitting down, the men took off their dark fedoras and white cowboy hats and put them on racks that hung from the ceiling. Each man then hitched up his trousers and sat down, staring straight ahead while he waited for the service to begin.

There was no music or chatter. Throats were cleared and shoes were dragged across the wooden floor with a hollow scrape. The man who sat next to me burped with a suppressed, gaseous sigh. Then a door swung open and six middle-aged men entered in single file. They climbed the two steps to the dais and sat down. Hans was one of the song leaders, and once again I was surprised at his transformation. The heavy overcoat, cowboy hat, and gloves were gone. Now his white forehead glowed above ruddy cheeks, his hair slicked into a severe side parting. The men opened their songbooks in unison. Hans called out a number. The rustle of turning pages filled the church. Hans began to sing in a mournful, nasal tone and the congregation joined in.

Unaccompanied "long melody" singing, where the leaders start each verse with call and response, is a plangent form largely unchanged since the sixteenth century. It became the only music allowed in most Old Colony churches when they arrived in Canada, as leaders tried to erase the modernization that had taken place while they were in Russia. To me, it sounded more like a droning chant than hymns.

After several songs a group of three older men entered and took their seats beside the pulpit, and then one of them stood up to begin a one-and-a-half-hour sermon. He switched between Plautdietsch and High German, his tearful pleading read line for line from a book before him. He begged the congregation to live holy lives and extolled the youth to turn away from their sinful ways. Never did the preacher smile, never did his demeanour offer a ray of happiness, joy, or grace. He was delivering the laws of the church, and that was nothing to be happy about.

The service had begun at eight o'clock, and by nine the church was stifling hot. There were no fans—indeed no electricity—and the air was torpid. The smell of sweating bodies bundled in heavy clothing lay thick across the sanctuary. The chirp of birds could be heard through the windows, only underscoring the sombreness of the service inside.

Around me heads began to loll. Men leaned forward, elbows on knees, heads on hands. Chins slipped from their perches and bodies lurched forward in drowsy clumsiness. At one point the entire row of song leaders took out their songbooks, in unison, and propped them on the low wall in front of them and rested their heads on them for a quick nap, even as the preacher droned on. A few minutes later the men sat back up, again in unison, blinking and yawning as the sermon continued.

The church was a rectangular one-room building filled with unpainted benches and white walls. Not a picture, a Bible verse, or a cross broke the austerity. Through the windows I could see horses still harnessed to their buggies, stamping their hoofs and shooing at flies with their tails. When a horse shifted and rattled his buggy the men craned their necks to peer out the window to see if it was their horse causing the ruckus. Chickens wandered the yard, pecking at holy crumbs.

Three times the preacher gave the command to pray. Each time I was caught off guard as the entire congregation stood up, turned around, and dropped to their knees in perfect unison. The church became silent as the congregation fell into individual prayer. Or they did as I did and inspected the ass and shoe bottoms of the person in front of them while listening to the flies buzzing in the corner. After each prayer the congregation stood up, dusted off their knees, and returned to their backless benches for further lecturing.

I watched, both detached and intrigued. Here was what these Mennonites would proclaim as the heart of their culture. Faith: living it and expressing it in a severe and particular way. I looked at Hans in the row of leaders. The camaraderie we had established the day before was lost. I tried to make eye contact with him but he did not look at me. Some of the church services I'd attended on my journey had made me feel nostalgic and home-sick because they were so similar to the worship services I'd grown up with. This one made me feel like an outsider, but still, I felt a tiny thread of connection. Like an outsider who understood, who knew the secret of our shared history. The faces around me were familiar, not unlike the faces around the campfire on the banks of the Red River at the start of my journey. I shared my Mennonite genes with these people, both the ones I admired and those I despised. Mennonites were just like any other family.

Just when I thought it would be impossible to keep my eyes open for a moment longer the preacher's droning came to an end. I stumbled out into the sunshine and sucked fresh air into my lungs. Horses were untied from hitching posts, songbooks put back into their wooden cases with a hollow clunk, and the buggies left the churchyard one by one, trailing clouds of silent dust.

Back at the Loewen farm, Sunday lunch was followed by *med-dach'schlop*. The air hung still and heavy, aiding in the well-deserved and highly cherished Sunday-afternoon nap. I crept into my tent and lay down, drowsy from the heat. Helena and her girlfriends, made restless by the quietness, loitered in the shade of the plum trees a few metres from my tent. I could hear them speaking in whispers.

"He slept in that thing, but he came inside for breakfast," Helena whispered to her friends. "And he came to the barn to watch me milk the cows!"

"Oh! That must have been so embarrassing, to have him watch you work!"

"Ya, and he kept making jokes the whole time."

"But why is he here? Does your father know him? Is he a salesman?"

"No, he's a stranger. He's on a long journey. He told me he was a writer."

"He's a *weltmensch*?" one of the girls asked, her voice rising in surprise.

"No, he's a Mennonite. Well, I don't know. At least that's what he said, but he's not a Mennonite like us. He speaks Plautdietsch, and he says he comes from those Mennonites in Canada. So, I guess he's a Mennonite."

I smiled to myself.

Yes, I am a Mennonite.

Afterword

My motorcycle journey did not end on the Loewen farm in Argentina. I rode on to Tierra del Fuego, where I celebrated New Year's Eve 2012 and then tried, and failed, to sell my motorbike. So I turned north again, and spent several more weeks camping my way up the beautiful Chilean coastline until I arrived in the capital, Santiago. Here, I sold my motorcycle and flew home.

My eight-month trip spanned some forty-five thousand kilometres and took me through nineteen countries on two continents. I burned nearly twenty-five hundred liters of fuel, wore through four rear and three front tires, and developed a very calloused backside.

I have enjoyed keeping in touch with many of the people in this book. Of most interest have been the Mennonite men in Bolivia's Palmasola prison. Most are still behind bars, but Peter Wiebe, the self-taught veterinarian charged with creating the anaesthetizing spray, was released in early 2018 and he moved his family to a more inclusive Mennonite community to rebuild his life. Jacob Wall, the first man to be arrested, was also released in 2018, when he was diagnosed with terminal cancer; he died shortly after his release.

The Mennonites in Mexico who were planning a move to Russia scrapped those plans. They also explored creating a new colony in Angola, but those plans were also abandoned. However, Mennonites across the Americas continue to acquire more land and to move back and forth, north and south between countries and continents, as economic and social factors change.

Klaas Friesen, the gregarious kidnapping survivor in Belize, tragically died in a road accident in 2015.

It has taken me seven years to publish this book. Getting it all down on paper and finding a publisher were part of that, but asking myself probing questions about my identity took longer, and was more emotionally and mentally challenging, than I anticipated. The book languished for long periods of time as other, less personal projects, from ocean sailing to digging for dinosaurs in the desert, presented themselves as welcome distractions.

But I kept coming back to this story. I was encouraged and prodded into action by friends and family who persistently asked about its progress.

Today, in my home city of Hong Kong, writing in 2019 after a summer of protests that have made newspaper headlines all over the world, I am faced with new questions of identity, of who we want to be versus who others see us as, and at what cost. Hongkongers are fighting for the right to be themselves, to maintain their freedom and their wonderful and eclectic cultural mix. Again, it is a culture that I feel I belong to, but in which I find no easy fit. Many of the existential questions Hongkongers ask themselves remind me of my motorcycle journey to find my Mennonite identity. The search for our identity has no end; the true reward is in the beautiful discoveries we make along the way.

Acknowledgements

My journey took me to nineteen countries across two continents, covered some forty-five thousand kilometres and lasted about eight months. I rode from Manitoba all the way to Tierra del Fuego, then back north to Santiago, Chile, where I sold my motorbike and flew home. No one robbed, attacked, or chased me away. Instead, people took me into their homes, gave me a bed to sleep in and food to eat. They guided me to hotels and negotiated discounts on my behalf. They helped me back to my feet after I crashed, offered local remedies for my maladies, and pointed me in the right direction. They lent me tools and fixed my bike for me. On the colonies, they did all these things even as I kept asking uncomfortable questions, badgering them for insights into their lives. Thank you to the bikers who waved as they passed, the momentary friends made on ferries and dusty roads, to the farmers who let me camp in their fields, and all those who ensured my safety. Thank you to those who saw a vulnerable solo traveller and stopped to say hello, to help, to share a moment of my adventure. The world is full of very good people. Don't be afraid to travel and rely on the mercy of strangers, because when you make yourself vulnerable on the road you experience new places, people, and ideas.

Thank you to all those Mennonites who told me their stories, showed me their colonies, took me into their homes, and fed me foods that reminded me of my home. There were many exceptional stories and characters that didn't make it into this book, even though they all deserved it.

My dear friend Victoria Burrows joined me on her own motorcycle for about two months and six thousand kilometres, from Mexico City to Panama City. I'm sorry I couldn't include all of our raucous adventures in this book. Thank you for sharing those miles and experiences with me.

Among those who helped me on the road were (in the order of their appearance): Troy Dunkly, Stephen and Caroline Burns, John Friesen, Bram Siemens, Gary and Bonnie Dymond, Caprice Parks and Joe, Klaas and Greta Friesen and their family, Ed and Carolyn

Reimer, Norman Collins and the Panama Piratas MC, Sonja and David Tkachuk, George Dueck and his extended family, Richard and Suzanne Chang Jonfe, Dom Harris, Luz Dary and her mother, Ofelia, David and Lisa Janzen, Rudy and Erma Friesen, David and Sieglinde Toews, Jacob Banman and his family, Anton and Elwiera Kauenhowen, Patrick Friesen, Werner Bartel, David Fehr, Peter Fehr, Rudolf Harder, Randy Fehr, Dorian Funk, Andy and Rafa Thielmann and the boys of Steinkrug, Volnei Adriana Damaren, the bikers in Witmarsum Colony, Hans and Lena Loewen, and the Chilean family who abandoned their day trip to guard my motorcycle while I went searching for parts.

Thank you to my family, who helped me with research and contacts and who have been my most powerful word-of-mouth marketing tool. My father, Leonard P. Dueck, was a true Mennonite pioneer, and I am eternally grateful to have inherited his sense of adventure and his determination to push on when talent, resources, and expertise have long gone dry. You inspire me. I also thank my great-grandfather John W. Dueck (Johann) for recording his experiences so that I could discover them more than a century later. Thank you, Fiona, the love of my life, for pushing me to complete this book and brightening my every day as I did so.

I thank my early manuscript readers: Chris Maden, Edmund Price, Justin Hill, and Thomas McLean.

I owe deep gratitude to my editor, Janice Zawerbny, for taking on my manuscript and then forwarding it to the right people. Thank you to Dan Wells and your team at Biblioasis for believing in this story.

This book was made possible through the support of the Banff Centre for Arts and Creativity, the Vladimir & Yachiyo Wolodarsky Endowment Fund for Literary Arts & Music, the Canada Council for the Arts, and the Vermont Studio Center.